Studies in Deprivation and Disadvantage 2

A Cycle of Deprivation?
A Case Study of Four Families

Studies in Deprivation and Disadvantage 2

Despite substantial economic advances and improved welfare services in Britain since the Second World War, there has been a conspicuous persistence of deprivation and maladjustment. In June 1972 Sir Keith Joseph, then Secretary of State for Social Services, drew attention to this. In particular it seemed to him that social problems tended to recur in successive generations of the same families—to form a 'cycle of deprivation'. Subsequently the Department of Health and Social Security through the SSRC, made available a sum of money for a programme of research into the whole problem.

Academics and practitioners from a wide range of disciplines and professional backgrounds were invited to investigate many aspects of deprivation and the process of transmission. Their findings are now becoming available and many of the empirical studies, together with literature reviews and the final summary report on deprivation and social policy, are being published in this series of *Studies in Deprivation and Disadvantage*.

Studies in Deprivation and Disadvantage 2

A Cycle of Deprivation?
A Case Study of Four Families

Frank Coffield, Philip Robinson and Jacquie Sarsby

Heinemann Educational Books · London

Published by Heinemann Educational Books Ltd
22 Bedford Square, London WC1B 3HH
LONDON   EDINBURGH   MELBOURNE   AUCKLAND
HONG KONG   SINGAPORE   KUALA LUMPUR   NEW DELHI
IBADAN   NAIROBI   JOHANNESBURG
EXETER [NH]   KINGSTON   PORT OF SPAIN

First published 1980

British Library Cataloguing in Publication Data

Coffield, Frank
  A cycle of deprivation.
  1. Problem family – England – Midlands – Case studies
  2. Socially handicapped – England – Midlands – Case Studies
  I. Title   II. Robinson, Philip
  III. Sarsby, Jacquie
  362.8′2   HQ616

  ISBN 0–435–82145–8

Filmset in Great Britain by
Northumberland Press Ltd, Gateshead, Tyne and Wear
and printed and bound in Great Britain by
Richard Clay (The Chaucer Press) Ltd, Bungay, Suffolk

Contents

Preface

It is sometimes important to say what a book is not. This book is not a portrait of life in Kindleton, the pseudonymous city where we carried out our research: many different styles of life exist there, and in this book the lives of only four families are described. This book is not a portrait of deprivation: again the styles, the paths and the patterns that deprivation can take are too numerous and diverse for this study to cover. The book has no statistics to show how each family and its problems could be multiplied a thousand times and carved into wooden stereotypes for trainee social workers or teachers to assimilate. Our study is not directed at the people who live or have lived through the kind of problems it describes, but it *can* and, we hope, *will*, be useful to their more successful fellow citizens whose life styles and experience are very different but who nevertheless administer, teach, judge, counsel and represent these people.

To study society adequately one must not only discover the regularities which shape the behaviour of millions, but also focus inwards on the minutiae of everyday life. Intensive fieldwork and close day-to-day and week-to-week contact with the families who are the focus of this research are ways of getting to know more intimately the problems of family life among people whose life style and neighbourhoods are so different from our own. Such an approach helps our understanding of the conflicting aims, the decisions and struggles which are lost in the facts and figures of large scale surveys.

Social enquiry does not take place in a vacuum, least of all when it is paid for by a government department, and our study in Kindleton was part of the programme of research into the transmission of deprivation set up initially by Sir Keith Joseph, funded by the Department of Health and Social Security and monitored by the Social Science Research Council. This kind of work, funded by a Conservative government and later by a Labour one, can be conducted by people and institutions with very different theories about the nature and causes of deprivation. There are those, for example, who see deprivation largely in terms of crude, composite, 'problem family' stereotypes: the parents are supposedly sub-normal and have criminal tendencies, the house is filthy, the father is drunk and out of work, the mother inadequate and unable to cook, the children ill-clothed, dirty, and performing badly at school, etc. For such theorists, the causes of deprivation are, to a great extent, personal and the explanations they favour are maladjustment, individual inadequacy or genetics. At the opposite end of the spectrum, other theorists see deprivation largely as the result of divisive economic forces in society. The starting points of such research would be, for example, poverty, low pay, unemployment, redundancy, 'black' schools, or slum areas.

Our research occupies an anomalous position between these rough categories because we could not hope to isolate structural factors convincingly from our sample of four families and our research methods would tend to make individual and psychological factors figure prominently. Our intensive and long-term contact, however, soon provided us with evidence that the forms of deprivation and the multiplicity of factors leading to them did not fit the crude stereotype of the 'problem family'. Social workers were heavily involved with three of the families, who had difficulties with their children as well as in their marital relationships. The complexity of their present problems was matched only by the complexity of their past histories, and we soon discovered that the circumstances of each family were the result of the interplay of countless factors in the wider society, the region and the neighbourhood, as well as in the extended family, the marriage relationship and the individual. Our fourth family was not involved with social workers but was characterized by us as a family coming out of deprivation.

We contacted two of our families independently and were introduced to the other two by social workers. Neither method prevented us from carrying out long-term fieldwork over a period from eighteen months to two years or from making lasting relationships with them. Our problem was rather that they forgot we were doing research and this caused us ethical problems: they were too open, too honest, too intimate for us to believe that they were consciously providing material for our project rather than discussing problems as friends. For this reason, we have disguised them, changed significant details and omitted material on many sensitive areas.

The case studies that follow are accounts of life among the least advantaged families in our society. They had no educational qualifications, and were for the most part unskilled or semi-skilled and, with

one exception, lowly paid. They had no capital, no assets and no
incremental salaries. They have not written their own stories here, but
we hope we have helped them to speak because all too often the
vulnerability of poverty has attracted blame rather than a sympathetic
hearing. It was their misfortune and not their free choice to provide
work for the caring services: their problems were problems for *them* as
well as for the professionals who tried to cope with them. It is their
distress and not their nuisance-value, accordingly, which is the focus of
this book.

Kindleton itself is an industrial city in the middle of England. All our
families lived there, sometimes on its peripheral council estates, at other
times in the older parts of the city, with its little terraces, backyards and
corner shops and pubs. The local Social Work Department introduced
us to Elsie and Vince Barker and also to Ada Paterson, who lived as
neighbours in Bramwell. Ada exchanged her house for the Martins' flat
in Cardale, a council estate farther away from the centre of the city, and
thus we came to know Peter and Sally and their children. We also met
Dora and George Fielding informally, when they were living at Aulton,
and followed what happened to them when they moved to a better house
in Drayford. Finally, we got to know another council estate at Elsmore,
when the Barkers moved into a larger house there.

Those readers who do not want to be involved in a discussion of
our research methods should turn directly to the four chapters on the
families (Chapters 2 to 5). In Chapter 6 we list the general and policy
implications of our work, and in the Epilogue we describe how we
revisited the four families after an absence of some fifteen months.
The Appendix consists of a critical review of the evidence Sir Keith
Joseph advanced in support of 'the cycle of deprivation'.

Our first and enduring debt is to the families who gave so much of
themselves to us. No acknowledgement can repay the friendship which
they extended to us. We also want to thank the joint Committee of the
DHSS/SSRC whose comments and advice on earlier drafts have greatly
improved the final version of this book, particularly Chapter 6. Finally,
we want to express our thanks to our three secretaries, Joy Brock, Olwyn
Clarke and Catherine Bloor, who worked diligently and carefully
against the deadlines we were always setting them.

April 1979

1 Introduction

The idea of a cycle of deprivation is not a new one, although the phrase was made popular by a leading British politician, Sir Keith Joseph, in the early 1970s. As early as 1921, a book was published by Jamieson Hurry under the title *Poverty and its Vicious Circles*. This book contained a number of diagrams of different 'vicious circles', all of which were said to lead to poverty. Hurry himself traced back the earliest use of this term, as applied to social problems, to a book by De Gérando in 1839. To understand, however, the contemporary version of this long-established idea, we must first turn to a speech of Sir Keith Joseph. This chapter will then describe our own research project, discuss the methods we adopted, and end by giving an outline of the city and of the five areas within that city where our fieldwork was based.

In 1972, at a conference organized by the Pre-School Playgroups Association, Sir Keith Joseph first addressed himself to 'the cycle of deprivation', arguing that many social problems reproduce themselves from generation to generation. In his own words, 'inadequate people tend to be inadequate parents and inadequate parents tend to rear inadequate children' (1972a, para 41). Sir Keith expressed concern about a paradox in British society whereby serious deprivation and problems of maladjustment 'conspicuously persist' despite long periods of full employment, relative prosperity and improvements in all community services (such as health and education) since the Second World War.

Sir Keith was anxious not to be misunderstood as suggesting that there was 'some single process by which social problems reproduce themselves'. Indeed, he cited a number of causes which he saw as interactive and cumulative:

1. Economic factors (persistent unemployment, low income);
2. Living conditions (bad housing, over-crowding);
3. Personal factors (illness, accident, genetic endowment);
4. Patterns of child rearing (emotional deprivation or instability).

Having accepted that deprivation was both complex and imprecise, Sir Keith argued that 'in a proportion of cases, occurring at all levels of society, the problems of one generation appear to reproduce themselves in the next'. In more detail, he was referring to what he called the 'casualties of society—the problem families, the vagrants, the alcoholics, the drug addicts, the disturbed, the delinquent and the criminal' (1972a, para 19). More recently, Holman (1978, p. 117) has produced a model of Sir Keith's cycle of deprivation and this is presented in Figure 1.1.

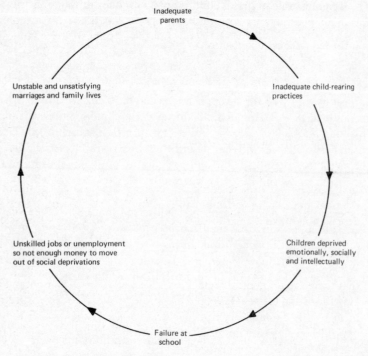

Figure 1.1   The Cycle of Deprivation

Source: Holman, R. (1978), *Poverty: Explanations of Social Deprivation*, London: Martin Robinson, p. 117.

On his own initiative Sir Keith Joseph, then Secretary of State for Social Services, asked the Social Science Research Council (SSRC) to explore the feasibility of research into this concept of the cycle of deprivation, and a joint working party from the Department of Health and Social Security and the SSRC was set up. For Sir Keith the purpose of such a research programme was primarily the development of preventive strategies. His own interim suggestions were fourfold:

1. The extension of family planning to reduce the numbers likely to be recruited into the cycle of deprivation;
2. Preparation for parenthood, to educate both children and adults about marriage, parental roles and children's needs;
3. Casework with parents who were themselves emotionally deprived; and
4. Playgroups to stimulate the intellectual, social and emotional development of young children.

In sum, Sir Keith advocated the strengthening of family life which is accorded so central a position in his explanatory system that there is no one-to-one correspondence between his four causes and his four solutions. Such is the concentration on all aspects of parental behaviour that the problems of persistent unemployment, low income and bad housing disappear from the analysis. The evidence which Sir Keith advanced in support of 'the phenomenon of transmitted deprivation' is discussed in detail in the Appendix.

Our Research Project
In discussing our own research, we start by arguing that the historical, political and social overtones which surround the concept of a cycle of deprivation make it clear to us that there is no value free social science. This will become more and more obvious as we begin to describe the methodological problems involved in studying a small group of families. We are here, of course, claiming nothing new or startling when we say that there are no neutral facts. Philosophically, we take our stand with Hawthorn and Carter (1976, pp. 43–4): '. . . facts are only constituted as facts by the explanatory and evaluative theory with which they are approached . . . we do not believe that there are any theory-neutral facts. There is only a theory-neutral world.'

In order to examine empirically the idea of a cycle of deprivation, we adopted an anthropological (or ethnographic) approach to studying a small number of families with problems. What follows, therefore, is a very brief account of the 'natural history' of our research project and a discussion of the various ethical and methodological problems we faced.

Our earliest ideas about an anthropological study of transmitted deprivation were to conduct a community study of a housing estate which had been defined by local officials and professionals as *the* area where deprivation was transmited from generation to generation within the same families. As can be seen from Figure 1.2, our intention was to 'home in' on a small group of 'problem families', after we had established relationships with key figures in the neighbourhood. Initially we thought that our main methodological problem would be one of gaining *access* to such families, having been alerted by West and Farrington's (1973) study that entrée becomes more and more difficult in almost direct proportion to the research importance of the family. This concern about securing access explains many of the decisions made at that time, although with hindsight we now wonder why it appeared to pose such a formidable task.

In March 1975 contact began with the Mothers and Toddlers Club on the estate we call Aulton. (All names of people and places are pseudonyms). At the same time that rapport with a group of young mothers was being established, we conducted a series of interviews with local officials in an attempt to familiarize ourselves with the official network of support services in the area and to inform these agencies of our research. As a result of these interviews we gained valuable contacts and useful information on the broad range of services in the area. Although we did not set out to make a detailed analysis of the views of the officials we interviewed in relation to our research topic, we were left with the distinct impression that the majority of them accepted that a cycle of deprivation does exist and that transmission does take place within 'problem families'. Very few of them, for example, spontaneously questioned this concept which seemed to be a conventional wisdom among such professionals. Many of the officials had no difficulty in specifying the most stigmatized housing estate in the area and they were able to call to mind families where they thought the cycle of deprivation was in evidence. Moreover, some officials, and they were in the main concerned with education, appeared to us to operate with a strongly psychiatric or psychological model of deprivation, where the main problems were seen to be those of disturbed personality, low intelligence and poor heredity. We wish to emphasize, however, that these impressions of official attitudes were formed as the interviews progressed and that an examination of official ideologies of transmitted deprivation was not the purpose of the meetings.

One interview in particular, that with the social workers, had a lasting influence on our research strategy. As has been mentioned, contact had been made in Aulton with a group of young mothers, but as yet there had been no invitation to visit any of the mothers in their own homes. The difficulties of access loomed large at this stage, and so we were pleased with the suggestion of the Principal Area Social Worker to

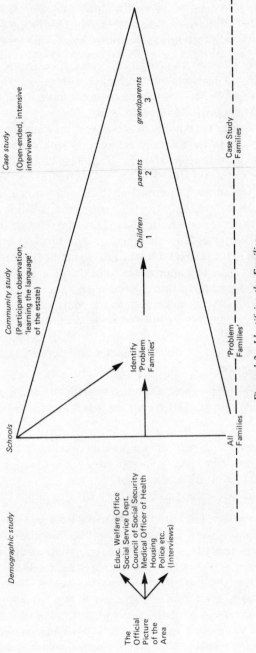

Figure 1.2 Identifying the Families

introduce us to a small number of families suitable for our research purposes. We withdrew to think further about his proposal and finally decided to accept it, producing the following reasons for our decision:

1. The proposal solved the problem of access. It also prevented us from putting all our eggs into the one basket of the informal approach in Aulton, which might have have been time-consuming and unsuccessful, but which turned out *not* to be so.

2. Being introduced to families by social workers would provide us with an interesting methodological comparison with our other informal method of introduction to families in Aulton. Philp (1958, p. 34) and Valentine (1968, pp. 184–5) both had alerted us to the dangers of appearing to our target population to be in any way associated with the police, the welfare system or any other official agency. We resolved to make our role (as researchers who were studying families who had experienced or were experiencing serious problems) as clear as possible to the families from the earliest moment of contact. Figure 1.3 sets out these two approaches to fieldwork and makes the point that the social workers' introduction did not prevent us from making contact with other families such as the Martins.

3. As the Department of Health and Social Security were financing the research, we thought it appropriate to study families who were considered by social workers to need a considerable amount of their time and energy.

Accordingly, at a subsequent meeting with the social workers, we produced the following criteria for the selection of two families:

1. That three generations should be known.
2. That the nuclear family should have a concentration of problems.
3. That the extended family should have some members who were successful and others unsuccessful.
4. That no other research was being done with the family or in the area.

These criteria were circulated among social workers in the area, and a number of families were suggested to us. It became clear to us that the social workers tended to have little detailed knowledge of all three generations of any one family or of the extended family and so criteria (1) and (3) received less attention than the others. Nevertheless, we finally decided to ask for an introduction to two families living in the same street in an older urban area, called Bramwell by us. The two families were Vince and Elsie Barker and Ada Paterson and her seven-year-old son. As confidence built up on both sides, we introduced each

Figure 1.3   Two Approaches to Fieldwork

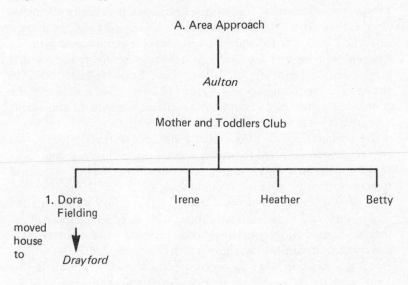

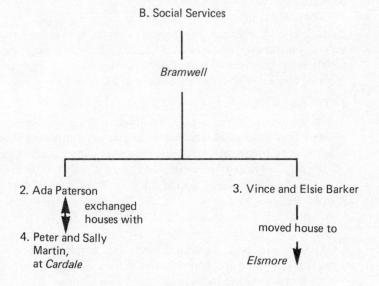

Notes

The four families chosen for intensive study have been numbered. Contact was also
established with other families in Aulton as invaluable points of comparison.

Aulton, Bramwell, Cardale and *Elsmore* are the four areas described later in this chapter.

other to all the families as it was obviously valuable to have three perceptions rather than one and the interaction between family members and researchers of different sexes was likely to vary. Six months after fieldwork started Ada Paterson exchanged homes with the Martins, who on first acquaintance seemed to exemplify the classical stereotype of the 'problem family'; and so we decided to include them in the small group of families who were to be interviewed intensively. We progressed slowly and capitalized on chance encounters and events whenever it seemed in the interests of our project.

The upshot of our decision to accept the social workers' initiative was that we became involved in two main areas rather than one, and those two areas eventually grew to five as our families moved or exchanged houses. So pleased were we at establishing rapport with four families, each with different problems relevant to the theory of transmitted deprivation, and at maintaining contact with other families at Aulton, that we changed our original intention of producing a community study and concentrated instead on a group of detailed case studies. We wish to emphasize, however, that we were introduced to only *two* families by social workers; the other families described in this report were initially contacted by ourselves informally.

The problems presented by each of the families spanned most of the main types of deprivation. We therefore decided to explore the complex web of individual and structural factors which had generated such problems in the lives of our chosen families. The main reasons for selecting these particular families were as follows:

1. The Barkers were a family with six children under the age of seven and an adolescent girl in care. Additionally there had been a sudden death of another child. The mother and children appeared to be eking out a poverty-stricken existence; they were in constant contact with the social services who considered them to be forever living on the brink of disaster. (See Chapter 2.)

2. Ada Paterson, when we first met her, was suffering the social isolation, grief and depression of widowhood. She was a woman in her late forties whose youngest child, a seven-year-old boy called Michael, was in a residential home for delicate children. Social workers had been deeply involved with the family for some years and they considered her to be inadequate. (See Chapter 3.)

3. Peter Martin had been unemployed for at least six months, and his rich fantasy life seemed to us to put him in danger of becoming unemployable. One of the Martin's children had been taken into

foster care for 'non-wilful neglect'. Peter and Sally Martin came closest to the classical description of the 'problem family'. (See Chapter 4.)

4. Dora Fielding was struggling to keep her family from experiencing the deprivations which she had suffered in the past. The importance of studying *discontinuities*, whereby people break out of cycles of disadvantage, had been emphasized sufficiently in the literature (e.g. Rutter and Madge, 1976, p. 6). Her family were also chosen because
   (a) All three generations of this extended family lived together within the city.
   (b) There were successful and unsuccessful branches within the family.
   (c) Dora was soon seen to be a central figure in a close network of friendship and visiting on the estate of Aulton. Whyte (1955, p. 300) had convinced us of 'the crucial importance of having the support of the key individuals' in any participant observation study.
   (d) Not least of all, the family were most friendly and welcoming, which were encouraging characteristics to researchers worried about obtaining access. (See Chapter 5.)

5. Contact was maintained, at different levels of involvement, with other families in Aulton who were invaluable points of comparison in relation to the four families studied in depth. We were interested, for example, in noting what problems or disadvantages these families talked about spontaneously. In other words, we were trying to measure deprivation by studying the self-perception and the values of families living on a stigmatized estate. Did they *feel* deprived of certain goods and services, although by national standards they were not so considered? Alternatively, did they see *themselves* as 'problem families' whether or not they had been so classified by social workers? Had they different definitions of deprivation from those held by administrators or social workers? Were they, for example, concerned about the standard of education in the local schools, or was education not seen as 'an important determinant of the life and livelihood of individuals'? (Halsey, 1972, p. 3).

Methods

Our research methods owe much to the influence of the anthropologist, Oscar Lewis, who produced a number of very detailed accounts of poor Mexican (1964, 1969, 1970) and Puerto Rican (1966) families. In an attempt to capture the adaptations and reactions of these poor families to their marginal position at the bottom of society, he invented the term 'the culture of poverty', by which he meant 'a way of life, remarkably stable and persistent, passed down from generation to generation along family lines' (1964). He later argued (1966, p. 5): 'By the time slum children are six or seven they have usually absorbed the basic attitudes and values of their subculture. Thereafter they are psychologically unready to take full advantage of changing conditions or improving opportunities that may develop in their lifetime.'

Such propositions and others contained in the 'culture of poverty' argument have been criticized by Valentine (1968), Leacock (1971) and many others, for blaming poverty on the poor and for legitimating policies which were aimed at modifying the behaviour of the poor rather than changing the social or economic structure of society. Lewis was also attacked for taking a few unrepresentative families as his basic unit of study, an approach which may have caused him to attach insufficient weight to structural determinants. The value to us of the debate on 'the culture of poverty' was that it made us realize that transmission of deprivation from parent to child may not take place within the family at all, but may be more concerned with being a member of a particular social class, ethnic minority, regional area, housing estate or school. Our intention, however, was to study the influence of *both* personal, individual factors *and* socioeconomic factors in the lives of our chosen families.

It may be thought expensive of effort, time and money to concentrate on a case study of four families, and yet the bare bones of statistical truth are hard to understand without the flesh supplied by the detailed study of day-to-day life. Our approach would be supported by Hess and Handel (1974, p. XI): 'Case analysis . . . translates abstractions into the concrete components of actual lives. The social scientist loses touch with his subject matter if he confines his work to disembodied responses and acts grouped into categories. Learning in social science must have a sensory base; tables of data must have some connection with people who can be seen or heard in action.' It is in the belief that the lives of our families are better viewed as a *gestalt*, as a whole rather than as a collection of meaningless parts or as a set of walking concepts that we present these case studies.

Having decided on intensive long-term contact with a few families, we set out to explore the transmitted deprivation thesis with these aims:

1. To produce detailed family biographies and genealogies;
2. To appreciate the accounts given by the main actors of their past and

present problems, and so provide some indication of the quality of their lives;
3. To study successful as well as unsuccessful members of families who had been in serious difficulties.

We wanted to enter the social world of a number of families experiencing serious problems. In so doing we were aware that we were changing that world, for inevitably in the social sciences, research disturbs the phenomena under investigation. The responsibility of the social scientist becomes that of gauging the extent to which his or her research may have distorted an individual's original view of the world. Our approach tried to reduce the gap between the subject and the enquirer, and to build a bridge from the theories of social science to the subjective, common-sense understandings of everyday life. Statistics do not necessarily bridge the gap between the models of social science and the world as perceived by individuals, and often masquerade as objectivity. In this project we have been conscious of Argyris's (1968) argument that research needs to be seen as an act of negotiation between the researcher and the subject: if the researcher exerts too much control, the subject may adopt a wide range of defensive strategies to protect himself.

The less structured, interpretive type of research which characterized this project attempted to reduce the distance between researcher and researched through involvement *over time*. As our involvement with the subject's world increased, so there was less space for him or her to present an inconsistent front. We came to know details of the lives of many individuals which had not been communicated to close members of their own families. When we started work, we were fully aware of Wright's (1955, p. 381) point: 'The individual is certain of disillusionment who imagines that family trees, let alone any reliable information as to the social performances of relatives, are readily elicited from the average problem family parent.' But, as our contact increased, so our relationship shifted from one of researcher to one of friend, and confidences were divulged on both sides. As these friendships developed, members of our families began to assume that we had finished our work. It then became difficult to remind respondents that we were still engaged on fieldwork. Some, such as Dora Fielding, forgot how we had first met; others, such as Vince Barker, would comment about that time in the past when we were doing research, or 'that survey', as he called our work.

Such a change in relationship increases the obligation on us to protect the identity of our families and counsels us to be circumspect in our use of the information given. Our first consideration is that this research should not harm our families in any way. We have given them all pseudonyms, we have changed dates, or deliberately left them vague, and we have changed other details which might lead to their being identified. We have also omitted important data rather than endanger the cover of a particular family.

Radin (1933) has argued that only long-term observation of the lives of specific individuals can enable the researcher to reach an understanding of their view of the world from their position. This type of research is best seen as a dialogue, an interaction which takes place within the micro context of an individual life and the macro context of the historical and social setting of that life. While there is a dialogue between the micro and macro variables, Radin pointed out that research is also a dialogue between the social scientist and the subject: 'Our ideal may very well be to secure all the possible facts, but every investigator soon realizes that the facts he is likely to secure depend, to a marked degree, not merely upon his competences, his knowledge, and his interests but to a factor frequently overlooked, his personality.' (1933, p. 113). We, as researchers, were not a *tabula rasa* upon which the world of our families made a well-formed impression, but a complex of prejudices, opinions, knowledge, past histories, careers and biographies which blinded us to some aspects and made us too ready to see other aspects of the lives of our families.

One aspect of this research dialogue is that we were largely restricted to the accounts of the world given to us by members of the families. The fieldworker's knowledge of his subject's world can be distorted, as the researcher has no natural place in the world observed and is constantly interpreting the picture which is presented to him. We had to learn the language, symbols, values and conventions of each of our research areas, before we could begin to understand the messages we were being given; but we were hampered in learning the language because we were not integral members of that society. Thus at first we did not appreciate, for example, the rationality of some of Dora Fielding's child-rearing practices which intitially appeared strange to us.

We were temporary participant–observers entering the lives of our families, sometimes for a short visit and on other occasions for a whole day; at times we just talked to members of the families and at other times joined a birthday party, a family christening or other family celebrations. Initially for us, the research relationship was easier to handle if there was a mutually acceptable reason for the visit. Therefore we took photographs of her son for Ada Paterson, helped to ferry Elsie Barker and the children to the clinic, gave plants to Peter Martin, and were initially attracted to Dora Fielding, not only because she lived next to a 'problem family', but also because she was friendly and amusing and helped us to be at ease in a novel situation.

Rigorous research copes with this unease by having a special task for the subject to perform, for example, a questionnaire to be completed, an attitude scale to be filled in, or a laboratory test or experiment in which to participate. These may be seen as trivial, bizarre or insensitive games, divorced from the everyday life of the subjects, but at least the participants have clearly defined roles in relation to each other. We, on the other hand, had to establish a relationship in a short period of time, and in doing so we broke a cultural norm, namely, visiting people in their own homes. In the areas we studied, female neighbours did not visit when the man of the house was present, though members of the extended family did apparently visit at any time. And we were neither kin nor neighbour. There was an unease in our relationship because, although our families knew about 'surveys', the idea of long-term anthropological fieldwork was unfamiliar to them. We told each of our families that we were engaged in a research project into families experiencing problems, yet our work appeared to them to be nothing more than 'having a chat'. As the project progressed, so the context of the 'chat' changed; we began to reassess early impressions and early information, as the gap between us and the families narrowed.

The central problem in all research is that of validity, and our central problem is the veracity of the accounts presented in the following pages. In rigorous research the problem becomes one of statistical validity; care is taken to ensure that the instruments used are valid and reliable. But the highest level of statistical validity cannot compensate for distortion in the subject's answers. The usual hope is that by randomizing the sample, subject bias will be lessened. Our assumption was that, with involvement over time, many inconsistencies would be resolved and omissions rectified as respondents moved from presenting what they considered to be a socially desirable response to one which represented their own views. Thus, when Elsie Barker was asked how many brothers and sisters she had, her answer in the second interview was that she was the third child out of six, and some time later she told us that in fact she was the youngest of four. Ada Paterson told us on our second visit that she had three children, on the eleventh visit she mentioned a fourth and on the thirtieth gave us details of each of her six pregnancies. It may be that, at the beginning of our contact with her, Ada felt that her child-bearing record was no concern of ours; it may be that she had good reasons to omit mention of three of her children; whatever the reason, we were only given what became the consistent figure of six when she was confident in her relationship with us.

Any research which tries to recreate the past runs into the problem of bias through reinterpretation and rewriting of the data. We can all give the correct dates when various key events happened in our lives; the difficulty comes in explaining the motives for our actions. The past is so much a part of our present that it is impossible to view the motives for our actions without distorting the present. We are all able to present reasons why twenty years ago we got married, had children, left home or sought a divorce, but the explanations we give now are coloured by the knowledge of the consequences of that action, while at the time such consequences were part of the future.

As well as the inevitable bias arising from reconstructing the past, our methods were open to two further distortions. Each visit was written up as soon as possible; on many occasions we tape-recorded notes as we drove back from a visit. Nevertheless, no matter how immediate the write-up, we were still selecting and reconstructing. Nietzsche has a phrase which could stand as a guiding principle for all such research: 'It is a popular error to have the courage of one's convictions: rather it is a matter of having the courage to attack one's convictions.' We tried to employ this principle among ourselves both by demanding firm evidence of each other for conclusions which appeared tenuous to the other two and by searching for that one piece of evidence which would disprove our generalizations (Popper, 1969). We each discovered our own perceptual biases; for example, our notes would differ even in relation to estimates of how long we were actually with a particular family. It is customary to deal with these problems of partial report and inconsistencies by taking the fieldnotes back to the subjects for verification. We felt this was not always possible as many of our notes contained information which was private to the subject about other members of the family and we could never be sure to see the informant by himself. We did however, visit at times with the intention of finding out specific facts, of ironing out inconsistencies, or of confirming past stories, though such was the ever-changing world of our families that it was not always possible to direct attention to past events in the face of a present crisis.

The second possiblity of distortion lies in converting the fieldnotes into a final report. Our method of working was to hold regular meetings to discuss the accumulated evidence on a particular family. For these meetings all our fieldnotes would be grouped together under a number of categories such as biography, health, relationship with neighbours, finance, and child-rearing. Such categorization was sufficiently fluid to allow for the formation of new categories if we had data which was not being used up by our existing categories; and, although we applied the same major categories to each family, there were some headings which were relevant only to certain families and not to others. Discussions centred on the interpretation of fieldnotes, their relevance to our existing knowledge of the family, and our emergent explanations of the current position of the family. This final version is part of our continuing discussion; it is not to be read as a collection of findings where a percentage of the variance of deprivation has been apportioned to particular factors, but as our best account at a point in time. We have not solved the problems of validity, but we think we have recognized them and have adjusted our research strategy to minimize the more gross distortions.

While every attempt has been made to reduce bias in our research, we are also frequently asked what generalizations can be made on the basis of four families. We have attempted, where possible, to show the magnitude of a variable, for instance that there are 1·08 million children in families of five or more children and 1·1 million in one-parent families. But having said this, and having given an indication of where our families lie in the social spectrum, we are still left with the question of 'so what?'. Clearly not every large family is similar to the Barkers, any more than all one-parent families are like the Patersons. Nevertheless, the Barkers and Patersons exist and social policy must deal with them as particular families as well as including them in the general cases of large or one-parent families. The value of the detailed case study such as this is that it presents a testing ground for policy; the central questions are not only about the typicality of the families, but also about the way in which a national policy can influence the particular cases which this study describes.

We turn now to consider some more specific methodological problems. In our involvement with the Barkers most of our evidence came from Elsie. We did try to obtain a more detailed picture of Vince's life, but on almost every occasion we saw him alone, he was in the pub, club or at work; in each of these locations he already had clearly defined, public roles and he presented us with autobiographies which varied in some important respects in these different settings. Consequently, his evidence has to be seen in relationship to the context of its transmission; for example his account of life in the circus was given to us in his local pub in Bramwell where he was seen as an accomplished and amusing

story-teller. Part of his story is no doubt true, but the context of its telling
was fertile ground for embellishment. (Helling, 1976, argued that auto-
biographical accounts tend to be inconsistent because they are a blend of
personal history, relatively stable elements of self image, and self-
presentation which is a product of the specific interactive situation of the
interview). Ada Paterson provides a further example of the limitations
of our research strategy. We were unable to see her alone after Stan
started to live with her in her flat in Cardale; not knowing how much
Ada had told Stan about her past acted as a constraint on what we felt
we could refer to, and we were also prevented from obtaining Ada's
evaluation of life with Stan. When we first met Ada Paterson she was still
coming to terms with the recent death of her husband and was
preoccupied by financial problems and the desire to leave her house in
Bramwell. The present was so pressing on her that she could not discuss
the past until she had talked through the events of the funeral, the
welfare of her son and her plans for future happiness.

Our data is qualitative in that we have attempted in what follows to
present a view, as close as possible to the actors' subjective perceptions,
of the world of families coping with a variety of social problems. It
remains true, however, that our approach was more likely to highlight
individual and personality factors rather than structural ones, but we
hope that our prevailing interest in the dynamic interaction between
these two sets of factors may have helped to counteract any such
imbalance. In sum, we were seeking not so much to sympathize but to
empathize with our families, and at the same time we were attempting to
avoid the dangers of either romanticizing their plight or condemning
their behaviour.

We would also like to set our interpretive approach in the context of
other methods. There is no *one* royal road to truth in the social sciences
or to an understanding of the cycle of deprivation. All methods have
their strengths and weaknesses and all are, in varying degrees, messy and
unsatisfactory because life is messy and unsatisfactory. We do, however,
suggest that our preferred method may be particularly useful at an early
stage of an investigation of a problem, when it is unclear what the crucial
factors are. The crucial factors which emerge from such a detailed case
study as ours can later be tested to see if they are general by using survey
methods.

The Research Area
We carried out our fieldwork in Kindleton, our pseudonym for a
manufacturing town of about a quarter of a million inhabitants in the

heart of England. Industry has had its home there for more than two centuries and with the constant demand for labour and traditional skills, the people who live and work in the city have a distinct sense of belonging. In spite of the huge engineering works, the mines, the factories, and the gas-works, nowhere are you far from little farms or open land. The reclaimed slag heap gives way to the lines of terraces, and these in turn give way, at one moment to a green valley, at another, to the dusty yards of a brickworks.

There is a sense of self-containment about the area which various authors have remarked on from the 1930s to the present day. It is a separateness which has helped to preserve the strong feeling for tradition within the city. Recently, there has been much slum clearance, and people have been moved from the centre of the city to the new, peripheral estates, leaving isolated pockets of terraced housing. There have been bold and imaginative attempts to rescue the face of Kindleton from the ravages of industrial growth and within its admitted ugliness there is also beauty. From almost every part of the city it is still possible to sense the nearness of the countryside.

Since 1960 the city's population has declined slightly as young people have moved out into the surrounding region. This outflow has not been compensated for by any significant immigration either from other parts of the United Kingdom or from overseas. The age structure of the population is similar to that of Great Britain as a whole, but the social class distribution of the area is very dissimilar: the middle class group is only half the size of that for Great Britain as a whole while the proportion that is working class is correspondingly greater. The city has twice been unsuccessful in its application for intermediate development area status, largely because unemployment was low.

While there is considerable restriction on the range of opportunities offered in Kindleton, the chances of gaining employment are better than either those in the Midlands generally or those in Great Britain. The financial rewards for labour used to be less in the city than in the rest of the Midlands; but the wage policies of the mid 1970s, which tended to give fixed rather than percentage wage increases, have had the effect of bringing the average level of wages in the city closer to the national average.

One of the perplexing features of Kindleton is that despite a distinguished record of investment in education the city has one of the lowest rates in the country of young people voluntarily staying on for further or higher education. The explanations for the persistently low rate of staying-on can only be speculative. It has been suggested that the general high level of employment in the city has meant that there is no great pool of surplus labour so that new firms have not moved into the area. The absence of a large variety of careers may mean that children see little point in extending their education credentials, and so they follow traditional career patterns.

It has also been argued that local traditions are strong and that children see school ending at sixteen and work beginning. If this were the case, the administrative division of education at sixteen can only amplify the tradition. In the city the sixteen-year-old school-leaver cannot simply drift back to his old school to spend a year taking extra qualifications: he must register at a new institution. Whatever the variety of reasons needed to explain the low rate of staying-on in the area, our families do not see education as a powerful and central determinant of life chances.

Each of our families was housed in local authority accommodation, but only one of them was severely overcrowded, and that while living in Bramwell. Towards the end of our fieldwork, this family moved to a larger house in Elsmore (the effects of this change are described in Chapter 2). In general, housing in Kindleton is not a major problem, although some 40 per cent of the housing stock was built before 1914, a fact which may explain the high percentage of households without exclusive use of hot water, fixed bath and inside toilet. A study of local housing statistics highlighted both the relative disadvantage of those households in the private rented sector and the desirability of access to either council or owner-occupied accommodation. Each of our families had lived in rooms; that is, they had been dependent upon the private sector at some stage of their lives. It was beyond the resources of all of them to buy their own home and thus have a valuable asset to bequeath to their children.

The Four Housing Estates

We turn, finally, to see how each of the areas in which our families lived fits into the structure of the city. We do not present detailed descriptions of, or statistical tables for, each area because of our desire to protect the identity of the families. Each area was a council estate, with many identical houses, few trees or public gardens, and little colour to break up the feeling of anonymity. The estates had comparatively low rents so that there were greater numbers of families whose income was low either because of low wages, large families or physical incapacity.

Aulton

Aulton was one of the peripheral estates built by the local authority after the Second World War. Originally it provided accommodation for people affected by slum clearance projects. The estate gave an impression of space yet there was a certain bleakness about it. Its remoteness was reflected in the large number who had to travel to work by bus each day in contrast, to say, Bramwell where, in a way reminiscent of the 1930s in Kindleton, the majority still walked to work. The families we visited lived in one corner of the estate covered by the same enumeration district. As one would expect from relatively new council housing, the amenities in the homes were good: over 90 per cent of all households had exclusive use of amenities, and the average housing density was less than one person per room. If we look at car ownership as an index of living standards in 1971, we see that more than three-quarters of the households did not own a car.

The estate itself was built in lines of semi-detached houses with front and back gardens. There were no trees. A pub and social club was a source of entertainment for the adult population, and a weekly youth club disco for the teenagers. There was a playground for the children. Behind all this loomed slag heaps and another estate. Local schools, shops and a church completed the picture; there was no doctor's clinic on the estate itself, but one close by.

The houses in our part of Aulton were not considered as attractive as some others on the estate. The interiors were being modernized and were now much better than in the old days when Dora Fielding and her mother (see Chapter 5) had slept with dogs in their bedrooms for fear of the rats. The new houses, said several mothers, were lovely inside and were centrally-heated, but they were hot in the summer and you could hear your neighbours. Poor sound-proofing seemed to be a continual cause for complaint among the families and their neighbours in the local authority housing we visited.

Some of the mothers felt that those in authority were 'against' the people of Aulton or that others deprived them of goods and services. For instance one mother complained that finance firms would not accept her as soon as they heard her address. Another said that the local nursery school was biased against children from the estate unless one of the parents was a policeman or a nurse. Another claimed that you could not get a telephone, as the GPO said it was a high risk area. In this case, however, there was some doubt as to the reliability of what this woman said: another resident already had a telephone which she hid from social security officials. It *was* possible to obtain hire purchase agreements if you lived on the estate, just as you could rent televisions; but of course if you were a bad payer, or the company suspected that you were, you might have difficulty in finding a firm who would accept you.

Several mothers talked of the disadvantages of having to send away for furniture and other items which then had to be paid for by weekly instalments. Others talked of shoddy workmanship. The problem they perceived was not that of living in a stigmatized area, but of having one's economic choices greatly reduced in the first instance by the smallness of one's income and then again by needing goods before one had the money to pay for them. Moreover the families found it difficult to travel to the large stores which had relatively lower prices, because the estate was on the periphery of the city.

There was some marked unfriendliness among families on the estate. For example one young girl of mixed racial parentage was twice called a 'black bastard' by women neighbours; once a fight ensued. One of the problems in fieldwork was that the bonds among members of a friendly group or network were strong, but so also was their antipathy towards other families to whom they did not speak. One could not move easily across this gulf and at the same time maintain friendships in the first group.

The schools were also the scene of difficulties and animosities. New children going to the upper school were alleged to be given a difficult time by the older pupils: there were rumours of children having their heads held down in the lavatories. One girl, whom we knew, had her raincoat taken from the school cloakroom; it was later found in a dustbin. There was also the disgust and shame which some children felt when they caught head-lice from one another; one mother said that she always put powder in her children's hair to prevent their catching head-lice; another described how her little girl would cry if you mentioned that she had caught them. Vandalism was common. Dora Fielding (see Chapter 5), for instance, complained of the noise which children made throwing stones at the next door house when it became empty. The Mothers and Toddlers Club, which was held in a school building, had its own iron box of toys which was locked and barred so that no young people could break into it. When visits were made to the Mothers and Toddlers Club, the cloakrooms for this building had no running water, soap or towels for the basins and no paper for the toilets.

The area was virtually without old people, whereas the largest age group was the ten to fourteen-year-olds. Given the physical isolation of the estate, and its general lack of facilities (despite a youth club), it was not suprising that members of this age group frequently drew the attention of the police.

Bramwell

Bramwell was close to the centre of Kindleton. It was a small council estate which had been built adjacent to traditional, nineteenth century, 'two up, two down' terraced housing. The area had a unity and an identity which was reflected in the active community association and in the well frequented public houses, which were small and cosy, each serving its own local clientele. On the occasions we went with members of our families to the pubs, we were always introduced to everybody and came away with the feeling we had joined a private party rather than having merely spent the evening in an anonymous public house. In this older property, just over half of the households had exclusive use of all amenities and just under half had an inside toilet. The lower housing density was a consequence of the great number of one and two person households in Bramwell in comparison with Aulton.

Cardale

Cardale was part of an estate of some 15,000 inhabitants. The estate was built in the mid 1950s with the aim was that it should become a self-sufficient unit. It consisted of a residential area complete with churches, a community centre, schools, shops, games areas for infants, youths and persons of more mature years, and public open spaces to provide a breath of the country. A previous research study of the estate in which Cardale is situated argued that the estate was too big for a sense of neighbourhood identity to develop. Its facilities were few, and though it had a central shopping area, the design of the estate made it inaccessible to many of those who lived there.

As one would expect, almost all the households had exclusive use of all basic amenities. A housing density of less than one person per room was slightly better than that for Aulton, but not as good as that of Bramwell or Elsmore. This was an area comprised predominantly of young people, and the elderly were much under-represented.

Elsmore

Elsmore was the area we knew least, as one of our families moved there only towards the end of our fieldwork. Like Cardale and Aulton it was a large estate, with almost all the houses being owned by the local council. It was older than the other estates, having been built in the 1930s. More than three-quarters of the households had sole use of all basic amenities, though just over 10 per cent were without use of an inside toilet.

This, then, was the world in which our families lived. It was not one of severe overcrowding, housing decay or exploitation. It was a traditional world, where people had strong loyalties to their own community, where friendship and family networks overlapped through long histories of association. In this established world it was more difficult to identify the nature of deprivation. The problems which our families experienced were less easy to disentangle, as they were not so obviously the fault of the environment, of living amidst slum property, or of experiencing the rootlessness caused by rapid industrial change. Kindleton is a supportive community, yet each of our families had different and intransigent problems, and to these we now turn.

2 The Barkers: A Large Family

In Chapter 1 we explained that the Barkers were one of the two families which we contacted after discussions with the local Social Work Department. We were first introduced to them by their social worker, Hilary Minton, and we subsequently visited them in their own home over ninety times over a period of eighteen months. Fieldwork with this family was extended for longer than had been originally intended for two main reasons: the Barkers moved house from Bramwell to Elsmore and, at the same time, their eldest daughter began absconding from the Children's Home where she had been placed under a care order. We were anxious to see how both of these events would change the basic pattern of their lives which we had observed until then.

In the main our contact over this period consisted of visiting Vince and Elsie Barker in their own home or having a pint with Vince in one of the local pubs. We also attended Mr Barker's birthday party; one of us was invited to become a godparent to their youngest child whose first steps were witnessed later in the year; we saw the family celebrate Guy Fawkes night; we visited the mine where Mr. Barker worked to gain some impression of his working conditions; we were invited to their wedding anniversary party; and we helped them move house.

When we first met the Barkers, they were living in Bramwell, two doors away from Ada Paterson, in a rather dingy street of red-bricked, terraced houses belonging to the local council. The small community of Bramwell is bounded on two sides by large industrial works and a long-disused canal, and on a third side by a major trunk road which was less than a hundred yards from the Barkers' front door. A small wooden fence protected a tiny garden, the central point of which was a dried up rose bush set in a sea of black earth and discarded toys. While Ada Paterson, the subject of Chapter 3, lived as a widow with her seven-year-old son in one house, there were six children and two adults living in the Barkers' home, which was the same size. Downstairs consisted of a living room, kitchen, bathroom, pantry, coal house and outside toilet.

The living room, as can be seen from Figure 2.1, was no more than thirteen feet by nine feet four inches, giving each person a living space of less than four square feet; and that calculation omits the space which was taken up by the furniture, the fireplace, the baby's pram and the television set. Upstairs, Vince, Elsie and the newly-born baby, John, slept in one bedroom; in the other, Alice, who was two years old when we first met the family, slept in a single bed, while her older sister, Julie, aged

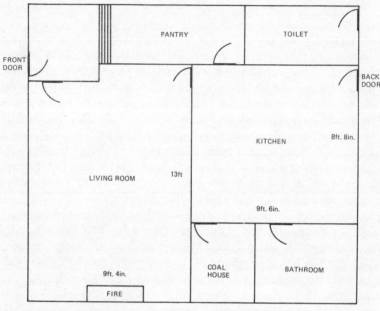

Notes

The toilet could only be reached by going outside the back door.

The floor area of the living room was 121.3 sq. ft. for two adults and six children under the age of seven. Spencer (1973, p. 84) quotes the space standards for statutory overcrowding from the 1957 Housing Act and he writes that they 'are accepted as representing an extremely low standard'. The standards permit two persons to live in a room with a floor area of 110 sq. ft. or more.

Figure 2.1   Plan of Barkers' House

six, and her brother Eddie, aged three, shared a double bed. In a little box-room, there was only space for a single bed which was shared by Steve, aged seven, and Tom, aged five. When the oldest girl, Tracy, then aged fourteen, spent an occasional weekend with her parents away from the Children's Home, they were nine people sleeping in two bedrooms and a tiny box-room. The floors in these bedrooms were covered with linoleum which the parents had found in empty houses nearby which were awaiting demolition because subsidence had produced large, visible cracks in the outer walls. Similar structural defects began appearing in the walls of houses in the street where the Barkers lived, and their occupants were transferred elsewhere as our fieldwork progressed. Elsie pointed out to us cracks of a less serious nature which started to affect her own home. Until they were finally pulled down, the condemned houses provided a fascinating but highly dangerous playground for all the local children. Moreover, both Ada Paterson's home and the Barkers' were damp and periodically infested by cockroaches.

No matter how hot it was outside, there was always a well-banked fire inside, something which in this part of the country is a sign of good house-keeping. On the walls there were pictures of children with huge eyes brimming over with tears. The furniture was old and battered, apart from a colour television set. The mantelpiece held photographs of the children taken at school, of the parents' wedding and of their subsequent two-day honeymoon.

To describe the Barkers as officially overcrowded (having more than 1.5 persons per room) would be an understatement. For the earliest and most enduring impression made on all three of us while visiting the family was of being cramped and confined. One report included the remark: 'I was literally scared of stepping on a child or an animal' while another had the comment: 'I didn't think I could bear it much longer' (after a visit of one hour). We found the conditions particularly difficult when we returned to the family after a short break from fieldwork. Of course, it was not only the overcrowding which produced this effect in us, but also the noise of the children fighting, of their mother shouting, and of the television blaring; and, added to all this, was the intense heat from the fire.

We, however, were only visitors: the Barkers had to live day after day, month after month in these conditions. The living room felt particularly cluttered in the winter months, when rain forced the children to play indoors. As the kitchen was so small (nine foot six inches by eight foot eight inches), the family were obliged to eat every meal on their knees in the living room. The lack of space also prevented the children from playing with what toys they had; so the doll's house which belonged to Julie and the boys' car racing track had to be left upstairs, unused.

There were also a number of accidents in the home during our period of contact. Although the parents had a strong fireguard, Julie fell while climbing over her younger brother and sisters and received a bad burn along one arm. On another occasion Alice pushed the fireguard over onto her mother's legs; fortunately neither was injured; Elsie already suffered from varicose veins and other pains in her legs from being on her feet too much. Less seriously, perhaps, the dog knocked Elsie's radio into the fire; the radio, which had given Elsie much enjoyment, was not replaced because of lack of money.

The Barkers lived in this house in Bramwell for six years before an exchange was arranged by which they moved to Elsmore. Elsie, however, could remember a period in her life when she had lived in even more trying circumstances. That was when she, her first husband, and her six-year-old son, Matthew, had lived in a car for six months. This, however, anticipates an orderly presentation of the biographies of Elsie and her husband.

Vince Barker's Biography

Before presenting Vince's account of his life, we feel we must, for the record, express our doubts about its truthfulness. Apart from certain inconsistencies which we were never able to resolve, we suspect that what follows represents a particular image of himself which Vince was keen for us to accept.

Vince said that he had been born just after the start of the Second World War of a Welsh, Roman Catholic mother and a man in the forces. His parents soon drifted apart, and Vince claimed he did not meet his father until he was eighteen when a man approached him in a pub and asked him his name. According to Vince, the man then produced a marriage certificate and a photograph to prove his relationship with Vince who became convinced of his authenticity. Vince did not say how his father had traced or recognized him.

When he was five years old, Vince's mother moved to southern England and began an association with a local miner. Vince described the period when he and his mother were on their own as happy, but the arrival of the stepfather, who had 'no time for' Vince, put an end to that. A half-sister, Hazel (see Vince's family tree in Figure 2.2), soon arrived on the scene and shortly afterwards the family moved to a mining village where Vince began to get into trouble. In his own eyes, the root cause of his delinquency was the treatment meted out by his stepfather. At the age of eleven he was put on probation for three years for stealing nails and a lock from a building site with some other boys of his own age. His next conviction was for assault. Vince recalled his feelings about this sentence by saying that no sooner had he gone into long trousers at the age of fourteen than he was suddenly forced back into short ones by being sent to a detention centre. When his parents failed to visit him at weekends, he began absconding frequently but he was always caught very quickly.

Vince attended the local secondary modern school, which was attached to an older grammar school. He remembered mixing with the grammar school children only at play-time and dinner-time; *they* were forced to wear uniforms, but there was no such ruling for the secondary modern children. In Vince's estimation, the only important difference in treatment had been that the grammar school boys played rugby and the secondary modern boys football; the grammar school girls had played hockey and basketball and their secondary modern counterparts were only allowed to play rounders. Vince himself was always getting into trouble at school for either being late or being absent. The only school subjects he was good at were woodwork, metalwork and religious instruction. He attended church regularly as a young boy and still claimed to enjoy biblical films or stories.

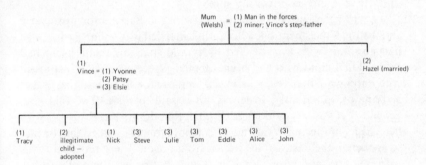

Figure 2.2   Vince Barker's Family Tree

When he left school, he tried to join the armed services but failed certain eye tests. Instead, he began working at a local circus because one of the workers had vouched for him in court and had taken responsibility for him. Vince started following the circus on its annual circuit from Birmingham to Nottingham, to Hull and Stratford-upon-Avon. He had loved the excitement, the noise and the colour of the circus, and the dangerous work which he undertook to impress the girls. He had enjoyed making them scream and laugh: 'I had some good screws', he said.

During the winter months, when he was employed in painting and repair work, Vince began associating with a young girl, Yvonne, who had been in care for most of her life. Yvonne used to hitch-hike over to see Vince and spend the weekend with him. Once she set off for home after drinking heavily with Vince during the day and, on the return journey, she was attacked and sexually assaulted. The following day the police questioned Vince, as he was her boy-friend, but the case was never cleared up.

Yvonne was described by Vince as 'something of a country girl', who had lived on farms all her life and who was being fostered out at the time Vince married her, when he was twenty-one and she seventeen and pregnant. Their first child, Tracy, was born while Vince was serving an eighteen-month prison sentence for theft. Vince explained that the charge had actually been for armed robbery, but all this had meant was that he and his two co-defendants had had one knife among them. Vince was now in his early twenties and sporting a Tony Curtis haircut; when Elsie, his present wife, saw a photograph of him from this period she said: 'It sent shivers down my spine.'

We had been engaged in fieldwork with the Barkers for just over a year before Vince mentioned that, while married to Yvonne, he had also had an affair with a girl called Patsy and that this relationship had resulted in a child who had been adopted. Vince eventually lost touch with Patsy who, in his eyes, had been far more fun to be with than either Yvonne or, apparently, Elsie. As Vince said to Elsie: 'I've told you, haven't I? If Patsy was to come through that door now, I'd be off with her.' Elsie, muttering 'You and your fancy women', agreed that he had so spoken in the past. On his release from prison, Vince returned to his wife, Yvonne, and baby daughter, Tracy; but he left them after a few months as he 'had had a bellyfull'. Later, we were to understand that by this phrase Vince meant that his wife had been unfaithful to him while he had been in prison. Some five years later, he returned to his family and a second child, Nick, was born. But as Yvonne's infidelity continued, he left them for good and later divorced her.

As well as working for the travelling circus, Vince had tackled a number of other jobs at different times in his life. When he was fifteen, he had trained for a year in the mines as a face worker; three years later he gave up the job after a serious pit accident which has left permanent scars. As a result of this accident he had been in hospital for some months and off work for even longer. When he fully recovered, he joined the building trade before returning to work with the circus. In his late twenties, he was again working as a builder's labourer in Kindleton. While in the city, he met and began living with Elsie who was a year younger. After two miscarriages and the birth of one child, and while

Elsie was pregnant with the second, they were married in the local registry office.

Vince's work and life style

In the first years of his marriage to Elsie, Vince had a number of jobs in between periods of unemployment. While working as a builder's labourer in the early 1970s, an injury severed part of one of his fingers, and he was off work for six weeks. In compensation he was offered a lump sum or a regular weekly payment; he chose the lump sum of £200.

Early on in our fieldwork, Vince once described the local pit where he worked, as a 'hell-hole'; but it became clear that he loved the excitement and ever-present danger of his work and he preferred it to the 'boredom' of work in the local factories. The visit we made to the colliery where Vince was employed convinced us that, despite modern mechanization, hard, physical labour and thick, penetrating dust are still very much part of the modern miner's job. In the previous year there had been over two hundred accidents in Vince's colliery, a rate slightly higher than the average for the county, but in turn considerably less than the average for Great Britain. Vince has had his share of minor injuries to his back, feet and hands (these do not appear in the official statistics because he failed to report them), but some of his workmates have received broken bones, dislocated shoulders and head injuries.

Vince did complain about shiftwork. The work of the colliery was organized by a continuous three-shift system, the hours of which were from 6 am to 2 pm, from 2 pm to 10 pm, and from 10 pm to 6 am. Of the three, Vince preferred the night shift. Earlier in his working life he had become accustomed to working at night and had discovered that this was the time of day when he felt best. His team, however, was expected to work in a three-week cycle, moving from one shift to the next at the end of each week. Vince disliked the early shift (for which he had to be out of the house by 5 am): he claimed that he never managed to sleep for more than four hours before an early shift because of waiting for the sound of the alarm. As a result he took every opportunity to switch shifts with his workmates. He regularly worked two afternoon shifts and one night shift.

Both Vince and Elsie noticed that when Vince re-entered the mines they quarrelled far more during weeks when Vince had to work the early shift because he would return home exhausted and bad-tempered. Elsie was ambivalent about the night-shift: sometimes she would lie awake wondering whether Vince had been injured, while at other times she enjoyed going to bed early in a house which was peaceful once Vince had left for work. It was, however, the system of shiftwork in general, with its irregular and unsociable hours, about which Elsie complained most, for she believed this to be the cause of her being left alone, without support from her husband, to cope with their six children. In fact the organization of Vince's work was partly (but only partly) responsible for Elsie feeling like a prisoner, trapped in her own home; when he was not working, he often chose to sleep or to be at the pub, and thus rarely helped her. One compensation which the whole family derived from Vince's work was the ten hundredweight of coal delivered to his home for every twenty days worked. He very often sold some of this coal when money was short. A less agreeable part of the job was that he sometimes had to work a double shift within twenty-four hours when, for example, underground fires broke out. Once, an outbreak lasted for one week and Vince was able to snatch only from three to four hours sleep each day.

At the time of our study, Vince was a man in his late thirties of considerable charm, as interesting to men as he was attractive to women. He described himself as an 'adventurer', as a tough hard man who could walk into a strange pub and, after two drinks, have the whole bar in uproar. On another night, he might drink eleven or twelve pints on his own without speaking or being spoken to by anyone. Vince was the kind of man who was very much in his element in a pub, where he appeared to be far more debonair and far more at home than he was in his own house. Certainly he was much more interested in the role of local man-about-town than in the role of father or husband. He enjoyed the reputation of being a rogue male, a snappy dresser and a big spender; without doubt he was a generous host who bought rounds of drinks and passed plates of food around the pub at his birthday parties and wedding anniversaries. In sum, Vince was a married man with seven children who miraculously regained his bachelor status as soon as the pubs opened.

Vince liked his pint. His average lunch-time consumption was between four and five pints, and in the evenings he often drank twice that amount. He and an eighteen-year-old friend, Brian, claimed that each of them had drunk twenty-five pints of beer in one session. When this claim was questioned, it was admitted that some glasses of Pernod were included in the total. Vince's beer belly explained why he was two stone overweight. He also reserved his scorn for one of Elsie's male relatives who neither smoked nor drank – 'a dog's life' was Vince's comment. He himself smoked between sixty and eighty cigarettes per week.

We noted that Vince's closest male friends were much younger than he; they were men in their late teens or early twenties who looked up to him. Although he had many bar acquaintances, Vince appeared to be less self-assured in the company of men of his own age and we gained the impression from his workmates that they did not take him and his constant string of jokes too seriously. During one of the family's financial crises we asked Elsie whether Vince could borrow money from one of his mates, and she replied, 'He hasn't got any mates.'

The ability to deliver crushing retorts, to indulge in smart repartee, was highly valued not only by Vince but also by his workmates and other drinking companions. Vince excelled at this art, on one occasion explaining his belief that it was important to have the ability to string people along. He also thought that in conversation you needed 'to be fast. You've got to get your answer in quick.' Waving across the street to one of his favourite old haunts, he explained its closure and broken windows by its impending demolition and then added to the delight of his audience, 'They only serve draught beer over there now.' At their wedding anniversary party, Elsie was carrying round plates of food and offered Vince a salmon roll: 'I'd better take it', he replied, 'it's the only roll I'm going to get tonight.' On another occasion, Vince had been delighted by the spontaneous repartee of his favourite son, Tom, who was then five years old. The boy had been imitating the star of a television programme and boasting to his father that he too had 'bionic arms and legs'. When Vince had heard enough of his prattle, he gave Tom a clip round the ear. Immediately, Tom had retorted: 'I haven't got ruddy bionic ears.' At times Vince's wit had an aggressive, cutting edge, the object of which seemed to be to show how smart, how omniscient he was, compared with his less clever and more gullible wife and children. It is not difficult to understand why he frequently sought to better us in conversation, but in outsmarting his young children, he often left them looking foolish and hurt.

Vince also enjoyed telling stories of his involvements with the police: how he had tricked a policeman into believing that he had a bad cold, when stopped as a suspected drunken driver and how he had received four endorsements, been fined over £50 and finally banned from driving for three years. The stories consisted of exciting car chases while under the influence, with Vince suddenly changing direction and so crashing into cement bollards or other cars.

Throughout the period of our fieldwork, Vince was in one form of trouble or another. One Saturday evening he went to the assistance of his landlord who had been booted in the face by a young customer. Vince threw a punch at the boy, missed and hit the publican straight in the eye. He also took revenge on the group of youngsters who had beaten up his eighteen-year-old working and drinking companion,

Brian. Vince marched into a circle of some twelve boys, called out Brian's main attacker and laid him low without the others daring to interfere. Brian had immense respect for Vince's physical prowess and courage, both of which came to his aid in a fight with no less than 'five men'. This scrap landed Vince in the police cells where he was detained overnight. He returned to his family after five o'clock the next evening, sporting two black eyes and claiming to have been kicked in the 'goolies'. Talking about the fight, Vince first assured us that he had given as good as he had received, and then commented on the lack of excitement in his everyday life. He felt the need for things to happen or the need to make them happen just to prove that he was alive and enjoying himself.

Vince's search for excitement included not only drinking and fighting but also sexual adventures. Twice during our fieldwork Vince talked of sexual encounters with women whom he had met in local pubs and night clubs. We also learned very early in our fieldwork that Vince had spent £60 on a projector so that he could show blue films, which he kept urging us to see and which turned out to be, technically and artistically, of the poorest and crudest type. Vince tried to show these films to his mates at the colliery's social club but the committee refused him permission, a decision which he thought stuffy and conservative. His girlie magazines or 'comics', as he euphemistically called them, were kept on the top of a dresser where they were found one day by the children who were not allowed to read them. Elsie, who claimed to have received no sex education from either her parents or her school, was very embarrassed by the magazines and the films which had her racing from the room with crimson cheeks. Vince's openness about all sexual matters never failed to embarrass her. Once, as he left to join the afternoon shift, he said to her (perhaps for our benefit): 'Now don't forget. No nightie tonight!' At times he tried to create, with us as his audience, an image of himself as a 'randy lad'; he also complained of Elsie's lack of sexual response in recent years. Elsie had lost interest in this aspect of their relationship as a result of exhaustion, depression, continual pregnancy and resentment at being kept short of money and help.

Elsie Barker's Biography

Elsie was born in Kindleton in the early 1940s. Both her father and mother came from an area of high unemployment and from very large families; her mother, for instance, was one of thirteen children. Her father, who was a miner for most of his working life, died a few years ago in his late fifties, having suffered from bronchitis, '10% dust in his lungs' (pneumoconiosis), and a heart condition. His deteriorating health forced him to leave the mines. He then worked at less demanding jobs, but even these became too much for him. Because of his ill-health he was unemployed for the last four years of his life. When we first met Elsie, her mother was sixty-one and had not worked for sometime, as she had had a stroke some ten years earlier and currently suffered from heart trouble. Elsie was the youngest of four children, although when she first listed her siblings, she appeared to be the third in a family of six. Elsie later explained that the three girls, who were ten years younger than herself, were in fact the children of her parents' first child, Brenda (see Elsie's family tree in Figure 2.3). For reasons we shall shortly explain, Elsie at first omitted all mention of Brenda, giving us instead the names of her two brothers, Colin and Ian, and of Brenda's three daughters, Marie, Kathy and Clare.

Brenda, who was born when her mother was seventeen, gave birth to her three daughters before she was married and all three girls were brought up by their grandmother, so much so that Elsie had always thought of them and continued to think of them as sisters rather than nieces. At the age of thirty, Brenda married Tony, a soldier who, the family alleged, was looking for a home rather than a wife. Brenda did not take her daughters with her when she married because her mother had reared them as her own. She and Tony produced no children, a barrenness for which she was held responsible by him despite the evidence of her earlier fertility. The marriage continued to deteriorate and Brenda eventually committed suicide.

The pattern of teenage mothers conceiving illegitimate children was continued by two of Brenda's three daughters. Marie, the oldest girl, was married with three children and her life was relatively trouble-free, compared with those of her sisters; and yet her husband was temporarily out of work and the family were deeply in debt as a result. Kathy, the middle girl, gave birth to two illegitimate children, the first of which was adopted on her grandmother's orders; the second, a little boy, was rejected by Kathy's husband, and so lived with his great-grandmother and only visited his mother during the day. Kathy and her husband had two other children, the first of whom was born just before they were married; both of these children were accepted by him. He worked hard as a bus conductor and together they built-up, in Elsie's words, a 'beautifully decorated home with fitted carpets'; the marriage, however, was turbulent and unstable, according to Elsie, and Kathy was punched when they rowed. As a young girl, Kathy ran away from home before she left school and was put on probation. She broke the probation order

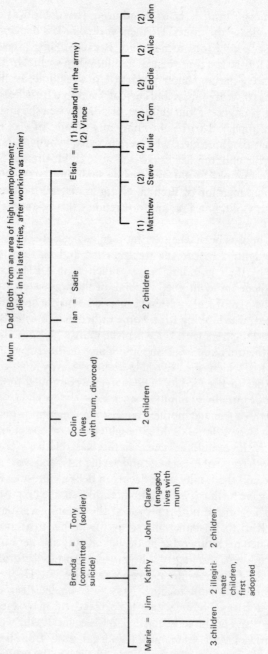

Figure 2.3 Elsie Barker's Family Tree

by running away again and living in a Salvation Army home where she was taught to be a nanny, a career she had always hankered after, but which her grandmother opposed. Clare had twice been engaged, was still unmarried, and lived with her grandmother.

Elsie's elder brother, Ian, led a reasonably harmonious life with his wife and two children; but her eldest brother, Colin, was divorced and he and his two children lived with his mother as he had always done. Colin was some ten years older than Elsie, who remembered him as being very kind to her when she was a little girl. When she was living in Bramwell, however, she complained that he let her walk the mile and a half back and forth to her mother's house in Elsmore, pushing a pram full of washing and with her young children trailing behind her, although he had a car and could have given her a lift. Elsie's complaint was that it never occurred to him to offer her a lift, whereas he had always been thoughtful in his dealings with his other sister, Brenda. Elsie felt that she had been and even now was the black sheep of her family. For example, she was the only one whom her father punished, and she described herself as 'a right varmint' as a young girl. While she lived at Bramwell, she believed that her family, particularly her mother, had shunned her because of Vince's prison record. But later, when they lived close to one another, Elsie visited her mother regularly and talked about her mother's complaints that Elsie's children did not come to visit her.

As a child, Elsie recalled being far closer to her father than her mother. Her Dad used to hand over his wages to her Mum who in turn gave him his pocket money. Similarly, when Elsie began working in a factory for £2.15s. per week, she was allowed to keep 15s. for herself to buy clothes and other personal items, but gave the rest to her mother. Elsie attended the local primary school but was not entered for the 11 + exam; she supposed that she must not have been considered clever enough. She had liked school until this point, but at her secondary modern she lost interest in school work because, she alleged, the children repeated the same lessons over and over again. Her poor level of achievement in school was partially a result of a number of illnesses which affected her hearing; first she had quinsy (inflammation of the throat) and then, at the age of ten, serious sinus problems which left her hearing impaired. The condition was not, however, noticed at school until one teacher realized that Elsie could not hear her watch. But by this time she was already attending special reading classes. She was given drops and other medical treatment to prevent her ears from being 'all bunged up', but she never recovered the lost ground. We noted that when she suffered from a heavy cold, her ears became affected so that she could not hear properly.

She was embarrassed about her poor educational skills and was forced to send her children to their father for help with their spelling or their school work generally. The only subject she enjoyed and was good at was netball.

When she left school, Elsie wanted to train as a hairdresser but her mother would not let her because the starting wage was too low. Elsie mentioned that she still resented her mother for this because it was the kind of job she could have continued after her marriage. Her relationship with her mother had always been stormy. When, for example, she was refused permission to go dancing at the age of fifteen, she put her fist through every pane of glass in her mother's kitchen. On another occasion she hit her mother and was given 'a good hiding' by her father. Elsie readily confessed that she had always had 'a terrible temper'. Elsie was convinced that her daughter, Alice, had inherited this ferocious temper, for she too used to go purple in the face with rage and frustration.

When she was sixteen and pregnant, Elsie married a soldier. The marriage lasted nine years, but resulted in the birth of only one son, Matthew: 'Nine years married and only one baby', Elsie said in criticism of her former husband. To this Vince promptly and proudly added: 'Now seven years married and six children.' When she was first married, Elsie had had to live in her mother-in-law's home, which, she felt, had put her in an awkward, inferior position. She was bitter that in her case, unlike that of all her siblings, the norm of starting married life in the house of the bride's mother had been broken. She spoke as though beginning married life at Mum's was the *proper* way to proceed. Quarrels soon drove the young couple out, but then Elsie often found herself alone with the baby in a strange town, while her husband was away on exercises and manoeuvres. For a long time she knew that her marriage was not working but she decided to persevere. When her husband, however, was released from the Army because of a nervous skin complaint, they had nowhere to live and so they went to Elsie's mother's house. After a month, there was a quarrel and Elsie's mother threw them out. For six months, Elsie, her husband, and Matthew, who was six years old at the time, lived in a car, while they walked the streets during the day, searching for accommodation. Eventually Matthew had a fit which was blamed by their doctor on the strain imposed by their living conditions. They acquired a council flat, but Elsie's situation finally became intolerable when her husband started beating her up. She left him and her son and returned to her mother. The fact that it was *she* who ran out of her first marriage continued to weigh heavily with her and strongly influenced her decision to remain with Vince. Matthew visited her from time to time, although Vince had always refused to give him a home; recently, the boy had begun stealing small sums of money from her purse so that he could go to football matches. As a consequence Vince ordered Elsie to ban Matthew from further visits. The latest news of him she had was that he had joined the Army on becoming sixteen, just as his father had done.

Shortly after the break with her first husband, Elsie met Vince in Kindleton. Previously, Vince had been going out with Elsie's niece, Kathy, and even at one point had thought that Elsie might be Kathy's mother. He then turned his attentions to Elsie who had two miscarriages before bearing him an illegitimate son, Steve. When she discovered she was pregnant with Steve, she left home and began living with Vince until their previous marriages were dissolved. Elsie divorced her first husband on the grounds of cruelty, and was seven months pregnant with Julie when she married Vince. Four more children followed in as many years – Tom, Eddie, Alice and John.

Elsie's work and life style
When we met her, Elsie was a woman in her mid-thirties whose body had become exhausted after nine pregnancies, eight of which had been very closely spaced, but she had a young, handsome red face with beautiful teeth and a lovely smile. She had varicose veins in her legs which were usually bare, and she suffered from high blood pressure,. Only twice did we record in our reports that she had found time to spend on her personal appearance: once when a neighbour cut and permed her hair (she spent 57p on this) for the wedding anniversary party, and another time when she wore a lilac two-piece suit, borrowed from her mother, to attend a local festival.

Her daily round of chores included two full washing lines every day. She first soaked the clothes in the bath, which made her hands raw, and then she stored the clothes, again in the bath, which prevented its being used. Her ring finger in particular became very sore, but Vince would not let her take the ring off. When the old-fashioned washing machine broke down, she had to trundle the washing in a pram for a mile and a half to her mother's house. If relations with her mother were strained, she washed everything by hand at home every second day. In bad weather, the clothes were left to dry in the bathroom, which again became unusable. Elsie then ironed the clothes on top of the washing machine. In addition, she swept the rooms clean every morning without the aid of a vacuum cleaner as her own was so old that it had broken down. Later she bought a new vacuum cleaner through a mail-order catalogue, and when this broke down, she could not get the parts to repair it. There were also eight people to be fed three times a day, and Elsie had neither refrigerator nor freezer. Moreover, at one stage Elsie had three children under three years of age and three others to get to school, six children whom she had to make sure were washed etc.

It is, therefore, in no spirit of criticism of Elsie that we report that the children were often dirty and their clothes grubby. At times we noticed that the underclothes they wore beneath their pyjamas were grey; their feet and hands were sometimes not just unwashed but black with ingrained dirt. The children's bed linen was not washed too frequently; and, although all the children were enuretic, there were no rubber sheets on the beds. Elsie just could not even keep up with the washing.

Nick and Tracy

Steve was two years old, Julie was one, and Elsie was pregnant with Tom, when Vince received a telegram from his first wife, Yvonne, saying that she could no longer look after their children, Nick and Tracy. Vince went to meet her and returned with the two children. To quote Elsie, 'They were dumped on me without warning because their mother didn't want them.' Against the advice of her own mother, who warned that Tracy, who was eight, and Nick, three, would be too much for her, Elsie took the children in. Her home at the time, in Castle Street, consisted of one large, furnished room which they rented from a private landlord. Elsie, who was pregnant, Vince and their two children shared a kitchen and a bathroom with five other families. Tracy still had the marks on her arm of cigarette burns made by Yvonne's second husband, who was also alleged by Tracy to have produced the burn on Nick's hand with an iron. Within six months, however, of joining the Barker household, Nick died. Shortly afterwards, the Barkers moved to the council house in Bramwell, where we first met them.

With a history of a death in the family and of violence between husband and wife in addition, Elsie felt that the authorities were almost waiting for an excuse to take her children into care. Tracy was, in fact, taken into care, but we were unable to reconcile the differing testimony of all those involved in this decision. According to the officer in charge of Tracy's Children's Home, Tracy, 'bruised and battered', was brought into a place of safety by social workers. One eye was badly discoloured, her lips were cut, her nose and both her legs were bruised, and her back looked as though it had been strapped. Despite enquiries, it has never been finally established who was responsible for these injuries.

Elsie's account differed in many important particulars. She was quite open about the bad feeling between herself and her step-daughter which sometimes brought them to blows. In her view, this was caused by Tracy's increasing 'naughtiness' and rough treatment of the other younger children. According to Elsie, the girl neither kept herself nor her clothes clean; at times she was as black as 'that fire-back'. In their previous home in Castle Street, Elsie had to boil kettles to bathe the children, but, even having persuaded Tracy to get into the bath, she could not make her wash. To Elsie's mind, there was a malicious and spiteful streak in the girl – this was exemplified by her destruction of all the china figures Vince had given Elsie as presents and her discarding of good food such as sugar and bread. Elsie summed her up by saying she was 'an expert at manipulating adults' and she had been the cause of many a quarrel between Vince and herself. Indeed, Elsie said that Vince had been violent with her either because he was worried about Tracy or because she, Elsie, had spoken harshly to the girl.

As to the particular events which caused the social workers to intervene, Elsie's explanation was that she moved to hit Tracy who dodged out of the way, hitting her head on a door and so blackening her eye. Elsie felt that the child must have done something to make her eye worse because she knew that Hilary Minton, the social worker, was coming the following day. By then, her eye was huge and she played, as Elsie alleged she always did for the benefit of the social worker, her role of 'Cinderella', by going into the kitchen and pretending to do all the work of the household.

Elsie felt that the social work report was biased against her and in favour of Tracy. It spoke of Tracy as a 'drudge', who did more housework than was commensurate with her age and ability; it also said she was frequently absent from school because of being kept at home to look after younger children. The report emphasized Elsie's psychological inadequacies and ended by stressing how Tracy reminded Elsie of Vince's first wife, Yvonne, and so aggravated Elsie's feelings of insecurity in her own marriage. Elsie thought that such psychological theorizing was beside the point: it was Tracy who was the problem and neither Yvonne nor Elsie's relationship with Yvonne.

A care order was finally granted in court, where Vince apparently defended himself with confidence and some style. Hilary Minton suggested that Vince's earlier appearances in court had made him quite familiar with legal procedure. She, on the other hand, had felt nervous and inexperienced, especially when Vince had cross-questioned her.

Tracy was put in the care of the Social Work Department until her

eighteenth birthday. But exactly as her father predicted, she 'went from
bad to worse'. Before Tracy was finally taken into care, Hilary Minton
convinced Vince and Elsie of the importance of regular contact, even
arranging for one of them to telephone Tracy every Saturday at a
specific time. The Home, however, was over thirty-six miles from
Bramwell, the Barkers had no car, and the cost of travelling regularly
was prohibitive. They each telephoned twice in the first six months and
then not at all. Elsie, despite her poor command of written English, sent
Tracy four letters, received no replies and became discouraged, while
Vince said he did not write because he had no time. But, when he *did*
write to her, saying that they would not turn their backs on her, she
absconded the very day she received the letter and made her way back to
Bramwell. Vince made the train journey once to see her, while Elsie took
her mother on her first visit and three of the young children on the
second. Despite the high quality of care in the Home, Tracy's behaviour
continued to deteriorate.

On her arrival in the Home, Tracy was said to come under the
influence of older girls who involved her in shoplifting. Soon they were
all caught, taken to court and given conditional discharges. Tracy had
never been charged with stealing before this, although her father
admitted in court that she had been pilfering in the local shops at
Bramwell. Vince told us that they kept her in the house in an attempt to
prevent her getting into trouble, but the neighbours began talking of her
as a 'prisoner at home'. By the time she was fifteen, Tracy had been
expelled from the local comprehensive school (after a number of
exclusions and re-instatements), and a long series of abscondings from
the Home began. The abscondings led to further thefts and to sexual
encounters with older men. Even when it was explained to her that she
could easily become pregnant and that the men could be sent to prison
for having sex with a girl under the age of consent, Tracy's response was
fatalistic: 'It cannot happen to me.' It therefore became a matter of
urgency to prescribe the contraceptive pill for her, but, because of her
age, parental consent was necessary.

This was Hilary Minton's job and she readily secured the agreement
of Elsie, who also promised to broach the subject with Vince. Miss
Minton expected difficulties in convincing him, but he agreed straight
away. Vince also adopted a very sensible attitude towards Tracy's
boyfriends in preferring her to associate with boys of her own age rather
than with boys of eighteen or older. Elsie, however, told us that, when
Tracy was allowed home for a weekend, Vince paid her so much
attention, and so excluded the other children from their company, that

the children, and particularly Julie, became jealous. This caused Elsie to blurt out that she was no longer prepared to have Tracy at home for a weekend if her own children were to be pushed out: Vince hit her, just as he had previously done when they were fighting over Tracy. With this major exception, the weekends Tracy spent at home went reasonably well.

At the Children's Home, however, Tracy's behaviour continued to deteriorate. Unable to attend the local school because of her expulsion, she spent the day performing routine chores and threatening to abscond. Eventually it was decided to transfer her to a Community Home for girls. Vince's prediction that institutional care would only increase Tracy's difficulties was borne out. Tracy's maternal grandmother (whose regular visits, Vince now alleged, were his main reason for staying away) brought presents for her fifteenth birthday which purported to come from Tracy's mother, Yvonne. The presents reduced Tracy to tears and, asked what she would do with one of them, an apron, she replied that she would frame it. At this point, Hilary Minton had said to her, 'It must be very difficult for you being torn between two families like this.' Tracy had replied, 'I'm not. I'll never go back to my mother. Not after what she did to my father.' On one occasion Tracy ran away from the Home, and managed to get back to Vince and Elsie; she pleaded to be allowed to spend the weekend with them. All three of them were reduced to tears and the parents were tempted to give in, but then Elsie telephoned Hilary Minton. The next time she absconded, Tracy went instead to Elsie's mother, having spent the night with a girl-friend whose sister, a prostitute, was entertaining clients in another room. Vince missed one day's work looking for Tracy whom he then returned to the police. The other children had cried while witnessing this and had asked: 'Why has our Tracy got to be taken away?'

Marital Relationship

In the struggle to keep the children well-fed, healthy and entertained, what help did Vince give Elsie? Elsie's usual definition of a good husband was someone who earned plenty of money, who gave his wife presents, and most important of all, who was kind to her. How did Vince match up to this definition? At the beginning, the couple presented us with a united front, being kind and gentle with each other, and joking when they were unable to agree. In the early interviews, when they recounted their own biographies, Elsie was always very loyal to Vince and supported him in everything he said, being careful never to put him in the wrong. Very soon, however, resentment bubbled over in his absence.

Although Elsie reproached Vince for being unfaithful, violent, drunk, selfish and mean, she was still prepared to say that she 'thought the world of him'. On another occasion, she called him a 'bugger', but a likeable one. Vince, for his part, was not the kind of man to pay his wife compliments in public; it was not his style. Instead he either ignored her totally or made her the butt of his jokes. For example, he referred to her as 'rent-a-gob', and, more cruelly, as 'a fat slob'. But he twice brought home small presents (of a brush and comb set and of an ornamental coal-miner) for her.

One of the major causes of friction between them was sex and choosing the most appropriate form of contraception. Elsie's earliest explanations of her lack of interest in sex ('I haven't been much that way lately') tended to blame her contraceptive pills which Vince tried to throw on the fire one night because she wanted 'nothing to do with him'. On reflection, however, she thought that sheer exhaustion, resulting from looking after six children all day, was the more likely cause. She had had numerous arguments over contraception with Vince who for years had prevented her taking the pill and only the intervention of Hilary Minton had convinced him. The contraceptive pill, however, could not be a long-term answer to their problems because Elsie had become overweight and her blood pressure was so high that for over a year her doctor had been recommending that she stop taking it.

After the birth of John, Elsie's seventh child, the local health clinic offered to sterilize her without consulting her husband. But she had not dared to undergo the operation without his knowledge for she knew how deep-rooted his objections were. At the party to celebrate their wedding anniversary, Vince explained to the assembled company that he was simply not prepared to let Elsie be sterilized because she would then be able to gallivant all over town. Elsie listened in silence and did not defend herself publicly, but in private she railed against his continual, corrosive jealousy: she was so tired in the evenings, she explained, that she hadn't time for *him*, let alone other men. Once, he kept her out of bed until 3 am, waiting to see what man would come to collect a bicycle which had been left in their garden; he then remembered that a workmate had called to see him and had forgotten it. He particularly accused her of entertaining 'fancy-men' when he was working on the night-shift. Elsie called on Steve (who was seven at the time) to tell his father whether she had male visitors in his absence or not and he had denied the charge. She summed up her defence with the words 'I'm not *you*.'

Vince ended discussion of Elsie being sterilized by promising to have a vasectomy himself. Hilary Minton had persuaded him that if he were opposed to Elsie's sterilization such a move was the best solution to their problems. He took great delight, however, in telling us how he tried to embarrass the social worker every time she raised the topic. Eventually, in his account, she had asked him bluntly and directly what contraceptive methods they were using. He replied that they were using two – brewer's droop and coitus interruptus. When Hilary then questioned the safety of the latter method, he had agreed, saying: 'No, it's not safe because I've put on so much weight recently I find it difficult to roll over.' She persevered with her argument, however, and finally he borrowed the £15 from Elsie and went to the local hospital to have the operation under the auspices of the National Health Service. To his consternation, the doctor who interviewed him was 'a big Paki' and when he asked Vince to strip and began examining his genitals, Vince was unable to continue any further and raced from the room. He also backed up his opposition to the operation by citing the example of a fellow miner who was forced to take so much time off work as a result of a vasectomy that he had lost his job.

Having thus disposed of efforts to sterilize himself and Elsie, Vince began pestering her to have another baby now that she had had 'a bit of a break'. Elsie did not know how he could propose such a course of action when they had both been told that another child could seriously damage her health and when they both knew how stretched their finances were already. Vince, however, kept saying to her, 'Let's have Henry VIII', and Elsie thought that he wanted to keep her 'tied' to the house by means of another baby. She herself remained opposed to the idea, but she also knew that it was dangerous for her to continue taking the pill. She claimed to be unable to stand up to her husband in a matter of this importance out of fear of his temper.

Elsie often spoke of being punched or in some way physically assaulted by her husband. When she was pregnant with Alice, for example, Vince had 'kicked her from one end of the garden to the other'. Their next-door neighbours had heard her screams but only Annie, and not her husband, had gone to Elsie's aid. Annie, who also gave us her account of the incident, had shouted to Vince that he would not dare hit *her*, which he promptly did while continuing to kick Elsie. Eventually the police arrived but Elsie sent them away. She had been surprised not to lose the baby. There was also the occasion when he struck her on the back with a poker. Although once or twice Elsie claimed that he had stopped 'knocking her about' since Tracy had been taken into care, we noted the times when, for example, she reported that he had hit her twice round the head for calling him 'an idle swine', when he bruised her upper arm and hit her on the face, when he punched her on the body and face with his fists, when he winded her by knocking her under the ribs and so on. She told us that one of his attacks on her had made her so angry that she had turned on him and seized him by the throat. 'Now you know what it felt like when you got me by the throat', she had said to him. She had been surprised at her own bravery because usually she was physically afraid of him. Her action brought immediate results – Vince brought some beer for himself and for Elsie into the house that evening instead of going out to the pub – but it did not last. Within a month the old pattern of repeated marital violence had been resumed.

At times of crisis and depression, she contacted Hilary Minton and pleaded for somewhere else to live with the children because she 'could not stand it with him anymore'. Each time the marriage was patched up and Elsie returned to make the best of it, but she received little help from Vince in keeping the family going. During his summer holidays he took to fishing every day, leaving her to cope with the family without a break, and throughout the fishing season he gave up making the Sunday dinner (as had been his custom) to pursue his hobby. When she tried to explain to him how miserable her life was, his only answer was 'Why don't you swine off, then?'. If she replied in kind and told him in no uncertain terms to pack his bags and go, she was reminded that the council house was in his name and so, if any one left, it would be *her*.

Finances

Apart from Vince's reticence about what he earned, we had other problems in assessing exactly how much money he was making at any one time: the wage rates varied according to the shift, night work being slightly better paid, the rates themselves increased during our period of involvement with the family, and, rather frequently, Vince missed a day's work as a result of illness, a minor injury or a family crisis. Sometimes we could not discover the reason for his absence from work. In addition, Vince's employers agreed at one point to give him a loan to help him pay off outstanding debts and were deducting £8 from his wages every week. But for these two factors his wages would have been higher. When we first met the family in the middle of 1975, Vince's weekly take-home pay fluctuated between £46 and £52, of which he gave between £25 and £35 to Elsie as her 'wages'. By April 1977 Vince was earning between £70 and £80 per week after deductions, and he was handing between £40 and £54 to Elsie. Her household budget for a typical week in mid April 1977 is presented in Table 2.1.

Table 2.1

Elsie's 'wages' from Vince	45.00	Food and household necessities	23.50
Child Benefits (6 children)	8.50	Milk	5.00
	£53.50[1]	Rent	8.00
		Charge for redecoration[2]	0.50
		Insurance: fire and accident	0.25
		Life Insurance for Vince	0.50
		Goods bought through catalogues[3]	4.50
		Weekly instalment on new carpet	2.18
		Weekly instalment on new cooker	1.62
		TV weekly rental and slot payment	4.00
		School meals for three children	2.25
		Private debt company	3.00
			£55.30[4]

[1] One additional item of income was the ten hundredweight of coal Vince earned for every twenty days worked. In April 1977 the price of one hundredweight of coal from local coal merchants was £1.64 for the lowest quality of coal and £1.99 for the highest.

[2] When the Barkers moved from Bramwell to Elsmore, their former home was redecorated by the housing department who charged the family £150, which they wanted repaid at a rate of £1 per week. Elsie telephoned them to explain that, with six children, she could not afford to pay more than 50p, and Hilary Minton's intervention was necessary to secure the department's agreement. Vince spent his leisure time over four days painting their home in Bramwell prior to leaving, but an official from the housing department criticized the quality of his work, and implied that he was wasting his time as the decorating would have to be redone. The house remained boarded up and unoccupied for some months after the move; the Barkers, however, will continue to pay off this debt until 1983.

[3] The goods were mainly clothes and presents for the children.

[4] This total does not include any calculation for gas or electricty.

This tabulation of Elsie's financial situation presents too rosy a picture; for it omits the crippling effect of debt accumulated from the recent past. The first large debt we heard about amounted to £100, which Elsie owed Helen, the owner of the local shop in Bramwell. Eighteen months later, by which time the Barkers had left the area for six months, Elsie was still paying off this debt, which in the meantime had been reduced to £30, increased to £140, and then wiped off completely by dint of Elsie's careful management in paying £10 per week. During Vince's summer holidays, however, their finances were again in a desperate state: out of a take-home pay for three weeks of £145, Vince gave Elsie £90, with which she paid a number of outstanding bills (including a final instalment of £30 to Helen) and spent £20 in buying shoes for all the children. She had understood that the £90 was to cover not three, but two weeks; by the third week, therefore, they had no money whatsoever, Vince having spent the money he had retained in the local pub and clubs. They first appealed to the local Social Security Office, who sent them a letter saying they were ineligible for help because Vince earned too much. Next, Elsie turned unwillingly to her mother for help; her mother delivered a lecture to her on Vince's faults, past and present, without offering any money. Having no one else to approach, Elsie contacted Hilary Minton, who suggested that the account with Helen, which had just been cleared, should be restarted. This was more than Elsie could face because she felt so humiliated. As she put it, 'It's always me that has to go crawling round on my hands and knees to ask people for money.' Hilary re-opened the account with Helen on Elsie's behalf and within two months the bill was again as high as £135. They were reduced to selling Helen bags of coal from Vince's allowance.

If only their debts to the local store had been the sole drain on their resources, they might have been able to muddle through. Vince, however, refused to pay bills until they received the final demand notice and, three times during our fieldwork, their electricity was cut off. Each time it cost them £1.50 to have it restored. The first time it happened, Elsie talked of her embarrassment ('the whole street knows'), but also of the fun it had caused. They had lighted candles and gone to bed early where they had talked to each other and played draughts and snakes and ladders. On the third occasion, however, the electricty was cut off for three days, one of which was her birthday. This time she had gone to bed on her own in a state of such depression that she had contemplated suicide. They were continually in the position of not having paid the electricity bill for the first quarter when the bill for the second arrived. Their old, draughty house with its settlement cracks was certainly no help in keeping the bills down.

Vince incurred other debts. He had to pay almost £20 for driving without 'L' plates and over £50 for other motoring offences; he also appeared in court for non-payment of the latter fine. Moreover, he was prosecuted for not having a television licence. Such pressures had driven him to use a local loan company – with whom Ada Paterson was also involved – and from which he borrowed £200; he was currently repaying this at a rate of £2.50 per week, and was still paying it two years later. His other attempts to raise extra money consisted in a brief spell of working in his spare time as a chimney-sweep (he bought the equipment from a mate at work) and selling part of his allowance of coal to neighbours, from whom he also borrowed money.

The Barkers also had continuing commitments, some of which were in Elsie's name and concerned purchases made before their marriage, to the 'Clubmen'. One November they were still paying the 'Clubmen' for the presents they had bought their children for the previous Christmas. Their reputation as bad debtors, however, was making it difficult for them to find firms who would let them buy articles 'on the club'. Elsie did not object to visits from the 'Clubmen' when Vince was at home, for then they would take no for an answer. But when she was on her own, she claimed that they so harassed her that she had been reduced to tears.

Elsie thought Vince niggardly where she and the children were concerned. On one occasion, he remonstrated with her for spending his money on underclothes for herself. She had, in fact, paid £1.60 for three pairs of pants and a brassiere.

The very first time we met Vince, he was tinkering with a new projector, which we later learned was for showing his blue films. It cost just over £60 and Elsie was left to find £8 a month from her housekeeping money to pay for it. Later, he chose a rifle worth £35 from Elsie's mother's catalogue and gave Elsie strict instructions to make sure it was ordered; it never arrived. He did, however, acquire for the new house in Elsmore an aquarium with tropical fish which cost £25. And he had grandiose plans to build a bar in the living-room at the cost of a further £40. At one stage, when they were deeply in debt and had no money for the weekend, one of the few objects in their home which was worth selling was Vince's fishing umbrella which he had bought for between £7 and £8; he sold it for £1.50, but not before he had forced Elsie to sell her 'new', second-hand dress back to the neighbour from whom she had just bought it. As soon as the crisis was over, Vince persuaded Elsie to order, again through her mother's catalogue, another fishing umbrella for his birthday. When she attempted to discuss how he spent his money, his answer was always 'I bloody work for it.' Elsie showed us how the children needed shoes and how thin the girls' dresses were for winter. Most of the children's and Elsie's clothes were second-hand and the new shoes that she bought for them were soon worn out because she was obliged to buy cheap ones.

In all the years she had been married to Vince, Elsie had never bought herself any new clothes, only 'cast-offs'. To attend her husband's birthday party in the local pub, she had borrowed a dress from a neighbour. On the other hand, in their seven years of marriage, Vince had bought himself two suits, the latest of which cost £28. For all her poverty, Elsie still showed remarkable generosity in parcelling up garments for the children of her neighbour, Sally Martin, and in giving away the baby clothes which John had outgrown. She had held some of these baby clothes up to Vince and asked, 'We won't be needing these any more, will we?'

Both of them called her weekly housekeeping money her 'wages' and many of their quarrels were about money and their continual financial difficulties. Elsie did not know how much her husband earned and felt very foolish about not knowing when asked by an official who was trying to ascertain whether the Barkers should be contributing to the cost of Tracy being in care.

The main consequence of her small 'wages' and the debts was that Elsie was often left on Saturday morning with £15, and sometimes even less, with which to feed a family of eight until Tuesday, when she received £8.50 in child benefits which was also spent on food. Much of her energy was therefore taken up in struggling to keep the family going from day to day and to talk to her about planning for the future would have been a cruel joke. She attempted, nevertheless, to save a little money each week for Christmas.

Sometimes, Vince protested about the amount of income tax he was paying and, in this matter, Elsie supported him. She was convinced that 'they' were 'all against big families'. Both of them were aware that, when we first met them, they did not qualify for Family Income Supplement because Vince's wage was slightly too high. By the end of fieldwork, his wage was comfortably above the starting level for Family Income Supplement. When they compared their financial position with that of their immediate neighbours (such as Sally and Peter Martin with three children, or the malicious gossip, Margaret, with her three children, or Ron and his six children), they considered themselves to be worse off even though Vince was the only father from these four families who was employed. Elsie reminded him that the whole family had been better off when he was unemployed and, in this mood of despondency, Vince would talk of 'packing it in', of getting into trouble at work and being sacked. During his period of unemployment, he had accepted one day's casual work, been found out, and Elsie was forced to refund £9. His first job after being unemployed had been as a labourer in a foundry, where he was paid £20 per week, but they had not been able to keep a family of their size on such money and so he had followed the trail of higher wages into the pits. We calculated (from the November 1976 rates) that, if Vince suddenly became unemployed, the family of two adults and six children would have received £58.38 and a percentage of their rent would have been paid; if he and his family had become totally dependent on Supplementary Benefit, they would have received £44.45 and their rent would have been paid in total. In November 1976 Vince's take-home pay was fluctuating between £70 and £80 per week. It was only when Vince fell ill with a stomach complaint that the children were awarded free school meals for six months. Vince and Elsie still felt that they were being treated unfairly by various authorities in financial matters and continued to complain about the more favourable position of their non-working neighbours. This cannot divert attention from the large amount of money which Vince kept for his own use.

Child-Rearing

The granting of free school meals for six months was not only a financial blessing but also a welcome relief for Elsie, who did not have to cope with all the children at lunch-time. The noise and fighting were at their height in the late afternoon, at weekends and during the school holidays when the children were all together. Once, in Bramwell, as the noise level rose, Vince turned and asked rhetorically 'And you wonder why I go out to the pub?'

Before discussing the child-rearing practices of the parents, it is worth remembering that they were bringing up six children in seriously over-crowded conditions, Elsie had no spare cash to provide diversions and entertainments, and they lived in an area where the school playgrounds, for example, were closed in the evenings, at the weekends and during the holidays. Six young children rendered her practically housebound. Lack of money also hindered the youngest child's development. John, at the age of eleven months, tried to feed himself, but the family had no high chair to encourage this advance, and Elsie had no money to buy either a new or a second-hand one.

Elsie, for the most part unaided by Vince, carried the burden of rearing the children, three of whom were at school in Bramwell, thus leaving three under the age of four at home every day. The fourth child, Eddie, was three-and-a-half when we first met the family, but only began attending nursery school some months later. Hilary Minton arranged for a young female student teacher to act as a home help for a few hours every week, but the arrangement did not last long.

In a spirit of gentle self-reproach, Elsie told us that Eddie had said to her, 'You keep calling me Tom, but I'm Eddie, aren't I?' Without doubt, affection was shown to the children by both parents. Vince, for instance, always kissed all the children before leaving for work, and he was adept at amusing them with silly jokes or frightening them in a way the younger children found exciting. He could, at times, be very attentive to them, ferrying them cold drinks on one occasion when they were waiting in a hot sun to be judged in a fancy dress competition.

His pet name for the baby John was 'tadpole', and when he asked Eddie how much he loved his daddy, 'two sugar lumps' had been the child's answer. In Elsie's words: 'The kids adore him.' For her part, Elsie was very nurturant, cuddling the children a lot and sitting them on her lap. She certainly loved them all but she could not love (in an active, giving sense) all of them at one and the same time, and so the children fought each other for her attention and, at times, literally screamed for it.

The children were not the only ones to shout and scream. Both parents, but particularly Elsie, were loud and abrupt when talking to their children; they shouted comments to them as though to puppies in training. Perhaps as a result of Elsie's impaired hearing, she often bawled at the children when she spoke to them, even if she was only trying to convey some simple information such as 'I've not got any sweets.' At times, her shouting reached a crescendo which gave her pains in the head. The children had become used to Elsie's shouts and took no notice. If Vince were not present to back up her attempts at discipline, she was often unable to make the children obey her: they were out of her control and they knew it, often laughing at her, and sometimes abusing her verbally, and even hitting her. As soon as Vince left for work or the pub, the children became more boisterous and demanding. Vince complained that she did not hit them often enough. Neither parent, however, explained the reasons behind their requests or commands, thus leaving the children at the mercy of what must have appeared to them as arbitrary or illogical rules. An example may help to explain this point. When the family were moving house, the children begged to be taken back in the empty van and car from Elsmore to Bramwell. Instead of telling the children that the space was needed for transporting furniture, they were simply forbidden to go near the vehicles and, one after another, they broke into tears.

On certain matters, the parents had no common policy and, individually, they changed their stance from one moment to the next: such inconsistency might have contributed to the children's confusion about how to behave. Many examples could be quoted, but these are three incidents. Elsie allowed them to play with Vince's felt-tipped pens in his absence, but, when he was there, she forbade the children to use them. Learning to respond differently to the same pens in Vince's presence and absence seemed to be a difficult lesson for all the children. Elsie would also change from wielding the stick to offering the carrot. Eddie, at the age of four-and-a-half, was slapped for being in a bad mood and for running off down the road; three times Elsie had to fetch him, by which time he was in furious temper tantrum, jumping up and down in rage and tears, so Elsie, in desperation, gave him money to buy sweets. Eddie was therefore rewarded for losing control of himself. We also saw very sudden switches of mood on Elsie's part which took the children by surprise. Her anger would break out very suddenly ('I got my hair off'), but these flashes of temper were not deeply felt for, a moment later, she would be laughing and joking. Alice was, for instance, just under three years of age and had been off colour all day. Elsie was explaining this, and the child was whimpering in her arms, when Elsie in a sudden flare of temper slapped her for sucking her thumb. Alice began screaming and Elsie responded by consoling her with caresses and kisses on the head, as though it had been someone else who had made the child cry.

The parents sometimes hit the children and often shouted at and threatened them, but not always with any obvious or serious intent; they had a style of interacting with their children which could be surprising, and even shocking, but it was not in the main unkind. The children were becoming as physically and as verbally aggressive as their parents; they handled John, the baby, and each other in the same rough manner in which they were treated by their parents. All the children, and not only the boys, were positively encouraged to be good fighters and to stand up for themselves. When Eddie had been tormenting Alice, Elsie counselled her as follows: 'You've got to learn to hit him back, Sunshine. Hit him back next time.' This was the standard advice issued by both parents. When Vince returned from the pub, we saw him arrange wrestling matches among the boys. He egged them on to fight harder, to use Kung-Fu strokes and to punch each other in the ribs and stomach until one child was defeated. We heard him forcing Tom to admit that his younger brother Eddie had beaten him, and we saw him play so roughly with his younger sons that they burst into tears.

Elsie had exhausted her repertoire of techniques for disciplining the children and had nothing new to call on. She repeatedly threatened the children that she would put on her coat and leave them for being so naughty. She warned them that they would be taken away by a policeman or by Hilary Minton to whom she said: 'You'll take them all off me in the end.' The children did not react to these threats.

Before concluding this section, some individual discussion of the children is necessary.

John

Unlike the others, he did not need to fight to secure his fair share of attention, for, being the baby, he enjoyed a privileged, if temporary, status. Elsie informed us with a smile that Vince spoiled the baby 'because he *is* the baby'; and, indeed, both of them treated him with much gentleness and leniency, although he was not spared the physical punishment which was meted out to everyone except Vince. He was smacked, in the main for 'yarling', but not often and only after he could walk.

Alice

The treatment of Alice, the second youngest child, was less permissive in comparison. She was reminded that she was not a baby any more and therefore no longer eligible for the attentions accorded the Benjamin of the family. Her parents seemed to imagine her as a delightful, naughty child whom they thought of as more like a little boy than a little girl. According to Elsie, Alice was so like Vince that she 'ought to have been a boy'. Alice enjoyed hearing stories of her own misbehaviour (for example, pouring a bottle of Camp coffee down the sink) and gleefully accepted her 'naughty' image. Once when Vince was looking after the children while Elsie was out shopping, she swallowed six of Elsie's contraceptive pills, but she came to no harm.

Eddie

At the age of three-and-a-half, Eddie was already acting the role of 'hard man' (for instance, refusing to be kissed), and generally producing the tough, masculine responses for which Vince rewarded him. He was the most aggressive of all the children. He frequently made attacks on Alice and on Tom and was not afraid to spit at his mother or hit her legs with a bat. Elsie commented to us: 'He's just like his father. He's never happy unless he's hurting something or somebody.' Like his father, he could also be very charming.

Tom

Vince said of Tom that 'He's more like me than any of the others', and Tom beamed with delight. Vince also claimed that he had treated Tom differently from the other boys in that he had not been rough with him or forced him to fight and yet he had become the toughest of them all – something we did not observe. As Vince expressed it: 'He'll be the first one to give me a hiding.' He also told us, and chuckled with pleasure as he did so, how Tom at the age of five had been caught stealing from the local shop and the bread van. Tom was his favourite and it was Tom whom we most often saw on his knee. Vince told story upon story about Tom's spontaneous wit, his smart repartee – in Vince's eyes, he was a 'card', just like his Dad.

Julie

Elsie worried about Julie's lack of balance in that she kept falling over, and she wondered whether it was connected with the meningitis she had contracted when younger. Julie also returned home with nits in her hair after playing with the Martins' little girl, Ruth. Julie appeared to be particularly upset by Tracy's comings and goings and would cry when she returned to the Children's Home. Although Julie at the ages of six and seven burst into tears, like all the others, when thwarted, and although she was smacked like all the others, she seemed more stable and less aggressive than her brothers. She did, however, give the impression at times of being a worried child. Unlike her brothers, she was helpful to her mother; for example she ran errands to the local shop and attended to the younger children.

Steve

Over the period of fieldwork with the Barkers, there was a marked change in Steve's behaviour. At the outset, he appeared to be a shy, sensitive and good-natured boy of just under seven years who said he wanted to go 'on the dole' when he grew up. Within three months of visiting we learned that Vince did not accept Steve as his child and was constantly needling Elsie about her alleged infidelity. Someone had told him that Steve was not his: that was the total substance of his charge but it was enough, in Vince's opinion. It took us some months to see how differently Vince treated Steve from the others. Vince called him 'timid' and Elsie thought him 'nervous'; then Vince, in anger, told him he was a 'bloody queer' and, Elsie, always supportive of her husband, added that he was 'like an animal'. At another time, Vince was convinced that Steve was 'becoming a real big head'; and he taunted the boy with the phrase 'mardie-arse', when Steve was hunting for his dummy on return from school. Steve took to hiding a dummy behind the storage heaters so that he could always lay his hand on one. On two consecutive years, Steve received nothing from his parents for his birthday except a card. Although there were no presents for Julie and even Tom on their birthdays, only Steve was tormented by Vince who kept saying to him, 'I've got something for you, son.' Elsie told him to stop.

During the course of an evening, we saw him being reprimanded over and over again; he was ordered to do something and then punished for doing it. His father made whining imitations of his voice, contradicted him whenever possible, and tried to diminish him in the eyes of the other children. He mocked him for taking a toy lamb to bed with him, which grieved Elsie so much that she later flew at Tracy who was also accustomed to cuddling a toy animal in bed. In short, Vince seemed to single Steve out for ill-treatment and to find his every action irritating.

The boy's reactions to this treatment varied. He stayed out late, at times returning well after dark. After a spell of being baited by Vince, he would retreat to his dummy or to a baby's bottle, and once even sat in the baby's chair. At other times, he stormed out of the house. We once heard him shout: 'Nobody in this house wants me! I'm leaving home.' Vince replied: 'Well bugger off, then!'; and Elsie added: 'You know where the door is.' Vince waited some minutes before fetching him back.

On her own, Elsie was more protective of the boy, explaining that he was 'a bag of nerves because he's seen Vince hit me'. Steve, for his part, either ignored his mother's requests, or defied her openly, or sometimes reduced her to tears with insults such as: 'You're nothing but a repulsive pig.' Later in the year he began swearing at her, using phrases he had picked up from an older boy in the neighbourhood. She threatened him with Vince, with his head-teacher and with the police; she warned him that he would be the next one to be taken away by Hilary Minton. He replied, 'I'll tell my Dad, and then he'll hit you.' Elsie claimed that Steve could no longer be controlled by being slapped, and needed the slipper.

Steve imitated his father even to the extent of sitting in a chair in the same manner. When Elsie commented adversely on his misbehaviour by saying, in her standard phrase, 'He's just like his father', Steve immediately brightened and interrupted to say: 'Yes, I am, aren't I?' Steve took every opportunity to insist that his behaviour closely resembled his father's, and he repeatedly made attempts to acquire the required masculine image.

At the end of fieldwork, he was accused by a little girl of stealing her bag and was severely punished twice by his parents for hitting the baby. Hilary Minton arranged for him to attend a junior youth club in Elsmore, but Elsie was soon threatening him that he would not be allowed to attend because of his misbehaviour at home.

In contrast to their behaviour at home, the three eldest children, the head teacher in Bramwell told us, presented no educational, emotional or social problems in school. All three were considered to be bright children, as the following reading ages (based on the Burt reading test) make clear:

	Steve	Julie	Tom
Chronological age	7 yrs. 6 mths.	6 yrs. 7 mths.	5 yrs 6 mths.
Reading age	9 yrs. 2 mths.	7 yrs. 2 mths.	5 yrs. 2 mths.

The only complaint the head teacher made against the family was that she had needed on a few occasions to ask Elsie to bath the children. Eddie and Alice both took to their nursery school in Elsmore and proudly showed us examples of their handiwork.

The Move to Elsmore
Partly because they received news of their 'exchange', we decided to extend fieldwork with the Barkers for longer than we originally intended. We had accorded the overcrowding in Bramwell such an important role in explaining the level of violence in the family that we were particularly interested to see whether living in a larger house would produce any change. But the aggressive patterns of interaction which had been established in Bramwell were transferred to their new home in Elsmore.

The particulars of the new house were given in a letter from the local council as: parlour, kitchen, scullery, four bedrooms, bathroom and toilet. The arrival of the letter changed the mood of the house in Bramwell. It brought Elsie out of a spell of depression, and she talked of a better future. Although the new house was far more spacious than the old one, there were, in fact, only three double bedrooms upstairs and a medium-sized bedroom downstairs, which Elsie thought would be better employed as a playroom. Vince tried but failed to make the children eat their meals in the kitchen. The new arrangements allowed the two girls, Julie and Alice, to have, for the first time, a room of their own where they slept in single beds; the three boys shared the second double room where they slept in two single beds pushed together (Elsie: 'They start fighting as soon as they open their eyes in the morning'); John, the baby, continued to sleep in his parents' bedroom. Other advantages were that Alice and Eddie began using the inside toilet, whereas before they had urinated into a small plastic bucket. The bed-wetting, however, continued unabated. The hand basin in the bathroom encouraged the children to clean their hands; the outside toilet in Bramwell had had no such amenity. Moreover, the greater space downstairs provided room for the children to play with their toys. When the Barkers took over the house, the back garden boasted, in addition to a lawn, a vegetable patch, even if it was a little overgrown. Eight months later what grass remained was covered in sand, discarded furniture and broken toys, Vince's talk of planting potatoes had come to nothing, and the vegetable patch was indistinguishable from the surrounding earth. Although there were over a dozen steep steps from the back door to the pavement for Elsie to negotiate with her pram, and though the interior was in need of redecoration and had a certain air of dilapidation because of the cracked linoleum on the floors, and although the house had no central heating and no power points upstairs, Elsie summed up her delight in her new home in these words: 'John is in his glory.'

They ordered a purple fitted carpet for the sitting-room from Elsie's mother's catalogue at the cost of £46 which they repaid at the rate of £2.18 per week. Before they completed the payments, however, the carpet was worn and threadbare. Vince coloured the sitting-room walls with lilac paint and built a cabinet to hold the fish tank. Their attempts at creating a homely atmosphere were spoiled, however, by a fire caused by the children playing with matches. The new carpet, an armchair, a settee, a clothes-horse draped with nappies and bedclothes and the ceiling tiles in both the sitting-room and the hall were all badly damaged. No one was injured except for Vince, who fought the blaze until the fire brigade arrived; he was burned, but not badly, by a falling ceiling tile. The Barkers replaced the essential items which they had lost in the fire at a cost of £25. Their lack of fire insurance (which they now possess) highlights how serious small accidents can be to families living on tight budgets.

When the Barkers moved house, the poverty of their possessions became evident. Their furniture was rickety, old and dirty; the mattresses were soiled and smelled of urine; all their clothes were carried in a few plastic bags, but they did have a number of books, which turned out to be sixteen bound volumes about the occult, which Vince referred to as his library. (Elsie claimed that none of these books had been read; certainly, we only once saw a newspaper in the house). In short, they had next to nothing worth selling in an emergency. Vince and Elsie had to buy a new bed for themselves as the old one broke during the move.

Within two weeks of moving house Vince was tormenting Steve, and rowing violently with Elsie just as before. His sexual jealousy remained strong and unreasoning: after six months in Elsmore he began accusing Elsie of having sexual relations with Pakistanis. Elsie claimed that she was no longer afraid of him and that she now fought back when he hit her; she was encouraged in this by her mother who said that Elsie was 'big enough to eat him'. Trouble still played a part in Vince's life: he appeared in court to give evidence about yet another fracas in the street and he opened the door of his home only to be punched in the face by a stranger who quickly disappeared in a car. They acquired a large, black dog to protect Elsie when Vince was on the night-shift because she had become frightened by knocks on the door.

Vince's behaviour underwent one major change, however, after the move in that he became much more home-based than at Bramwell, where he habitually retreated to the pub both at lunchtime and in the evening, partly, no doubt, in order to avoid the noisy and overcrowded conditions in his own home. At Elsmore, however, to Elsie's surprise, he visited the local pubs on only one occasion, claimed not to like them, and began staying at home. The increased space in the new house and the fact that there was only one child (John) at home during the day may also have influenced his decision, but at the same time he began suffering from a stomach complaint shortly after the move, and he was advised by his doctor not to drink.

The children's behaviour showed little change: they squabbled and shouted and were hit. The older children also encountered some difficulties in changing school: the teaching methods were different, and Julie claimed that her new classmates were picking on her. At one stage she stayed away from school, complaining of a headache. Elsie, anxious as always about being accused of neglect, acceded to her wishes, and so the children saw how they could gain more control over her and avoid doing anything they did not want to do. Elsie became depressed, and her doctor prescribed valium. In time Julie made friends with a girl of her own age and began playing at her friend's house.

The Community Home, to which Tracy had been transferred, permitted her to return to Elsmore at weekends more frequently, but this brought problems in its turn. Although Vince gave her strict instruction to be home by 10 pm as she was only fifteen years old, she stayed out until midnight and returned one evening, falling drunk through the door. Her father then discovered that she was frequenting pubs which were the haunts of local prostitutes. He was equally worried about her association with a much older youth who came from a reputedly 'dirty' family on the estate, and who was also unemployed and in trouble with the police.

Elsie's Mother

At a number of points throughout this chapter, reference has been made to Elsie's mother, who appears to have had a considerable effect on the lives of her daughters and some influence on the course of the Barkers' marriage. She prevented Brenda, her eldest daughter, from marrying when she first became pregnant and Elsie from taking up hairdressing as a career. She raised Brenda's three children, Marie, Kathy and Clare, and then she prevented Kathy from training as a nanny. She was prudish about all sexual matters: she made Elsie 'feel dirty' because she had had seven children, although she herself had given birth to four. Before Clare was born, she insisted that the baby, the third illegitimate child, should be adopted, but then relented; she made sure that Kathy's first illegitimate baby was adopted. She paid for an abortion on one occasion and advised Elsie not to accept Tracy and Nick. She remained the focal point for family gatherings and Elsie felt indebted to her for using her washing machine, her catalogue and her house for John's christening party. Elsie wanted her mother to be concerned for her but was not prepared to accept her advice.

Furthermore, Elsie asserted that her whole family 'turned against' her when she married Vince. Her mother spoke better of her first husband, now that he was no longer there. She was a source of friction between Elsie and Vince; for example, she refused to come to their wedding anniversary party because she 'could not stand' Vince, while, at the same time, she complained that he never visited her. As Vince saw the situation, Elsie told him on the one hand, that her mother 'loathed his guts' and, on the other, that he ought to visit her. Elsie was seemingly caught between them, feeling that she must partially reject Vince in order to gain her mother's help and affection.

One of the main reasons Elsie advanced in favour of the move to Elsmore was that she would be 'closer to Mum'. This turned out to be a very mixed blessing, for Kathy quickly arranged to leave her two young legitimate children with Elsie so that she could go out to work. Although Elsie was paid £6 per week for this task, it meant that she still had four young children in the house after her own four eldest had gone to school. Elsie accepted this plan readily, arguing that the extra money would enable her to buy the children Christmas presents. She may also have agreed to look after Kathy's two children in an attempt to reinstate herself with her own family. The arrangement, however, proved too much even for Elsie and she had to abandon it after two weeks.

Elsie was also sensitive about the lack of attention shown by her brothers, who did not remember her children's birthdays, and by her nieces and sisters, who were not prepared to babysit for her, but who helped each other out. Contact between Elsie and her own family was always initiated by Elsie; her relatives talked about her 'dirty home' as their excuse for not visiting. As a result, Elsie began a friendship with another mother on the estate who had a similar reputation. Nevertheless, Elsie still involved her family in her troubles: the first time Vince hit her after the move to Elsmore, for example, Elsie went straight to her mother and Clare returned with her to give Vince 'a telling off'. Vince's answer was 'I've got no-one to stick up for me.' In sum, the move brought Elsie nearer her mother who provided moral support, practical services and at times unwelcome advice. It appeared that Elsie would have liked to have been further integrated into her own family.

Relations with the Social Worker
Hilary Minton provided the whole family with a large range of material help from furnishing curtains for their new home to finding a pram for the baby. She also arranged loans when they were deeply in debt, ferried Elsie and the children to hospital and to Elsie's mother, and secured the services of a young female student to help Elsie with the children. Eddie and later Alice were both found places at nursery school, and Steve was introduced to a junior youth club. Elsie turned to Hilary Minton in emergencies which were either financial or concerned Tracy, Steve or Vince's treatment of her. Elsie also needed someone to talk to and Hilary filled that important role on a regular basis, often acting as an escape valve.

Despite all this help and this commitment of time and effort, both parents had the conviction that they and their children were in the power of the authorities. Elsie was very ambivalent in her attitudes to Hilary Minton, at one moment expressing her gratitude for the support and sympathy she received, and at the next resenting the criticisms made of her (in the report on Tracy, for example). It was, however, the power of Hilary Minton to advise that her children should be removed which riled Elsie most. Jordan accurately described Elsie's position when he wrote: 'Having once embarked on a career as a social work client, she is in constant jeopardy as a mother, for her every action is being observed and judged not only (as in social security) for its deservingness, but also for its parental quality' (1974, p. 132).

Vince's attitude to Hilary Minton became increasingly hostile and critical. He spoke bitterly of what he described as 'intrusions' into their private life, of her attempts to tell him what to do, of his quarrels with her over Tracy, and of her habit of siding with Elsie and against him. Many of their difficulties and disagreements were created by Vince who held what, in our opinion, was a distorted image of her, namely that of a naive young girl in her early twenties who had little experience of life and even less of raising a large family. This image seriously militated against the development of an effective case work relationship between them, but because of Vince's possibly low regard for women in general, any other female social worker would very likely have been confronted with the same emotional defences. On the other hand, the Barkers would really have preferred to have been involved in discussions about the plans for Tracy's future, and their exclusion became a criticism levelled at the social worker.

Commentary

One of the comments of Sir Keith Joseph about the cycle of deprivation, namely that 'inadequate people tend to be inadequate parents and that inadequate parents tend to rear inadequate children' (1972a, p. 8) may appear to have been substantiated by this description of the Barker family. Such a judgement on the Barkers would be too harsh and too simple and would not do justice to the complexities of their situation: we wish to place the debate in a wider context.

Would the Barkers, for example, qualify as one of the 'socially disadvantaged' families, as that term was defined by Wedge and Prosser (1973)? Their three criteria for deciding whether children were to be classified as 'socially disadvantaged' were

(a) coming from a one-parent family or a family of five or more children

and (b) receiving free school meals or supplementary benefit

and (c) living in an overcrowded home or one lacking hot water.

The Barkers would certainly have been included within category (a), and category (c) applied to them while they lived in Bramwell. The children were awarded free school meals but only for six months, and so category (b) referred to them for just a brief period. The family can therefore be pictured as moving in and out of Wedge and Prosser's categories of disadvantage. Parker made a valuable point in this connection: 'There is no distinctive group of the most disadvantaged who are somehow detached from the rest of society. They are at the end of a spectrum. Adopt a more or less generous definition of poverty, of overcrowding, or of what constitutes a large family and the point of demarcation shifts one way or another along the continuum.' (1974, p. 15).

Wedge and Prosser found that 6.2 per cent of the children in their nationally representative sample were socially disadvantaged because they were in all three categories. As they pointed out, 6.2 per cent means that one child in every sixteen, or two children in every British classroom, have experienced all three of the factors mentioned above. If policy were to be directed at relieving the suffering of this most deprived 6.2 per cent, the Barker family would not be helped in any way. Such policy issues will be discussed in Chapter 6; for the present it is worth recalling that at the age of seven or eleven 18 per cent of Wedge and Prosser's sample (or more than one in every six children) lived in a family where there were five or more children.

To present the information in another way, the 1971 Census (10 per cent sample) gave the number of families with five or more dependent children as 196,000 with 1,083,000 children in such families (*Social Trends*, 1976, p. 69. This large group of children is therefore comparable in size to the total (1,110,000) of dependent children in one-parent families, of whom so much has been heard since the publication of the Finer Report (Department of Health and Social Security, 1974a). The trend to smaller families, which, according to Land, started at the turn of this century, appears to have continued since she wrote: 'In 1966 there were about 1,450,000 children in such families.' (1969, p. 9). She has summarized (1977, p. 163) the present position by saying that, although the number of large families in Britain has been declining in the last ten years, 'there are still a substantial number of children who are currently members of a large family'.

It is also clear from the extensive literature on the subject that large family size is connected with a wide range of different deprivations, but only the studies most relevant to the Barkers will be referred to here. For example, Packman's study of children taken into care showed that 25 per cent of committals to care, 11 per cent of long-term admissions and 22 per cent of short-term admissions came from families with five or more children (1968, p. 47). Lafitte used figures, issued by the Ministry of Social Security on families in poverty in 1966, to conclude: 'The proportion in unrelieved poverty rose from 2 per cent of children in one- or two-child families to 11 per cent of those in five-child families and to 20 per cent of those in larger families.' (1973, pp. 28–9). Similarly, West and Farrington (1973) listed large family size as one of the five factors judged to be of special importance in relation to delinquency. They carefully pointed out, however, that the association between large family size and delinquency was part of a cluster of factors which included overcrowding, irregular work by fathers and physical neglect of the children. Rutter, Tizard and Whitmore (1970) have also shown that children from large families are twice as likely to develop conduct disorders, and numerous studies have reported that such children have lower verbal IQ and reading scores than children from small families

(Douglas, 1964; Douglas, Ross and Simpson, 1968; etc). Poor nutrition (Lambert, 1964), overcrowding (Land, 1969; Spencer, 1973) and placements in schools for the educationally sub-normal (Chazan, 1964) have all been found to occur more frequently in families with five or more children.

Certainly, if Sir Keith Joseph were looking for one detailed case study to exemplify the cycle of deprivation the Barkers would at first glance appear to be the answer. For, at a superficial level, examples of transmission abound. We have seen the oldest son imitating some of his father's most aggressive tendencies; the eldest girl of fifteen has had a turbulent history in institutional care, a history described by her father as 'me all over again'; both parents claimed to have suffered disturbed childhoods and their own children were experiencing many of the same difficulties; the mother of the family claimed to have been treated as the 'black sheep' in her family of origin, and one of her sons was treated as a scapegoat by her husband; both parents had minimal education and had very low educational expectations for their children; and in the extended family a pattern of illegitimate births and early marriages was repeated in the lives of adolescent girls in two generations. Let us, however, examine certain aspects of their lives in more detail.

It is worth reflecting on Vince's view that the aggressive tendencies which he inculcated in all his children are exactly what they need if they are to survive in the streets and in the schools of the neighbourhood, in that 'jungle of might-is-right' which, according to the Newsons (1968, p. 133), awaits many working-class children outside their back door. There is a great deal of sense in his argument because life for the Barker children is in many ways a fight for survival, in which the values of co-operation are down-graded in favour of individual competition. Certainly, Wilson's argument (1974a) that middle class and child-centred methods of child-rearing are inappropriate in the milieu of poverty is applicable to the Barker family. So it remains a possibility that the children's behaviour and the parents' child-rearing practices are in some senses very well adapted to their social situation.

The amount of suffering and personal distress among the children suggests, however, that the adaptation (if that is what their behaviour represents) is only achieved at some considerable cost. Knowing the Newsons' finding about the prevalence of 'comfort habits' among their Nottingham sample of 700 families, namely, that '50 per cent of our sample were still using dummies at twelve months, whereas only 14 per cent were still doing so at four years' (1968, p. 311), it was not out of the ordinary for Alice at two-and-a-half years and Eddie at three-and-a-half years to make constant use of 'titties' and drink from babies' bottles. That Steve, aged six-and-a-half, should come home from school and regularly put a dummy in his mouth and become very distressed if it was not immediately available, was another matter. Even at the end of fieldwork, when Steve was over eight years of age, he still had need of his 'titty' and no amount of mocking from Vince could dissuade him. (Vince himself, according to Elsie, sucked his thumb until he was sixteen). The only reference to dummy sucking in the Newsons' third report, when their sample children were seven years old, talks of the habit being closely linked with withdrawal into sleep and of it appearing at moments of stress (1976, pp. 384–5); there is no mention of a child regularly using a dummy at that age.

The children were all enuretic – some, like Steve, being regular and others, like Julie, being only occasional bed-wetters. With Steve and Tom sharing a single bed, it was difficult for Elsie to tell who was responsible on any particular night. It is bad enough for a child to be forced to share a bed with a brother, but when that brother also wets the bed.... Wedge and Prosser commented on the 'staggeringly high' proportion of one in twenty-two of their disadvantage children who both shared and wet the bed. 'Even when disadvantaged children were in bed, the nature of their sleep was likely to be very different from that of ordinary children.' (1973, p. 26). The outside toilet in the house at Bramwell, of course, provided no incentive for the children to go to the lavatory in the middle of the night and this was especially true in winter. Elsie therefore hoped that the move to the new house with its upstairs toilet would help the children gain more control, if only to reduce her washing load, but there was no improvement. No rubber sheets were being used in either home. The Newsons (1968, p. 326) reported that 11 per cent of their sample at four years of age were 'chronically enuretic in that they have more wet nights than dry ones', and as many as 30 per cent of children in social class V homes wet their beds at least occasionally at that age. Surprisingly, there is no detailed reference to the subject in their book on the children at seven.

We are forced to conclude that the atmosphere of violence, the feelings of insecurity, the lack of a developing sense of worth among the children, and the inconsistent methods of discipline which are imposed without explanation are not in the long-term interests of the children. The scapegoating of Steve, for instance, if continued indefinitely, is unlikely to produce a stable personality capable of succeeding within the educational and social systems, even though he appears to have the intellectual ability to do so. We therefore accept the conclusion of the

Newsons: 'Thus the child born into the lowest social bracket has everything stacked against him *including his parents' principles of child upbringing.*' (1976, p. 406, emphasis as in original). In general, we thought the children were being socialized to obey orders and to accept an authority against which they constantly bridled; in this they resembled their parents' own attitudes to authority.

We began studying the strategies which the children adopted to cope with their problems. In terms of the minimum period of eleven years which the children will spend at school, perhaps the most important tactic they employed at home was retreating into themselves and insulating themselves from the threats and the noise. We saw that even the toddlers who had no experience of school or nursery class had learned not to pay any attention to adults who were shouting at them. They had already developed the skill of 'filtering out' threatening adults, and they are likely to adopt the same defence mechanism when confronted with difficulties at school.

The Barker children exemplify perfectly the conclusion of Mitchell and Shepherd (1966) that many children exhibit disorders of behaviour *either* only at home *or* only at school. Whether school continues to be an oasis of peace and intellectual excitement and perhaps even a ladder to better things, remains to be seen. If education were to play that role for the children, they would still be faced with an uphill battle. Unfortunately, Elsie had internalized a Galtonian view of heredity, which was evident from such remarks of hers as 'I'm surprised any of mine are good at anything because I was a dunce.' She expected that all of her children would 'end up in a factory like everyone else round here'.

Another tactic was mainly used by the younger children in the daily scramble for attention and affection. Alice, for example, at the age of two-and-a-half, threw things at her mother in such a determined way that she was bound to be smacked. Just as Elsie was on the point of hitting her, Alice would burst into tears and put her arms round her mother's knees. She ran the risk of being punished in order to be cuddled. In a manner not too dissimilar, the older children would become more extreme and persistent in their behaviour to get what they wanted, knowing that their mother's resistance or good temper would soon crack. By the age of fifteen months John had learned from the others to scream at the slightest irritation or just to attract attention.

It is important to add that the practices employed by Elsie and Vince Barker can also be explained by a breakdown or loss of culture from generation to generation, and structural, as well as individual, psychological factors have played a significant role in that breakdown. Both parents had deprived and disturbed childhoods in families which were uprooted either in time of war or in search of work. The support normally supplied by the extended family of grandparents, uncles and aunts had not been available to the Barkers. Vince in particular had a mysterious and difficult past, with no relatives to draw upon. This had in part been caused by Vince and Elsie breaking the norms of their society and becoming the 'black sheep' of their respective families. The break with their families of origin had also partly been brought about by the sheer size of the problems they presented and the regularity with which they presented them. They were not considered by their relatives as a social advantage and every interaction with them was likely to result in loss of money, time and emotional tranquillity.

This leads us to the more general point that modern British society is not geared to cope with families of six or more children who are brought up on non-professional wages. Houses, wages, holidays and cars are all understandably produced with the ideal, nuclear family of two parents and two children in mind. Husband and wife are thought of as a single unit, who are supposed to work as a united team and share the joys of bringing up their two children. The formidable task of rearing six children would test the capacities of any young couple and is clearly beyond the capacities of *any* one individual acting on his or her own. And yet that is what Elsie is struggling to do. Barbara Wootton has accurately summed up Elsie's plight: '... the parents of large families are faced with quite exceptionally difficult problems, failure to cope adequately with which might well be a sign, not so much of their own sub-normality, as of their lack of the supranormal qualities which the situation demands' (1959, p. 59). Elsie still does not have the basic household gadgets which every middle-class wife with a husband and two children would take for granted. No wonder that she already longs for the future when her children will have grown up, married and left home. In Hilary Land's (1969) study the richest respondents were able to cope with their large families by buying the accommodation and all the support services they needed; it was Elsie's inadequate resources which made her large family seem over-abundant.

The absence of any views on wider social issues (such as the optimum size for populations and families with limited resources) was also relevant to the Barkers' decision to have so many children. Their political horizons were narrow and their range of experience limited. In their attitude towards authority they were both firmly of the opinion that '*They* are against large families' and, in a very real sense, the Barkers were right. We concluded, however, that the six children were not so much the outcome of a conscious *decision* to have a large family as the result of a number of interacting factors such as Vince's *machismo* and refusal to allow Elsie contraception, her fear of defying him and her embarrassment about sexual matters, their own feelings of powerlessness and their insecurities as adults, the cost of another child becoming increasingly marginal (the number of children jumped suddenly from two, Steve and Alice, to five with the arrival of Tracy and Nick and the birth of Tom), their lack of a broad social perspective, and perhaps a lack of foresight and planning.

The Barker family fit the pattern described by Askham (1975), who explored the reasons why lower working class couples tend to have more children than skilled working class couples. She found that those with larger families tended to have experienced throughout their lives more poverty, insecurity and deprivation than those with smaller families and that this affected their view of the world and their attitudes to the size of families: 'Where deprivation is extensive the type of orientations which develop, and which guide behaviour, are a concern with the present rather than the future, a sense of the individual's lack of control over his own life and therefore a passive acceptance of events rather than use of individual initiative, and a relative lack of striving for material achievement' (p. 168).

The question which Askham's concentration on the situational factors of the lower working class raises is: should we expect people who live from crisis to crisis and who are at the bottom of the heap in society to behave rationally, generously and providently? Is it sensible to expect such behaviour especially from people who have suffered as much as Elsie and Vince? We have, in fact, given instances earlier in this chapter when Vince and Elsie revealed an exceptional generosity of spirit by welcoming Tracy and Nick into their single room and by giving away clothes to their neighbours. Elsie showed foresight in saving for Christmas, and she managed their debts as carefully as she could. She and her children eked out a drab and poverty-stricken existence, but she alone appeared to bear the burden of anxiety and to bear the brunt of the minor humiliations associated with penury. Debt and mismanagement of income loomed large in the lives of the thirty-three 'families without hope', studied by Tonge, James and Hillam. One of their conclusions – 'An impoverished family can avoid the millstone of debt, but only if the wife had a personality which is free of psychopathic traits such as impulsiveness' (1975, p. 88) – is simply not applicable to Elsie. She could be possessed of the most equable temperament in the world and still not be able to keep her head above water financially. Elsie was well aware that the goods in the local shop were far more expensive than in the supermarkets in the city centre. For example, she could buy the very same loaf which cost her $17\frac{1}{2}$p at Helen's in the centre of town for 13p. But as both Land (1969) and Piachaud (1974) have demonstrated, the poor are forced to buy food in small quantities, at frequent intervals, and often on credit so that they end up by paying more. The local shop cannot be pilloried for its high prices because its 'customers are poor and only make small purchases, (it) has a low turnover, cannot get bulk-purchase discounts from the manufacturer, and, despite low wages and rent, has to charge high prices to break even' (Piachaud, 1974, p. 3). Elsie also knew of the existence of the new hypermarkets which had recently opened in the region, but without a car, a fridge and a deep freeze, the advantages of bulk buying, of buying in season and buying special offers and 'loss leaders' were not available to her. As Piachaud argued, you need money to enable you to save money.

It is nevertheless tempting to summarize our discussion on the family by referring to the historical evidence which, in Young and Willmott's words, presents a kind of working-class man who is 'a sort of absentee husband, sharing with his wife neither responsibility nor affection, partner only of the bed', and his wife as 'struggling bravely on though worn out by children, loaded with hardship and old before her time, sharing a house but not a life with a figure pictured as neither a loyal husband nor a dutiful father' (1962, p. 19). The concern Vince had for his reputation as a big drinker, the facility for smart repartee, his love of excitement and danger, the exaggerated masculinity as shown by his physical toughness and his aggressive sexuality all suggest a close parallel with Miller's (1958) famous paper on 'Lower Class Culture as a Generating Milieu of Gang Delinquency'. Though originally written to describe the 'focal concerns' of slum life in American cities, and though mercilessly characterized by Charles Valentine (1968) as the projection of unresolved problems of the middle class onto the poor, the article is still relevant to an explanation of working class adolescent behaviour in Britain, as David Downes (1966, p. 113) readily acknowledged. Miller's six 'focal concerns' – trouble, toughness, smartness, excitement, fate, autonomy – or at least the first four, seem to summarize Vince's main interests and preoccupations. Rereading the article with the Barker family in mind, one is struck time and again by how apposite it is. For example, Miller wrote, 'A mother will evaluate the suitability of her daughter's boyfriend less on the basis of his achievement potential than on the basis of his innate "trouble" potential.' Elsie's mother did exactly that: her relationship with Vince was forever marred by her knowledge that he had been in prison.

Vince's compulsive charade of masculinity can also be seen in terms of *machismo*, which is not seen by Keller as an expression of masculine strength and power but of masculine weakness and impotence. The man who exhibits *machismo* lacks status in three important areas: in relation to material success, other men and women. As she commented: 'The stress occasioned by failure, and the sense of inadequacy and frustration accompanying it, propels men to accentuate those aspects of admitted masculinity that they can control.... Hence, a common theme in lower-class milieus around the world is for men who are failures in the world's eyes to berate women.' (1975, p. 21).

One of our earliest thoughts about the Barkers' marital relationship was that Vince believed in strictly segregated roles, whereby he felt that his work, with its shift system, was so physically demanding that he should not be expected to help in the running of the home or in the rearing of the children; those two tasks were, we thought, exclusively women's work, as far as Vince was concerned, and therefore Elsie's preserve. After four months, however, we began to change our opinion, as the evidence mounted that Vince had no fear of being associated with women's skills. We learned, for example, that he had helped to deliver Eddie, an incident which Elsie still recalled with embarrassment. At the time, he was a keen and skilful cook who prepared the Sunday lunch for the whole family. He was also clever with his hands, was able to sew and had made a necklace for Elsie, and a totem pole and fancy-dress costumes for the children. Moreover, he once created a scroll, complete with ribbon and seal (a beer bottle top), as a certificate for those who had been so many years 'on the dole'. But the longer our project continued, the more we returned to our original conception, as Vince withdrew whatever help he had been offering Elsie. His life at Bramwell seemed to us to revolve around his work, the pub and other masculine pleasures, which accounted for an increasingly high percentage of the family income. He appeared not to care about the additional stress to which Elsie was subjected because of constant anxieties about debt.

Any summary which made Vince out to be the 'villain of the piece' would contain a measure of verisimilitude but it would not be the whole story. For, to appreciate *his* situation, one needs to ask: what does the future hold for him? His job demanded that he remained in perfect physical condition and yet he was already in his late thirties, he was two stone overweight, and every day he ran the risk of injury, dust and disablement. If he should be fortunate enough to escape such fates, he can still look forward to steadily decreasing physical strength and a correspondingly lighter pay packet. In other words, the future for Vince was one of increasing gloom and he was too intelligent not to be aware of it. In such a predicament, living for the present *was* a rational and understandable reaction. Deferring gratification in terms of saving for the future would be a sensible strategy, only if you could believe that you were going to survive long enough and be fit enough to enjoy those savings. Liebow (1967, p. 6) described the working man at Tally's Corner who squanders a week's pay in two days, not because 'like an animal or a child, he is "present-time oriented", unaware of or unconcerned with his future. He does so precisely because he is aware of the future and the hopelessness of it all.' On the other hand, Vince's 'short-run hedonism' provided pleasures for himself and not for any other member of the family, and he did not live through creating happiness for his family.

Shiftwork presented Vince and his family with a number of different problems, and shiftwork, according to Young and Willmott (1975, p. 175), 'is clearly on a large, and increasing, scale' in British industry. Their sample of ninety-five shiftworkers contained, mainly because of the higher wages, 'relatively few young unmarried men and relatively more married, especially if they had large families to support' (1975, p. 183); Of this sample, however, 52 per cent said that their work interfered with family life. In just the same way that we saw Elsie behave, so Young and Willmott reported that 'Many of the wives felt frightened being alone in the house at nights, and made themselves anxious trying to keep the house quiet while their husbands were asleep in the day, avoiding the use of their vacuum cleaners, trying to hush the children and rushing to the door if anyone rang to stop it happening twice.' (p. 186). Although Young and Willmott did find some families who adapted well to the irregularites inherent in shiftwork, a study by Mott et al., quoted by Brown (1975), showed that 'shiftwork made it difficult to perform the duties attached to marital roles and, particularly for fathers with school age children, it made it difficult to fulfil the role of father' (p. 236). The physical and temporal demands made on Vince by his work certainly helped to throw the major burden of rearing the six children onto Elsie.

The immediate future for Elsie was just as bleak, if not more so. She was then deep 'in the first trough of the Rowntree cycle' of poverty (Young and Willmott, 1975, p. 183), and likely to remain there for at least eight more years until Steve became old enough to work. Moreover, unlike Vince, she had never experienced a period of relative affluence while she was earning money and before she was first married.

The repeated pattern of early marriage and even earlier illegitimate conception in her extended family is a powerful force, pushing adolescent girls into grossly overcrowded or inadequate housing, as happened to Elsie. There is then the incentive to have a second child because of the need for more housing points in order to acquire a council house. Such young families are then swept into what Ineichen called the vortex of disadvantage where 'the workings of the housing market put couples into positions which mock their own best interests' (1975, p. 303).

When looking at Elsie's psychological health, it is worth recalling Brown, Bhrolchain and Harris's report (1975, p. 246) a 'surprisingly high rate of psychiatric disturbance among working-class women with young children at home'. Furthermore, they identify four factors which increase the chances of developing such a disorder in the presence of severely threatening events or major difficulties (concerning housing, money or children, for example). Elsie has had her share of severe life-events and of major long-term difficulties. In addition her vulnerability was increased because, of the four factors – 'loss of mother in childhood, three or more children aged under 14 living at home, lack of an intimate confiding relationship with a husband or boyfriend, and lack of full- or part-time employment' – all but the first applied to Elsie.

The outlook for Tracy Barker was also grim. Her removal from home and her involvement in institutional care had, in her father's opinion, only increased her problems. To quote the famous dictum of Florence Nightingale – 'The first requisite of a hospital is that it should do the sick no harm' – is *not* to condemn or to criticize the excellent care provided by the Children's Home but to point to the enormity of the task faced by such professionals when dealing in a residential setting with a young girl who had suffered so much from such an early age. Despite the commitment of large amounts of staff time and specialized psychiatric help, her behaviour deteriorated steadily and she was eventually transferred to a Community Home. Our case study therefore adds weight to the growing body of opinion in the United States and in this country which favours a move away from custodial treatment. The arguments for such a change in policy are to be found in the work of Goffman (1968), Polsky (1962), Schur (1973) and Cornish and Clarke (1975) amongst others. The tenor of the movement can be judged from the following comment of Wheeler et al. (quoted by Cornish and Clarke, 1975, p. 50): '... it is not at all clear that doing something is better than doing nothing... we are finally beginning to understand that any intervention has the possibility of harm as well as help....' The closing of the training schools in Massachusetts (Cooper, 1976, p. 224) shows that 'a major shift from a custodial and large-scale institutional response towards smallness in scale and variety of provision' is possible. An extension of fostering, and a greater investment in community workers and in intermediate treatment generally (Leissner, Powley and Evans, 1977) would go some way to increasing the variety and effectiveness of our response to the types of problem which Tracy Bennett and many other adolescents like her present us with. Cohen (1979) has, however, spelled out the dangers implicit in any naive, utopian move to greater community control.

For the Barker children the primary school in Bramwell, although it was housed in old and inadequate buildings, was a place of safety, reason and intellectual excitement in comparison with home. All five children loved school and attended regularly and this was one of our most hopeful findings. It suggests that, despite the depressing conclusions of Jencks et al. (1973) about the long-term impotency of education with regard to eradicating the inequalities suffered by the children in the same class position as the Barkers, schools serving deprived areas may still play a crucial role in improving the quality of life for many individual children. There remains the problem of caring for such children during school holidays, which always became times of crisis for the Barkers. One is left, however, wondering what measures would *significantly* alter the life chances of the Barker children. For at present they and their parents, in Henry Thoreau's phrase, 'lead lives of quiet desperation'.

3 Ada Paterson: An 'Inadequate' Mother

We were introduced to Ada by her social worker, Denis Johnson, and visited her over eighty times during a period of eighteen months. She was described to us as 'inadequate' and as a widow with broken relationships and discarded children behind her; her problems seemed to be chiefly those of loneliness and dependence. Her world at first appeared to us to be chaotic with many threads crossing in an apparently random fashion. Ada herself attributed many of her problems to bad luck.

Ada's house was exactly the same as that of the Barker family, who lived two doors away in Bramwell. Although Elsie Barker said there had been significant contact in the past—she said she had fed Ada when she had had no food and had given the child clothes—the households did not seem to be in close contact, and the only link was a gossiping mother, Margaret, who visited various houses spreading tales of mischief from one to the other. The first member of the project to visit the Paterson home noted that '[the garden was] no better than a rubbish tip, part of the down spouting is cracked and broken, and the paintwork is peeling and crumbling—the house itself is in general dereliction'. Shortly after Ada left the area, the council set about doing repairs to all the houses on the estate. At the same time, because of subsidence in the area, a number of houses were demolished. There was talk among residents of the council's plans for the whole area 'coming down' and to rehouse the entire community, but nobody locally knew when this might be.

Ada talked of wanting to leave the house because of its size and its associations with her husband, Alf. She had been widowed earlier in the year, and she gave repeated and detailed accounts of Alf's death and funeral to each of us in turn. She told us that she had been very depressed after his death, 'terrible bad with my nerves', and she appeared to be suffering from depression when we visited her. Ada was taking valium, talked of having taken an overdose to kill herself and often looked haggard and drawn. Sometimes she would cry, her speech and movements would be slow, and a nervous tick would play about her eyelids. Stomach cramps, diarrhoea and vomiting beset her at intervals, and in retrospect it seems likely that they too were related to the emotional crises she was undergoing. Much later during the course of the fieldwork when the insecurities of this period were past, her demeanour and health improved considerably. Even during this period, sudden hopeful interludes would lead her to tend her hair, put in her teeth (except for eating), apply lipstick and eye shadow, and generally dress to be attractive.

The early relationship between Ada and the project was not easy. Almost from the beginning, crises in her day-to-day life demanded that we pay attention to her present problems. This made it difficult to ask about her life history, and in particular conversation would be riveted to one or two major preoccupations, problems that Ada herself could not solve. Her talk was often repetitive and depressing. Because we wanted to give as well as to take from her, we took her for an outing with her son, Michael, and took commemorative photographs. We also ferried them to the bus which was to take the child to the residential school he was attending. The chauffeuring became a pattern, useful to the project as well as helpful to Ada, but eventually a problem. At one stage, we feared that we had made her over-dependent on the cars, and guilt was only later assuaged by the social worker who told us how Ada had organized a similar private transport system with other visitors in the past, and had tried to organize *him* in the same way.

This aspect of the relationship was an example of a more general problem in the conduct of our fieldwork: namely that it was very difficult to participate, observe and yet not to interfere and seriously affect the situation. Ada seemed anxious to thrust problems, and more worryingly, decisions into others' hands, and the desire to help had always to be tempered by the need to hold back and leave the decisions for her to make. This problem was encountered more in relation to Ada than to any of the other families and caused the fieldwork in this case to be more of a strain than in any other. Another related problem was the unreliability of some of her statements and of her re-interpretations of the past which sought to engage our present sympathies and active support. Understanding of her situation and of the processes leading up to it evaded us while her problems swept over her and us alike.

During the course of the first full year of fieldwork the changes were so constant that we were not able to predict a more peaceful stage from the first months of interviewing, nor the downward turn of events eighteen months later. A long period of contact was absolutely necessary to form any understanding of the problems and to watch Ada's interaction with individuals and organizations.

Ada Paterson's Biography

Ada's parents were born at the turn of the century; her father, Mr Smith, was a local man and her mother came from Wales. Mrs Smith had worked in service with the family of a dentist; later, during the war, she worked in a munitions factory, and after the war she had cooked in the kitchens of a large, city hospital. Ada's father worked locally – in the pit; he had been married before, and he brought a daughter, Frances, to the second marriage. Ada's mother came from a family of seven, but four of her brothers and sisters had died in a fire one Christmas when the streamers from the tree caught fire. Ada's mother had gone on working until she saw one of the kitchen staff killed by a car (she herself was knocked down); after this her nerves deteriorated and she never worked again. She was then about sixty-five. She died several years ago in her early seventies – 'of a heart attack and old age' – while Ada's father had died quite recently. He was suffering from Parkinson's diease and was nearly blind when he had fallen from an upstairs landing and was killed.

Ada appears to have got on well with her parents and to have been particularly close to her mother. She would sometimes remark that if her mother were alive, she would not have let her daughter stay 'in this mess'. Her half-sister, Frances, who was four or five years older than Ada, was supposed to have been jealous of her, and they apparently fought bitterly as children. At about the age of three, Ada had been in hospital for three or four weeks as a result of chasing her older sister across a road and moving into the path of a bus. Her younger brother, Len, was brought into the same hospital with scald burns sustained at home during this same period. Frances left home to marry early and produced six children. Ada, when not quite fourteen, had to look after her brother, Len, another brother, Dick, sister Beryl and baby Tom because her mother did shiftwork. Ada was frequently absent from both her first school before the age of eleven and from her last school. She learned to read, write and spell, but little else. She went to school only when this fitted in with her mother's shiftwork schedule: her mother had to work because her husband (Ada's father) earned so little in the pit. He suffered progressively more from bronchitis as he got older. There were always problems in making ends meet, even though her mother worked, but Ada thought the happiest time of her life had been when she was a child with her parents in – as she recalled it – a clean, happy, well looked after home. Not only Ada's education but also her social life were limited by her child-minding role, something which she remembered with wry humour. This situation continued after she left school at the age of fourteen, in the early 1940s and was something of a trial to her when she was working and of an age to have boyfriends. She earned little, but gave her pay-packet to her mother out of which she was given ten shillings per week pocket money.

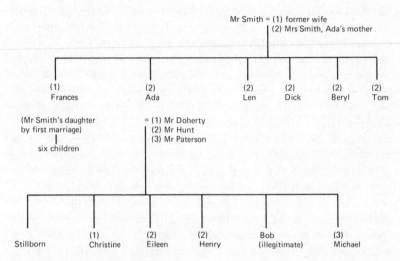

Figure 3.1   Ada Paterson's Family Tree

The first man in her life was in the armed services, and she had a child by him when she was seventeen. The child was stillborn, and Ada said: 'to tell you the truth it was a good thing she died'. ('To tell you the truth . . .' was Ada's standard conversational opening). Her parents had an understanding attitude towards pregnancy, but had thought her too young to have the child. The man had been pleased that the child died, and he was married shortly afterwards to someone else.

Ada's first job was as an unskilled labourer in a local factory. After five years, when she was nineteen, she moved to a similarly unskilled job in another factory, where she spent two years before becoming pregnant with her first daughter, Christine. Ada worked until the last possible minute before going into hospital, although she was carrying heavy loads every day.

Being pregnant when she got married, she was not able to have a white wedding such as her mother would have liked to give her. Her fiancé, Mr Doherty, was a Roman Catholic, but she did not convert to his faith. After a year, Mr Doherty deserted her for another woman, and Ada divorced him. The daughter, Christine, was adopted by a professional man, and has herself followed a profession allied to his.

Ada set out to hitchhike to London when she was twenty-three, but she met her second husband, Mr Hunt, in a transport café on the way. He was a long-distance lorry driver and was twenty-five years her senior; she returned with him to Birmingham, became his housekeeper and eventually married him. Altogether she lived with him for eight years, and then left him, giving as the reason than she was living too far from her parents and that her mother was ill. She later divorced him. She had two children by him, Eileen, who at the time of writing was seventeen and worked as a secretary, and Henry, aged sixteen, who was also working. Her fourth child, Bob, eleven-years-old, dated from the end of this period, after her return to Kindleton, and was the result of an encounter with a local man, Fred Bourne.

Before Ada's second divorce went through, she was already living with another man, Pete, in a caravan. He left her or, according to another version, her mother advised her to leave until the divorce from Mr Hunt was finalized, and Ada returned to live with her mother again. (We shall have cause to remember Pete later.) At about this time, Ada met Alf and conceived Michael, her fifth and last child. After the birth, she was divorced, and also at about this time had a hysterectomy to remove a malignant growth. Ada and Alf had council flats in Cardale and later came to live in the house at Bramwell, where we first met her. Michael did not thrive particularly well, and was in and out of hospital several times. The family lived on social security.

When Michael was four, Alf and Ada got married. Ada's social worker thought that the contact with the social services had been made by Alf who had volunteered himself and family as being in need of help. For a number of years Alf argued and fought with local authority officers, sometimes dragging Ada long as evidence of his sick dependent. Ada's psychological state of health was apparently brought down by this, and she underwent psychiatric treatment for depression. Ada attended a day centre for the sub-normal, but would only go there when chauffeured by a social worker. When Ada's husband died, the child was sent to a residential school. Alf had worked as an unskilled labourer during the last year of his life. Nevertheless, they had a reputation in the area for bad debts, as Alf was an erratic provider and an impulsive spender. After her husband's death Ada became a sort of 'merry widow', blossoming into cosmetics and outings again.

Social Services Involvement during Fieldwork

The involvement of social services in Ada's affairs had been fairly constant for some time, and it is probably worth noting those areas where their advice or intervention could be seen to spotlight her problems during our period of fieldwork. After Alf's death, she had agreed that Michael, her son, should be sent to a residential school, because of his general debility and the bad effect which his father's death had had on his health. Michael was small for his age, but his father had also been a small man. Both he and his father had had a history of childhood illness.

When we arrived on the scene in June, Denis Johnson, Ada's social worker, was helping her with the problem of a rent rebate form which the housing department had lost. Denis was called in again in August when Mrs Paterson gave all her money to her current boyfriend, Pete, with whom she had lived many years earlier in a caravan; he went off with the money leaving her penniless. At about this time the social worker gave her five pounds for food, and he had previously given her twenty pounds in food vouchers. When she exchanged her house for a council flat on a different estate, Cardale, social services provided her with a stove, but she did not get it connected because she claimed that she could not afford the connection charge.

At the beginning of October she again contacted Denis Johnson to discuss her financial arrangements. She had an electricity bill to pay and was expecting a very high gas bill. Shortly after this she said that something was wrong with the electricity meter and that she had spent the weekend in the dark, only getting the problem put right when she walked up to social services to get help. At this time she was also in debt to a loan company. Her boyfriend, Pete, had disappeared, and so she decided to throw out all her furniture, lately provided by social services, in an effort to force them to rehouse her. If she could not get a room, she reasoned, somebody would pick her off the street, even if it was only the police. She said that her social worker had taken her to the DHSS office in her new area, but he had been unable to persuade them to give her assistance as she was already receiving a widow's pension. At our next visit, an outing to Michael's school, the matron of the school said that she would telephone Ada's social worker for her because Ada had said that she must leave her flat. The reasons she gave were the malicious neighbours, the fact that she had no friends in the area, that she would have to live in town if she were to get a job, that she had no furniture, and that she must avoid her boyfriend, who would come back on Tuesday, as soon as he knew she had collected her pension. She also said that her doctor had advised her to leave.

The social worker at this stage advised her very strongly against leaving her flat because she would find it very difficult to get another council tenancy. He also offered to replace her furniture and pleaded with her to postpone taking any action for at least a week. Denis Johnson's advisory role was supplemented by material assistance of an essential kind. He managed to sort out a problem over Ada's pension which the DHSS office in her new area had reduced considerably on the grounds that her child was in a residential school. The ruling of the office in her previous area had been that she was entitled to provision for the child in spite of this. He provided her with furniture and carpets, with an electric cooker (unconnected – which proved to be another problem with which she could not deal herself), with an offer of a Home to go to for Christmas, with money (from a special fund) towards her gas bill, with money for bedding, with assistance with the crisis of her burgled meter, and with her rent rebate forms. In April, Ada said he had told her he could not help her with her bills any more, and she was cut off by the electricity board.

Health

For the first eight months of our involvement, a doctor was constantly supplying Ada Paterson with medication for depression, for repeated attacks of vomiting and diarrhoea, and, she asserted, for bronchitis and toxaemia. She complained repeatedly of depression. She went into the casualty department of a local hospital after what she described as an attempted rape. On one occasion she called the doctor because she claimed that she could not get her breath. She went again to hospital because of a very bad pain in her left side. She called the doctor again when she had another attack of vomiting and diarrhoea and also backache. Next she talked about the doctor worrying about her loss of weight. She said she had gone into hospital again, having taken an overdose. She again suffered vomiting and diarrhoea and visited the doctor, complaining of pains in her stomach and chest. She suffered migraines which, like the vomiting, she attributed at this stage to the gas central heating. She was again taken to the hospital, this time by ambulance, after she had collapsed in a pub: she claimed that she had had a heart attack (her social worker insisted that the hospital had said that there was nothing much wrong with her). Ada was still taking three valium a day when her next door neighbour heard her screaming and found her writhing in pain on the sofa with her 'nerve pills' scattered about: when the doctor was called in, he said she was suffering from deep depression and not drug poisoning and prescribed a sleeping pill. He returned ten minutes later to find that she had gone to the local club to meet her boyfriend, and he told the neighbour to tell her that she was wasting all their time. These continual crises in her psychological and physical health all occurred in a period of less than eight months. In the past she had been in hospital with a stomach ulcer, a 'repair' of this, for an appendectomy and a hysterectomy as well as for six hospital births.

Why, then, so many health problems during this period? We give below a summarized account of her main preoccupations as she herself saw them at this time: their multiplicity and inter-connectedness speak for themselves.

She was depressed after Alf's death and bored in the absence of his company and that of her child, who had gone to a residential school. Quite soon after the start of our fieldwork, an old flame, Pete, who many years earlier had lived with her in a caravan, moved in again, but she was worried about the instability of the arrangement. Almost immediately he was asking for – or just taking – her money and keys, and leaving her without warning for days at a time. She wanted to move from her house in Bramwell. She went out to look for Pete and was attacked in the street by a man in a car; the police were something less than sympathetic about this incident and seemed to think that she might just have been drunk and fallen over. But for whatever cause her leg was hurt and bandaged and she did receive out-patient treatment at hospital.

Pete returned after a week, and Ada bought him trousers, socks, after-shave and hair cream, but was preoccupied with the uncertainty of his movements. He humiliated her publicly at the club and hit her when they had rows at home. He 'took' all her money, leaving her without food. She felt suicidal: but she was also afraid he would come back. According to Ada, he hit Michael when the boy was at home on holiday.

Pete returned and tried to make Ada reverse her decision to exchange houses with the Martin family, who had a flat at Cardale. Under presssure from the Martins, Ada signed the forms, but then had serious doubts. In the end, the police were called to force her to go. She moved to the ground floor flat in Cardale but was very unhappy with the area and with the loss of her friends (although she complained about the social isolation in Bramwell, she did have some considerable contact with neighbours). Pete was apparently following a pattern of driving Ada in his van to get her pension, taking the money from her, going off for two or three days, and then returning – spending the time that he was with her either drinking or sleeping.

The next few interviews were full of Pete's comings and goings and misdemeanours and also full of distress at the 'filthiness' of the flat, at problems with the gas central heating and with the electric cooker which had not been connected. Ada said she wanted to return to Bramwell; during this period she was extremely depressed, she was taking valium, suffering from stomach and digestive disorders and complaining that she had no food; her relationship with Pete and the general pattern of her life had led to a quarrel with women neighbours, one of whom, Gwen, had been very kind to Ada when she had no cooker or hot water.

Ada went looking for rooms in the city – she no longer got on with Alf's relations because of Pete and his behaviour towards Michael. Pete disappeared, the electricity meter went wrong, and even though Denis Johnson had it mended, Ada threw out her furniture and carpets, and determined to leave. After Denis Johnson persuaded her not to do this, she was given more furniture, but was incapacitated by another attack of stomach or intestinal problems, which was followed by the problems of a burglary in which her radio and clock were taken as well as all the money from the electricity meter. Once again Pete disappeared taking her money.

At about this time, Ada was concerned about her relations with Alf's sisters and family; she made no effort to visit Michael at the school herself – knowing that they would be there – although she tried to get us to take her. Alf's niece and her husband had been talking of adopting Michael and of having him at their home over Christmas. Ada agreed to the Christmas visit but had a row with them during the holiday and took the child away; her main preoccupation during all this period, however, was with Pete and his 'intentions'. She tried to involve us and her social worker in talking to him to find out whether he intended to stay and make a home with her or not. She wanted it to be true, even though she alleged that he took all her money, was feared by the child, never took her out, was unfaithful, left her without food or money and denied her any part of a woman's role at home. She was getting deeply into debt.

In mid January she was in hospital again and maintained she had had a heart attack. She claimed that the housing department had insisted that Pete must go, but he would not. Relations with Ada's neighbour, Gwen, had been steadily improving all through December and January, until Ada seemed to be spending all her time upstairs in Gwen's flat. On one of Pete's returns from a visit to his sick father, Ada got Gwen to confront Pete with everything he had done, but when Pete said he was leaving she denied all the allegations she had made. Pete strongly denied that he had taken any of her money. There were more rows with, on one occasion, the police being called; another time the doctor was called when Ada feigned another overdose. Finally the meter was burgled again, and Pete disappeared from the scene. It was during this period that she told us she preferred being in hospital to being at home.

Relationships with Men

Ada spoke about Alf with some loyalty, saying what a good husband he had been and how he used to fight on her behalf with the housing and social services departments. She did not mention how she used to have to go down to his works to try to collect his wages before he spent them on the way home. Time had polished his image into that of the perfect husband, solicitous when she had a bad back and good fun when they went out for a Saturday night. Even his unending feud with the housing department was transformed in retrospect into an amusing anecdote. Alf's complaint was that the house was infested with cockroaches and was very cold, and he had withheld rent, saying that he was fighting for central heating to be installed. Ada's social worker suggested that her life with him was not so pleasurable and that she suffered from depression, but Ada either edited this out of her account for our benefit or edited it out of her memory for her own.

Some months after Alf's funeral Ada began living with Pete, her relationship with whom we have already described. After Pete's departure, she had a short relationship with an ex-paratrooper, and then she met Stan, a general labourer, who described his work experience as if he were a skilled man. He said he could do anything in building, but his decorating was so shoddy that we began to have doubts about his claim. He was able to earn good wages and to do without cards or income tax liability by living a semi-nomadic existence, working in different parts of the country. He had started life in Wales as a miner and then worked in a steel works, but he had found the 'sameness' of a local community boring. He had also been married and had children but he was restless and had moved about a lot. Neither he nor Pete came from the truly dispossessed class of society: both had inherited a house from their parents.

Pete, however, had several physical disadvantages: he was very short, he had a pronounced stammer which made his speech practically unintelligible, his parents were aged and in poor health and he had a severely sub-normal twin. Pete had a plastic leg bone following a motor bike accident when he was seventeen and this impaired his mobility in cold weather; nevertheless, he tended to do strenuous work such as heavy vehicle driving. Like Stan, he could earn good wages as long as his employment was not on the record and his wages consequently subject to tax and national insurance payments, but, on the other hand, this meant he had poor security of employment. He tended to move about in search of work, and to drop poorly paid jobs when he had a cold or was going out with Ada. Pete had twice been married and was waiting for a divorce from 'the old bag' with whom he had last lived.

Stan moved in with Ada almost immediately after they met, and Ada started talking about marriage and of what she would wear for an Easter wedding. When Ada had her electricity supply cut off again in March Stan put up with living in her flat without electricity for a month. But Easter came and went without a wedding. Stan's marital status, i.e. whether married or divorced, never became clear. Ada was relying very heavily on her neighbour, Gwen. She would spend all day in Gwen's flat, eat with her and use her cooker to cook Stan's tea. Also during this period, Ada suffered another break-in – the fifth, she claimed, in the seven months since she had come to the area – at a time when she was in debt and in need of every penny of her pension. Ada and Stan's relationship seemed very unstable for a while, with a series of rows and complaints from Ada. Michael came home on holiday, but had apparently not liked Stan. Stan was laid off work in May and remained out of work for nine months, for the rest of the course of our fieldwork. At the beginning he was very touchy on the subject of being unemployed, and one of the problems for Ada became the uncertainty as to whether or not he was going to leave her and search for another job elsewhere. But by the end of May, the tone of conversations had changed, Stan was buying trinkets for Ada to wear and for the living room, and was talking of redecorating the new flat they were in (Ada having exchanged flats with Gwen).

As Stan's status improved, the relationship with Gwen deteriorated, and women neighbours held an informal tribunal condemning Ada for thinking more of her man than of her son. She had apparently asked Gwen to tell Stan to go, and then had backed down, exactly as she had done in the incident with Pete: the neighbours now condemned her as a woman whose priorities were wrong. At this point there was a break in contact because Stan was unwilling for us to see Ada; indeed, we scarcely saw her alone after this. When we saw her again, she seemed much more settled: Stan was stripping the walls, they had a television and were generally presenting an image of conventional domesticity. Ada was even talking about getting a job, so that they could buy bits and pieces for the home and go away on holiday. Stan began to claim social security of £26 per week for himself, Ada and the boy, and Ada now lost her full pension. The flat was still in Ada's name and costing £2.50 per week. Although Ada and Stan's relationship seemed to be flourishing, the child, who was home on holiday, was apparently being dumped on neighbours and friends, and the alienated women neighbours were not slow to describe problems between him and Stan. By this time, Ada had stopped taking valium, and was not depressed, but at intervals talked of Gwen 'turning against her'; and of not liking the people in the neighbourhood. The child went to visit his aunts for the long summer holiday, and Ada talked about her social worker being determined to let the aunts adopt Michael when he came home from the school for good.

Ada's Relationship with her Son

At Christmas, Ada and Stan were leading quite a homely life (Ada, who had always been preoccupied with 'going out' and the 'good time', talked of taking up knitting), and Michael, who had finally come home to them permanently, was getting on well with both Stan and his mother. In the New Year, however, the idyll was over: over Christmas Ada had thrown Stan out and brought back Pete; she had taken Michael to stay with his aunts until the end of his holiday; she then got rid of Pete and reinstalled Stan. She talked of Michael refusing to eat, of his sleepwalking and 'not doing anything for' her, of his being 'deep', and not telling her what was wrong. At the same time, she mentioned that with all the coming and going over Christmas, they had run up large debts and were due to be evicted for non-payment of rent and to have the electricity cut off if they did not pay a £25 bill. The problems of Michael and money came together when Ada explained that she had written to one of the aunts asking her if she would look after the boy until they got straight. But she added, 'I'd like to go away, get a job somewhere else and leave my worries behind me.' Stan was planning to go south, and Ada wanted to go too; her child was no longer part of Ada's world.

Michael was the last of five children (although Ada had had six pregnancies) and the only one of those five about whom we had any real information, the others either having been adopted or living in other parts of the country. We knew that one was a secretary, another a semi-professional and a third working; but we knew nothing about their home life or their relations with other young people. Of the fourth child, Bob, we knew only that he had been adopted. We cannot say whether they have suffered from the loss of their mother as well as, in some cases, their biological father. We know only that two of them have had training, and that they have 'gone up in the world' in Ada's eyes.

Ada felt that Michael would also do well, as he took after his father. Alf, however, appeared to be the only sibling in his family who had not done well for himself. Alf had come from a local family of seven, all small in stature like himself. One sister had a shop and the other two worked in factories; all of them were moderately successful and had cars. His brothers were all miners, but Alf had had diphtheria and was sickly as a child, having only one good lung. He had rarely been to school, and he could not read or write. There was some intergenerational continuity between the lives of Alf and Michael in that the boy had also been sickly. He was small for his age now, but at birth he had weighed only four pounds and was kept in an incubator. In addition he had suffered from meningitis when he was a few months old. He had also had gastroenteritis as a baby. Ada's fastidiousness in relation to food and washing-up was poor, and she herself, each of her men-friends in turn, and the child suffered rather frequently from bouts of sickness during our period of contact. We felt these two facts might well be related, and that her lack of knowledge of hygiene might have contributed to the ill health in her household.

The first and last references to Michael in our field-notes are curiously similar. In both of them, Ada complained that the boy would not eat, would not go out, and would not go with her to visit a relative some distance away. In both cases he had returned from a period away at a residential school, and in both he was getting used to a situation in which his mother was accompanied by a man other than his father. In the second instance, when he was eight, Ada described other symptoms such as refusing to sleep in his room (opposite her bedroom), sleepwalking, weeping and refusing to get up to go to school. When we met him at the residential school which he attended for nearly two years, he appeared to be relaxed and pleased to talk to us. Nevertheless, his teacher suggested that he sought attention more than a child from an affectionate, stable home would normally do. The matron of his school thought that his strong personality would pull him through, although she had not visited his home and she did not know what the circumstances of his home life would be when he returned there.

Ada was proud of Michael, and in our early contact with her she talked about how he could sing and play the guitar in school concerts: this was something of an over-estimation of his talents at that stage. In material terms, Ada was not an efficient provider for him: she did not feel it was her responsibility to buy him clothes, and she did not see to it that he ate. He returned to school with blepharitis, a disease of malnutrition or stress.

The most serious attack made on Ada by her neighbours was that she was not a proper mother, and that she put her men-friends before her child. Ada realized how important a charge this was (she could scarcely fail to, as it resounded, in awful repetition, about the flats for week after week) and she vigorously attempted to deny it. She asserted that whatever happened to Michael, she would always care for him; nevertheless, she did not act as a staunch protector, any more than she was a careful provider. She told us that early in her relationship with Pete, Pete had hit Michael until the child locked himself in the toilet, shaking like a leaf. Neighbours gossiped of similar treatment from Stan, and were of the opinion that one should never hit anyone else's children. Ada bundled the child off to spend the day with neighbours or friends when she wished to go out with her men-friends, and he was constantly in tears, not knowing where he would be sent next for a day or a week.

While the child was at the residential school, she telephoned him regularly, and wrote to him very occasionally. She often asserted that she wanted or intended to visit him on visiting days, which were every other Saturday in the afternoon, but unless she had someone who would ferry her there she did not in fact go. She claimed that various people, such as Alf's sisters or Denis Johnson, had promised to take her, but when we checked with these people, they denied having made any such promises. Denis Johnson said that she had always claimed she had a fear of public places including, apparently, public transport. Her reluctance, if not her fear, was very real, and we felt it might have been lessened if the journey to the residential school, which involved her taking two buses, had not been so long and complicated. It was certainly not easy for parents without cars to get to the school, and the transport problems were aggravated by the fact that visiting day tended to coincide with the day that the local football team played at home. At the beginning and end of holidays, a bus took the children between the residential school and the city centre. (It would have helped many of the parents on low incomes, if, in addition to this, there had been one regular bus for them every second Saturday afternoon).

Ada did not put up Christmas decorations for Michael, and did not provide him with a Christmas as such, in either year of our contact. This was left to Alf's relations. According to neighbours, the child had asked for food from a woman across the street, and according to Ada's own account, she had had no food for him or for herself when Pete took her money. Neither did she make sure that Michael would have a roof over his head, because she got rid of his bed when she wanted to leave her flat, and intended moving into one room, which was for herself and not her son. From all these points of view, one can see why she was generally condemned as 'inadequate' in her mothering role. Ada gave the impression that her own mother was very important to her, but Ada herself was not the kind of mother around whom a family revolves. To understand her better, we need to look at the networks of relatives, friends and officials with whom she interacted in her day-to-day life.

Relations with her In-Laws
Ada's relations with her own siblings were fairly tenuous, but with her in-laws they were explosive. The matron of Michael's school saw them as decent, working-class people who budgeted carefully and who therefore had no time for feckless women such as Ada who had people 'running round after them all the time, and who did nothing for themselves'. Nevertheless, their protective interest in Michael's welfare meant that they had to come into contact with Ada. Ada dreaded meeting them and continually expected to be reproached by them. Sometimes there were very upsetting rows when again Ada's fitness as a mother would be roundly called into question. Ada could clearly not stand up for herself whether she was in the right or not. An incident which happened on a visiting day at the school serves as an example of this. Two aunts brought Michael presents and a cake, insisting that it was his birthday, and telling Ada off publicly for forgetting it; they were entirely in the wrong about the date, but Ada could not bring herself to argue it out with them, although she was obviously upset. It was only afterwards in private that she was able to tell us the date, which in fact tallied with the boy's birth certificate.

For some time, Alf's extended family visited Michael regularly, and this in itself may have contributed to Ada's reluctance to visit him. Their alienation from Ada dated especially from the time when she volunteered information to them that her boyfriend Pete was hitting Michael and generally disliking the child. This was very curious imformation to give to his close relatives, reflecting, as it did, so badly on herself, although we presume that her motive was to put Pete in a bad light.

Ada complained that her in-laws organized her life after Alf died. However helpful they may have intended to be, they also seemed to want to strip her of Alf by taking her marriage certificate from her and even asking for the one photograph which she had of him. Some married relatives of Alf's who had no children were eager to adopt Michael, and it was this couple with whom he constantly stayed. Although Ada alleged that they wanted to take him from her, evidence, first from her social worker and later from her own description, suggested that she was not their victim, but that she actively offloaded the child onto them when her own way of life could not accommodate him.

Relations with her own Extended Family

During the first part of fieldwork, Ada had consistent, if not frequent, contact with her own sibling group. She used to go to a club with her brother and sister-in-law on a Saturday night, and there was reciprocal visiting with one of her brothers and a sister. When she was in hospital, the sister visited her there. Ada complained, nevertheless, that her family neglected her because of Pete who had a police record: this of course was in line with her assertion that everyone had turned against her because of him. By the end of her relationship with him, however, and after several hospital trips (during which Ada did not fail to let her relatives know that she was in need of visits) there seemed to be a period during which there was not much contact; no one, for instance, remembered her birthday, which caused her some disappointment. She was still feeling some coldness from her relatives when Stan arrived on the scene, and she remarked that she did not think they would come to her wedding if she invited them. During the relative stability of the following autumn, contact with her sister was renewed, and the death of her half-sister's husband itself precipitated some friendly contact amongst the sibling group. Apart from any demands which Ada might have made on them (she wanted to move in with one of her brothers when life was particularly difficult), Ada's loss of contact was probably in some measure a result of the inaccessability of her new home. This council estate was pleasingly set on the edge of green fields, but it was also expensively distant from the older parts of Kindleton and from some of the other peripheral council estates where some of her relatives lived. Contact was re-established with a sister largely because the latter acquired a car.

Relations with Neighbours in Bramwell and Cardale

When we first met Ada, she wanted to leave Bramwell and saw Cardale as the fountain of all happiness. Once installed at Cardale, she missed her friends and the shops she knew, and said that she and Michael hated the new area; soon she was complaining about the neighbours too, just as they were complaining about her. She tended to see places in terms of people, rather than material comfort, aesthetics or status. Exchanging flats with Gwen, for example, was perceived as a service to Gwen, so that her daughter would have a garden to play in. She seemed to feel no security in having material possessions – quite the reverse – and made no real fuss when the new tenants of her old house did not let her have her own cooker; when she wished to leave Cardale, however, she marked the strength of her decision by throwing out all her furniture.

Ada's relations with her neighbours were on the whole intense and volatile. When she lived in Bramwell, her neighbour, Margaret, was constantly in her house; Margaret was the gossip who, nevertheless, performed acts of kindness such as feeding Michael and setting Ada's hair. Ada said that no one came to see her in Bramwell, but at the same time she claimed that she had 'so many friends' there. It was not very long before she had struck up a friendship with her nearest neighbour in Cardale, who was soon inviting her up for tea and a sandwich and who in turn did her hair for her. After quite a short acquaintance she relied very heavily on this neighbour, Gwen, and was using her cooking facilities and boiling kettles in her flat until she sensed that she was not so welcome. Shortly after this, the neighbours combined in a verbal attack on Ada, and there was talk of the first conflict between Gwen and Ada's man-friend. On this occasion, Gwen was supposed to have heard Pete spreading rumours and scandal about Ada in the pub and to have told Ada about it. Ada confronted him about it and, when he denied it, called upon Gwen to make her accusations in front of him, which she refused to do. Ada then turned on Gwen and her other new neighbours, and saw them as troublemakers, who 'want nothing, but to cause upset among people'.

For a while, all contact between Ada and Gwen ceased, and Ada took up with the old lady from across the road, who did not belong to the same visiting and gossiping group as Gwen. Ada began to rely on her heavily for support, and involved her as well in her relationship with Pete to the extent of leaving his suitcases with her when he went off for a while. In his absence, she also went out to pubs and dancing, and met another man and some women with whom she made further arrangements for outings. The outgoing, 'pubbing' aspect of her life, however necessary for her own well-being, was frowned upon by her married or widowed neighbours, who spoke disparagingly of the amount of time and money she spent on drinking. It was the daytime drinking which was most frowned upon.

Not long after this, Gwen was friendly towards Ada again and, according to Ada, friendly with Pete. On the whole Ada nurtured a very close and dependent relationship with Gwen. Not only did she spend most of the day with her, both eating and watching television in her flat, but she talked intimately with her about her relationship with Pete and her feelings for him. The same thing occurred, when Ada had Stan living with her instead. Ada's means of creating closeness, however, was to complain bitterly and constantly about her men-friends, thus creating hostility between them and her closest woman-friend – a hostility which had an element of rivalry in it. Ada pushed this to the limit and used Gwen to confront Pete (and later Stan) with complaints which she herself did not have the courage to voice. She then became desperate, denied the accusations and left Gwen without her object and ally to defend – and Gwen quite naturally became upset. Gwen went through these dramas on Ada's behalf at least three times and still spoke well of her, fed her and to a great extent looked after her. During much of our fieldwork, Ada would come from Gwen's flat in order to talk to us, and Gwen performed other favours for Ada such as washing a coat for her, lending her a radio, dyeing her hair and giving her some curtains. It was only after the third drama, when Ada asked Gwen to tell Stan to go, that a big rift occurred; but even then, despite the big rift, the quarrel was overcome in the end and informal services resumed.

Relations with Social Worker and other Officials

The relations between Ada and the 'providers' of public services were not always so agreeable; for example, Ada complained that even Denis Johnson had 'turned against' her and was conspiring with her in-laws over the care of Michael. Ada's account of these relationships appeared to us to be very unreliable. There was very little correspondence between what she said and what Denis Johnson, or the matron of Michael's school, or Pete or Gwen, said about events in which she played a part. These divergences often arose when Ada attributed to others decisions and assertions of her own. We did not assume that because the social worker, or other responsible public employees, gave a different description of events that their description was the correct one, but the pattern of difference was so consistent and so similar to our own experience of Ada that we often did finally discount her version and looked at it from the point of view of how her doctoring of the past made sense of the present. Some examples of this might be useful at this point: when Ada moved to Cardale and went through a very unsettled period with Pete disappearing and reappearing on pension days, Ada began to attribute all her misfortunes to a single cause: the move itself. She seemed to forget that Pete had been behaving in just the same way when she was living in Bramwell; instead she remembered Bramwell as the place where she had had 'all the luck in the world'. Towards the end of our period of fieldwork, when she was in a relatively settled period of her relationship with Stan, she recalled Bramwell as the place where she used to be ill and depressed, and seemed to have obliterated entirely her first months of constant crisis in Cardale. When Ada was faced with a decision about where Michael should go for Christmas, she asserted that one of us had said it would be 'alright' for Michael to go to his aunts: such a responsibility not being one which we had courted or accepted. It seemed that we were being dragged into the picture as authorities, when we had not intended to direct her in any way.

Other discprepancies were more puzzling: her social worker said it was very unlikely that the housing department would refuse a tenant's request to have a lodger, and yet Ada received a letter from them refusing her that right. Her social worker believed that Ada used the housing department to encourage Pete to stay or go according to her feelings about him at the time. More seriously, we were under the impression that it was the matron of the residential school and Ada's social worker who decided where the child should go for Christmas: Ada gave us to understand that she was the recipient of such a decision, and not that she had made it herself. She talked of not being allowed to have him and of not being able to understand why 'they' would not let her keep him. When we spoke to the social worker and the matron of the school separately about this, they both told us that it was entirely Ada's decision where the child should go, and also that there had never been any suggestion of his going permanently into care. When we visited the school and talked to the matron, it became clear that Ada had been offered these alternatives: (i) that the child would go into care over Christmas or (ii) that it would be better for him to go to one of his aunts instead. All this has important implications for the amount of control which Ada had over her own life and that of her child – was she giving him to his aunts voluntarily or not? We suspect that there might in fact have been genuine misunderstandings, for example such as that caused by the linguistic confusion of 'can't' with 'may not'. She talked of her social worker or the matron having remonstrated with her when she had the electricity cut off: 'You *can't* have Michael staying here without any heating!' She might well have interpreted this as meaning 'may not', or 'will not be allowed to'. In the end, we learned that she had eventually written to one of the aunts (after the boy had been home from the school for six weeks) to ask if she would look after him for her. Michael, like her other children, was to be given voluntarily into the care of others.

We have already described her involvement with doctors and

hospitals and a few months of her interaction with social services. Her first contact with the police, during our period of fieldwork, was on the evening when she suffered a sexual assault or attempted rape by a man in a car. She did not feel that the police treated her sympathetically, and in particular she was upset when they insisted that her child was 'in care' even though she was at pains to explain to them that he was just in a residential school for his health. She also believed that the police (for whose assistance she had dialled 999 at the time) suspected that her story was untrue and that she had been drunk and fallen over. In contrast the ambulance men had, in her opinion, been kind.

The police were called in again when Ada went to hospital with a pain in her left side; on this occasion, they called an ambulance for her and informed her sister that Ada was in hospital. The police (CID) came to see her when her meter was burgled, and to see Pete to sign a statement about his van. They returned when her meter was burgled again, and this time they took it away to test it for Pete's fingerprints. Ada said he was known to have burgled other meters before, but she would not tell them who had burgled this one, even though they were very annoyed with her lack of co-operation. Gwen also telephoned the police (and the doctor) when Ada feigned taking an overdose. The police were called in again when Ada and her neighbours were having heated arguments which were causing a disturbance, and on another occasion they were called in to investigate a burglary and, with heavy irony, they complimented Pete on his happy situation, paying no rent or board. Six weeks later the CID were called in for Ada's third burgled meter (not counting one which went wrong probably because it had been given a hefty bang). The number of occasions on which the police were called in, and the variety of reasons for calling them, were surprisingly large. Ada (and sometimes Gwen) dialled 999 and asked for the police and/or an ambulance whenever they could no longer deal with the situation, when they thought there was something seriously wrong physically, or when they could not manage relationships any longer. The category of 'burglaries' was more obviously the concern of the police. Such break-ins were reputedly common in the area, and whether or not a proportion of such events were inside jobs, the police were necessarily called in. At times Ada certainly needed help, and the people at the other end of an emergency dialling code were easier to obtain than any other helping agency (certainly easier than most doctors), and more certain to respond than anyone else. Ada had no-one to whom she could always turn, partly because she tended to saturate people with her needs. Her social worker, it has already been said, was very supportive, but he was also very busy and his role could include neither the kind of caring which a short hospital visit could provide nor the drama of a police visit.

From the opposite standpoint, the departments with which Ada had dealings, were sometimes remarkably unhelpful. Her rent rebate forms, for instance, defeated us as well as Ada. The social security office in her new area gave her problems by changing a ruling on whether her pension should include provision for her son. Nobody from the council housing or maintenance department made sure that her exchange went smoothly by helping her master the central heating or connecting her stove. At Michael's school, the social and teaching sides seemed quite separate, so that although the matron was aware of the boy's home problems, this did not seem true of his teachers. And there was friction with the housing department over her lodgers.

On the debit side, Ada demanded a great deal and obtained a good deal from the various services and departments, and she was obviously not an easy client. When she applied for her first exchange of house, for instance, she kept changing her mind until she had to be forcibly moved: she had signed and had to abide by that agreement. She did not pay for essential services and expected her social worker to help her out. She asked various people to rid her of her boyfriend, and then would back down. It is not clear even now whether she really wanted a permit for either of her men-friends to be a lodger, or whether she wanted to transfer the flat into their names. Her dealings with social security were complicated by the male comings and goings in her life; for example, sometimes Stan was claiming for her and sometimes not. When she was getting the full pension for Michael in his absence, she still expected 'the education' to pay for his clothes, and thought this was their duty rather than hers. There were also other dealings which Ada claimed to have had: she said that the council had not *allowed* her to go into rooms, when she decided to return to her flat; to have received a letter from Denis Johnson putting her on the emergency housing list; to have had her doctor write a letter saying she must be moved because of the toxic effect of the gas central heating; to have been informed by the matron and Denis Johnson that Michael was to go to his aunts. It is very unlikely that any of this was true: she was attributing to authority figures statements which she wished to be true. What was indisputable was that Ada needed emotional and practical help, and that she was like to continue to need full-time care from social services for an indefinite period.

Work

Ada's attitude to work was not marked by any compelling interest: she had, after all, the right to a widow's pension and did not need to work unless she wanted company or to raise her standard of living. She said that her mother had instilled the value of work into all her children and that her mother had been a good worker. Because her nerves were bad, Ada had not worked for years, but she told us on several occasions that she was about to start a job – either cleaning, or working in a bar, or in a factory. The factory jobs which Ada were offered paid £31 for a forty-hour week, and the cleaning job offered £6 for twelve hours. She usually told us afterwards that she had not started because she did not have the bus fare; somehow, Ada could never get where she wanted to go. She was able to muster the courage to go and meet people socially, but work was more problematic. Ada would worry that she was not able to perform her work properly.

Ada's Intellectual and Social Skills

We have briefly discussed Ada's health during the course of fieldwork, and its relationship to the crises and emotional problems which she was undergoing, but a little more needs to be said about her general disposition and her social and cognitive skills. Her social worker felt that she was poor at performing some intellectual processes: he had tried to explain the implications of certain courses of action to her (after Alf died) and allegedly she had not been able to follow him. She was, of course, in a depressed state at that time. He also attributed the fact that she allowed herself to be exploited by Pete, and to some extent by Stan, as a sign of low intelligence. We felt far less certain of her intellectual level, and thought it more useful to explain her subjection to the wills and whims of her men-friends in terms of an unusual system of values, or of priorities which were so pressing as not to allow her to fulfil, in a socially acceptable way, the responsibilities which she incurred.

The notions of left and right and of duration of time did not come readily to her, but she had a very good mental map of her locality. She described herself as having lost a lot of weight when she was nine stone, and having gained a lot of weight at eight stone: here again, it is more useful to see these statements in terms of a marshalling of information to fit in with a more important assertion – in this case, that she was or was not going through a worrying period in her relationship with Pete or Stan. If she had lost weight, it was Pete's fault, and if she had gained it, it was the result of Stan's good influence. Ada described herself essentially as a pawn, handled and disposed by outside forces.

Her speech was basically 'Kindleton' in syntax and accent, and also contained some idiosyncrasies. She came out with such remarks as 'Both my parents are from Kindleton, except my Ma was from Wales' and 'The car was the same colour as yours, only lighter and more different.' Another one was 'This is the worst life I've had in all my life.' She used words such as 'uterus' and 'saturated' correctly in their context and without hesitation, but she also coined phrases such as 'a needle for titanic' (which was an injection against tetanus) and 'I'll never get raped again.'

Ada was often a pathetic figure, prematurely aged with worry; she was unusual in her dress, favouring very short skirts and light materials which were somehow teenage in style. She would often gleefully show us new dresses which she had been given by charitable organizations, or a new long dress or coat from a man-friend. She was careful to remind us to look out for particular items which she wanted such as boots or a trouser-suit, or a bikini. Ada was much more active in the area of personal adornment than she was in furnishing or beautifying her flat. There was a marked absence of pictures, ornaments, cushions or of anything which she might have bought herself. The furniture and carpets had been provided by social services and were not unattractive. Stan was markedly more conscious of 'home' than Ada, and bought all manner of nick-nacks for the mantlepiece, as well as renting a television. Ada was not covetous and, if one took her a flowering plant, she would take it to her neighbour, if they were friends at the time. She was noticeably generous in economic transactions with individuals; for instance, when she had been given a good many tomatoes by her half-sister, Ada made up a bag-full and gave it to us. She was verbally generous in her thanks for the interest and time that we had spent with her and for the photographs of Michael, the outings and chauffeuring. She was careful to buy a toy for Gwen's baby for Christmas and to do shopping for her when she had a lift into town.

Ada smoked cigarettes regularly and often, but she was not quite a chain-smoker. She was not, to our knowledge, a very enterprising caterer or cook, favouring such things as tinned meat and potato pies, faggots or beef-burgers, but she knew the value of 'two veg', and would include them in her teas. She often complained that Michael would eat nothing at home. While Pete was living with her, she complained that he would not let her have anything to eat and that she was starving. It certainly appeared that she was eating nothing except for the occasional sandwich given to her by her neighbour. Her idea of a well-stocked larder was, for example, bread and margarine, a quarter pound of tea and a meat pie.

Ada's interest in her home was, as we have already said, minimal: it was not seen by her as an extension of herself, as an area of interest or self-expression. When she had got to know us, however, and when she was not in a fit of depression, she would make us tea, and she quite obviously had a sense of offering hospitality. She paid Pete to redecorate her first house, but she took no apparent pleasure in it. Although very scathing about the 'dirty folks' (as she described the Martins of Chapter 4) who had moved in there after her, Ada's own standards of hygiene were not rigorous. She used one towel to dry both herself and her teacups, and just as obviously she used it for a long time. Her clothing often needed cleaning, and Michael's underclothes and bedclothes were grey and unfragrant. Occasionally, there would be a little washing on the line. Apart from her clothes bundled up in the sideboard, she had very few possessions: at Bramwell she had one knife and two forks; at Cardale, there were only two cups while Pete was living there. On the other hand, neither of her homes was bright and new; in Bramwell, her lavatory overflowed onto the floor; windows were broken in Cardale, and both areas had a slightly depressing, run-down look about them, in spite of the individual efforts of some householders. Nevertheless, the area where she lived was very important to her, and she consistently imagined that she would be happy if only she were somewhere different.

Finances

The financial side of Ada's life was chaotic and problematic, bound up as it was with her unstable cohabiting relationships. For the first time in her life, she had the right (as a result of Alf's death) to a permanent independent income coupled with a home in her own name. When we first visited her, she was receiving £20.87 per week in widow's pension, which was reduced in three weeks to £16.80 (+ 80p Family Income Supplement) because Alf had not paid a national insurance stamp for a full year before he died. Eventually, this went up to £18.74, and her rent of £4.40 was reduced by 49p per week after a rent rebate was awarded. Ada's budgeting was not perhaps as sophisticated as is necessary to be able to pay winter fuel bills and to repay burgled meters, but of course even the most sophisticated budgeter could scarcely manage if the weekly income had been given away at the beginning of the week. Ada put a low priority on economic and residential security and a very high priority on entrusting all her material assets to her provisional 'spouse'. At first it appeared that such trust was inappropriate for Pete, but worked well with Stan. Our later discovery that this still resulted in non-payment of rent and bills for essential services and the dissolution of her home and her household with Michael, with a return to her previous depression, led us to think that such passivity was not an adaptive mechanism or, at any rate, was no successful recipe for survival for Ada. It did not work: it did not stabilize her relationship, and Stan left.

At the end of our period of contact, Ada and Stan were receiving £26 jointly and paying (or rather owing) £2.50 per week in rent. Their money came by post office giro, and they were sometimes worried that it would come late, and they would be left without any money at all for a day. The legacy of Alf's bad reputation for 'never paying a bill in his life' caused Ada difficulties when she tried to hire a television. On the other hand, she received credit for other goods and services, which she did not repay: rent, electricity, gas, television, a loan company and the milkman. The loan company harassed her and reputedly demanded her pension book; the others merely withdrew their services. When she was destitute, Ada sometimes tapped us for money which she always repaid promptly.

Commentary

Early in our relationship with Ada, she said that she was forty-seven, young, single and able to marry again, and what she wanted was a nice man who would not 'mess her about', but would take an interest in her and devote time and attention to her. This is a central factor in understanding her relationships not only with men-friends, but also with her son, her neighbours and relatives, her economic situation and with authorities, council departments and social services. Ada's chief preoccupation was to find someone who would make it his business to look after her and cherish her. In return, she offered her income, home, time, skills and companionship. Unfortunately she had no means of filtering out undesirables or sorting eligible candidates, and she offered a kind of total dependency which appeared difficult to bear. Although her men-friends ranked so highly in her priorities, she rarely described these relationships in agreeable terms. Both Pete and Stan were allegedly quarrelsome and difficult and 'treated her like a dog'. Stan paid for his board, bought her presents, and spoke well of her in front of us, and yet he too was on occasions thrown out. Even with her own home and income, she could not bear the single state; she was not proud, not even confident, although she was generous, grateful and had a good sense of humour. Being willing to accept almost anyone whom she met at the pub, she affronted her neighbours, who counted on their fingers the number of men who crossed her threshold. In her sexual morality she thus ran counter to the norms of the respectable working class among whom she lived. She also had a poor borderline between reality and unreality which alienated her from other people: Gwen, Pete, Stan and ourselves all complained that we could not accept her stories at face value and that she was inconsistent in what she said. On the other hand, she consistently overestimated the age gap between herself and the men she had known, clinging perhaps here also to the image of girlish youth which she expressed in other ways. During our period of contact, the importance of her widowhood and depression should not be under-estimated. Doubtless they accentuated a lack of confidence and strength which have characterized her dealings with men and children through-out her life.

From the focus of Ada's conversational preoccupations, her prob-lems were primarily to do with loneliness and the alleviation of this through her relationships with Pete and Gwen. Morgan (1976) attri-buted the lower morale of young widows in part to their lack of a reference group: their contemporaries are still married. Just as Marris (1958) saw income inadequacy as a major contributing factor, so the problems of mounting debts, lack of money for food (leading to poor health) and for essential services (gas and electricity bills) derived, according to her, from Pete's financial demands and her inability to stick up for herself. This caused her trouble and loss of esteem with her neighbours, with her in-laws, with the housing department, the gas and electricity boards, a loan company, the police and her doctor. Social services performed a very supportive role during this eight-month period which was the most crisis-laden of our year and a half of contact.

Davis (1970) has drawn attention to the large number of patients suffering from depression in the 45–9 and 50–4 age groups. At these ages more of the patients are women, and, as with Ada, likely to have suffered recently the deaths of both parents, and to be undergoing the meno-pause. Ada was of course also widowed, and less than 3 per cent of widows in this age group re-marry – few finding partners outside marriage either. Loneliness, because of social isolation, and a pre-occupation with the dead husband are common to many widows in Ada's situation.

It was suggested that Ada's apparent depression might in part be a mechanism for managing difficult situations. Although it was plain that she could put on a dispirited and hopeless look and way of talking when she wanted to make us feel sorry for her, it was also plain that Ada did go through a period of deep depression which interfered with her capacity to cope with everyday situations, and especially with the perennial problem of Pete.

Ada's feelings about her relationship with Pete or Stan – whether it was thriving or unbearable – found expression in the presence or absence of Alf's photograph above the mantlepiece. When Michael returned home, Alf's photograph was hung in his son's room – and this seemed to be the ultimate solution to Ada's ambivalent feelings.

The sudden end to her second marriage to Mr Hunt and her return to her parents in Kindleton was an early example of Ada's nomadic, non-materialistic tendency to uproot and leave whatever she has made of her life so far. It is tempting to see this desire to start afresh 'leaving my worries behind me', unembarrassed by possessions, as closely allied to her behaviour towards her children, all of whom have been left behind in the quest for the ever renewing life, the spring of second chances, symbolized in her eternally teenage clothes.

Ada was not totally passive in her physical surroundings, but she did not usually express the conventional norm of the mature woman. She did not seek the symbols of permanence: the bulky paraphernalia of the comfortable household. When she tried to leave her flat and take rooms in town, her total possessions were contained in two plastic bags. Her make-up and clothing affirmed another aspect of the same transience: the girlish image which focused on her personal desirability rather than her careful housekeeping and selfless economy. The negative symbols abounded in such things as the poor cleanliness and state of repair of her child's clothes, and the almost total lack of soft furnishings. When Stan showed us things which he had bought for her, he pointed to the ornaments and decoration of the room; when Ada drew our attention to his gifts, it was in terms of dresses, jewellery, or a hair brush set.

Ada was encouraged by her doctor and social worker to go back to work in the hope that such a move would help her depressions. She did in fact find a number of jobs for herself during our period of fieldwork, but she never managed to start any of them. We can only compare this with the lack of confidence which many other women experience when they have been out of work for some years in order to bring up children. For some, the return to work is not at all an easy process. Work is, of course, more stressful in that one has to conform to regulations about such things as punctuality and dress as well as performing set tasks, overcoming monotony and getting on with new people. We do not anticipate that Ada will ever be able to hold down a full-time job.

Work also posed problems for Alf, Pete and Stan. All three formed part of the pool of unskilled labour with intermittent employment, which has a choice between very poorly paid, low status jobs or the more attractive pickings of occasional well-paid jobs of short duration. This occupational sub-structure of their lives contributed in all probability to the transience of their home lives and lack of permanent involvement with Ada.

It seems unlikely to us that Ada will transmit her own disadvantages to her children. Perhaps it was her lack of confidence which directed her to give them into more capable hands, uncertain of her own ability to benefit them herself. Her education, like Alf's, had been neglected (an important point to which we constantly return in the accounts of all our families), and she knew that others were better equipped to deal with the world. Ada was singularly unaware of having any power to change her situation; she had a fatalism and passivity which led her to leave the organization and the clearing up of her life to others. She had neither the assets, nor had she had the good fortune, to attract a man who could take over this responsibility and relieve social services of theirs.

The evidence that we have suggests that Ada's parents did not have the problems she was experiencing. They appear to have been stable in their relationship and in work and to have had a pleasant home. Her siblings seem also to have escaped serious problems. Ada's council-owned flat had an independent hot water supply, an indoor toilet and three rooms, kitchen and bathroom: she was not overcrowded or disadvantaged in terms of amenities. Nevertheless, her problems were manifest and manifold, and her succession of discarded children and broken relationships was important. It is probably true, however, that we would view her divorces and widowhood in a very different light if she were as rich or as beautiful as Elizabeth Taylor: it was her poverty, her lack of assets or supportive family and her cost to the public which made her so vulnerable and which allowed her neighbours to cast a reproachful eye on her affairs. Her affairs became public business as soon as she involved public departments in her welfare – and this she most emphatically did. Even though Ada could not pay her bills, these would not have been so insuperable if she had had the support of relatives with middle class salaries; but Ada lived in a world where those who managed well had nothing to spare, and those who did not manage at all had nothing to lose. Ada had probably quite accurately assessed the fact that she could neither rise nor fall, but society would not willingly let her starve or freeze to death: she could merely endure.

We can only hypothesize as to how Ada developed a pattern in her relationships which seemed to work so badly for her. The teenage clothes, the visits to under-twenties' discotheques, the dyed hair and make-up and the lack of interest in mothering and housekeeping all seemed to point to a desire to stay at the narcissistic moment of girlhood when a woman is just waiting to start out on an independent life. We know that Ada spent part of that moment as a childminder, looking after her brothers and sister while her mother and father worked. We also know that her first affair ended with a stillborn child and a man who was about to marry someone else. Her adolescence was perhaps short and soured. Certainly her education would have been much better if proper pre-school provision had existed for her younger brothers and sisters.

It is possible that Ada was always unconfident and dependent. We cannot be sure. Much more important, however, is to observe how her dependence was magnified by the isolation of her position, by her need to seek help in the most fragmented section of the working class, through chance meetings with men who were themselves on the barely acceptable fringes of the local culture. Ada's situation might have been considerably worsened by her move to a new area; her need for community support was very great whenever her current man-friend stopped providing security, but at any time she showed signs of needing kinds of support which were not consistently available at the bottom of society where she was located. These problems were deep-seated and not susceptible to immediate policy, and yet other short-term solutions in terms of sheltered workshops and bussing to and from work would neither solve the basic problems for Ada nor be economically feasible for the rest of society. She evaded a single answer, except in terms of compassion and continuing support.

4 The Martins: A Long-Term Unemployed Family

The Martins were a vulnerable family whose position in society was so precarious that they reminded us of the man described by Tawney as 'standing permanently up to the neck in water, so that even a ripple is sufficient to drown him' (1932, p. 77). The major problem we encountered with this family was one of coming to terms with reality. Strange inconsistent stories abounded and consistency became a spectre in their ever-changing view of the world. We visited the family on thirty-six occasions over a period of twenty months. Our visits tended to be shorter than those to other families; all three of us found conversation with Peter Martin exhausting as we had to struggle to understand the logic of his accounts of his world. The difficulty was most acute when Peter discussed his health; we tried to make sense of, for example, his stories of coming back to life, of a twenty-four hour open-heart operation and of the success of a drug he called ZX. We had discussions about UFOs, line valves in televisions, and broken washing machines which always needed a belt to be 'like new'. Peter told us of a world where everyone was a Mormon, where the spirits of their dead grandmothers were said to visit their house in Bramwell, and where a lost father apparently appeared in the street as an ice cream salesman. Each visit to the family revealed a new complexity, a new mystery. These eccentricities in a family from a low economic position exacerbated their status as a 'problem family' in the neighbourhood. The difficulties they had in communicating with others often led to a total breakdown in communication, as both we and busy officials strove to understand them; they produced so many implausible and conflicting statements that we began to doubt the truth of all their accounts.

We met the Martin family without the help of the social service department. As we described in Chapter 3, after the death of her husband. Ada Paterson felt she wanted to move from Bramwell. She had told the housing department that she wanted to move and had also inserted a card in the window of a local shop, asking for an exchange.

The Martins saw the card and discussed the possibility of a move with her. We first met them after taking Ada Paterson and her son Michael to the departure point for the coach which took Michael back to the residential school. On our way back to Bramwell Mrs Paterson pointed to Peter and Paul Martin, saying that they were the ones who wanted to exchange houses with her. Our first description of them reads: 'The Martins are twin brothers, just over five foot in height, painfully thin, weighing probably seven to eight stones. One brother has very discoloured, rotten teeth, while his twin has not got any teeth at all. They are both unshaven, haggard, and dressed in dirty old clothes; Peter's blue jeans are held together at the waist by a large pin.' This was in mid July 1975 and immediately we entered the complex world of the Martins. Mrs Paterson told us that she had not agreed to the exchange and had not seen the Martins' flat, though she had allowed the Martin family to move some of their belongings into her house. Mr and Mrs Martin were no longer living at the flat they rented in Cardale (because of 'trouble in the street'), but with Sally Martin's parents elsewhere in the city. We were also told that they had three children: Mark, who was then aged five years four months; Ruth, three years five months; and Gary, seventeen months old. Gary, the infant, was in the care of the local authority because 'to tell you the honest truth, it didn't thrive at all at home'.

At this stage in our work our prime interest was Ada Paterson. We took her, together with the Martin brothers, to see the flat in Cardale. Our description of the visit reads 'The inside of the house smelled; there were piles of old clothes, broken toys and rubbish in every room.' We may have over-reacted to the disorder; after all, the family were on the point of moving. We also noted the derelict state of the garden, though Peter told us, 'There was a time when the rent collector was able to pick a rose for his buttonhole from the garden.' As Mr and Mrs Martin had only lived in Cardale for eighteen months, this was unlikely. (Later, the deputy head of the school Peter and Paul had attended in the late 1950s did comment on the brothers' interest in gardening, which suggests to us that Peter's comment was an example of wish-fulfilment). Having seen the flat, Mrs Paterson decided she would exchange with the Martins and we took both parties to the housing department to make the necessary administrative arrangements. We helped Ada Paterson and Peter Martin to complete their application forms, as both experienced difficulties with the questions and asked for help.

We next met the Martins five weeks later, again while visiting Ada Paterson. Mr Martin and Mrs Paterson had each received a letter from

the housing department, asking them to visit the department at 10.30 am
to finalize the arrangements for the exchange. Our fieldnotes read: 'Mrs
Paterson had told Mr Martin that she had been poorly that morning but
that she would be up at the department by twelve o'clock. So Mr Martin
had climbed the hill and waited. At four o'clock she still hadn't appeared
and so he had come back down again to ask her what she was playing at.
"They told me in Kindleton she was one for going back on her word."'
The move was finally made at the end of August, but even then only with
the assistance of the police. Mrs Paterson, having agreed to the
exchange, decided at the last minute that she didn't want to move after
all. Meanwhile, the Martin family had pressing reasons for moving. The
'trouble in the street', which had been referred to at our first meeting,
escalated into a fight between Sally and a neighbour, Freda Parker. Sally
claimed that she had been publicly accused of stealing Freda's purse;
Freda had pursued her, knocked her down, blackened her eye and had
bitten her 'in the chest'. We were subsequently to notice, scratched onto
the door of the Martins' flat in Cardale, the words 'Sally Cow'. Mr
Martin was also worried that his son, Mark, had found out 'how to
make his thing hard' and had consequently become concerned about
Ruth's moral safety; the little girl had been moved from the bedroom
which she shared with Mark into the parental bedroom. Finally, Mr
Martin claimed that he had been told by a social worker that their
youngest child, Gary, would not be returned from foster care until the
family had moved into a larger house.

We visited the family again, though we had not decided at this stage to
ask them to help us with our project. During the autumn, however, we
became more convinced of the value of the family to our work. In the
first place, they were a family experiencing multiple problems: unemployment, low skills (when we asked Peter how old Gary was when he
had been taken into care, Peter replied, 'I don't know. I'm backward.'),
housing stress, difficult relationships with neighbours and marital
problems. Secondly, they were local people, which gave the possibility of
contact with their extended family. Finally, though the family was in
contact with social services, we did not meet them through that
department.

Peter and Sally's biography

Peter Martin was the second of fraternal twins to be born to Sheila and
Cedric Martin towards the end of the Second World War. Sally, his wife,
was born eight years later, the daughter of Bernard and Barbara

Smithson. We found out little about Peter's parents. At the time he and his twin, Paul, were born, their father was serving with an infantry regiment, but soon after the war he left Mrs Martin. As children, Peter and Paul spent considerable time being looked after by their grandmother; Peter claimed that he was a 'weak child' and missed a lot of time from school. At the end of the 1940s, their mother, Mrs Martin, married Gerald Smithson. Gerald brought one child, Margaret, into the marriage and soon he and Sheila had a son, Michael. Both Margaret and Michael appear to have been more successful than either Peter or Paul. Peter referred to his step-sister as: 'her who has married a man who owns his own house, a snob, who works for himself and who has bad health'; and he claimed that his half-brother was earning just less than £100 per week.

Sally's father, Bernard, is the brother of Gerald Smithson. (See Figure 4.1 for the Martin's family tree). Bernard was born in 1930 in Kindleton and had the reputation of being a 'hard man'. When Sally and Peter moved into their house in Bramwell, a neighbour – the gossip Margaret – recognized Sally as being 'one of the Smithsons' and told us of the family's reputation for being dirty. At the end of her primary schooling, Sally attended a school for delicate children for three months, and we noticed throughout our period of contact with the family that Sally suffered from either a cold or a cough or some other minor ailment. She left school at fifteen to work in a factory, and married Peter when she was nineteen.

On leaving the school for educationally sub-normal children – or 'the school for daft children' as the brothers called it – at the age of sixteen, Peter Martin first took a job at a garage in Kindleton where he worked for almost a year as 'a motor mechanic'. It is difficult to record with any certainty what took place over the next ten years, or until Peter married Sally. Peter claimed to have had sixteen different jobs, including putting soap powder into boxes and working for a building firm, before being sent to prison when he was nineteen. He told us that he was arrested at a local football ground, where he had tried to prevent two other boys stabbing a policeman. The police had apprehended all three and discovered that Peter 'had a flick knife in my pocket and I was wearing a studded belt'. He then alleged that he was fined over twenty pounds, sentenced to three months' imprisonment, and that this was the only occasion in which he had been in trouble with the police. A month later, however, he told us that he had been 'the driver' in a bank-raid and as a result had been sentenced to three years in prison. This account is complicated further by Peter's later assertion that the offence was one

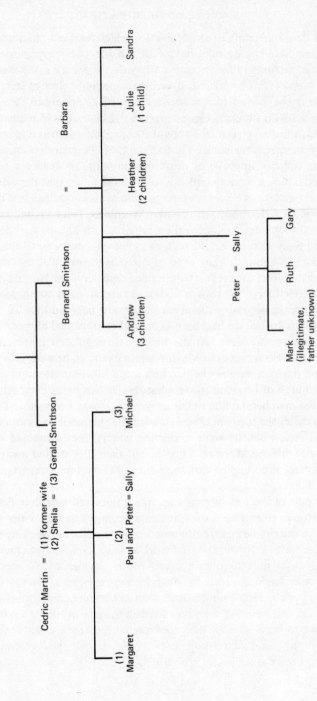

Figure 4.1 Family Tree of Peter and Sally Martin

which Paul had committed but one for which he, Peter, had taken the responsibility. His descriptions of prison life were very graphic; for example, he talked of nightmares allegedly caused by a cell-mate who used to scrape his fingernails down the walls until they bled.

During the period of our contact as well as previously, Peter was influenced by different religious groups. He claimed to have become a Jehovah's Witness 'because he could ask questions at their meetings and answer the preacher back'. He told us that the members of his new religion did not approve of drinking, smoking, or even sex between married couples; tea and coffee were forbidden 'because they stain the stomach and so we have tea bags and ovaltine instead'. When, in response to a doorstep visit of two Mormons, Peter invited them to return a week later to discuss their religion with himself and Sally, he assured Sally that all would be well as the Mormons were 'under the Jehovah's Witnesses'. They were baptized as members of the Mormon Church and for a time regularly attended their services. They referred to their co-religionists as brothers and sisters and stressed how much better they felt since becoming members. Peter now believed that we had all been spirits before we had been born and that we had all been on the earth in a previous life. At the time of their greatest involvement it seemed that Peter met only Mormons; for example, he went into a local pub and the man standing behind him was a Mormon. He went into the local Church of England to see what service was being conducted and again the man behind him in the congregation was a Mormon. For two months after the baptism (Peter claimed that his heart had stopped and he had died when he went under the water), they remained heavily involved with the Mormon Church, but then they drifted away when they became preoccupied with the return of Gary, the youngest member of the family.

For part of the time between leaving school and marriage Peter left Kindleton to go and work on a civil engineering project in Wales. On his return to the city he again had numerous jobs including working for the local authority as a dustman, and work as a mechanic and as a painter. It proved impossible to obtain corroborative evidence to support his employment record, a record which became even more complex when set alongside Peter's lengthy succession of accidents and illness. When they were first married, they had lived in the city in rooms which they alleged had been infested with cockroaches and rats, which Peter had been in the habit of feeding in the belief that they were cats. The buildings have since been demolished.

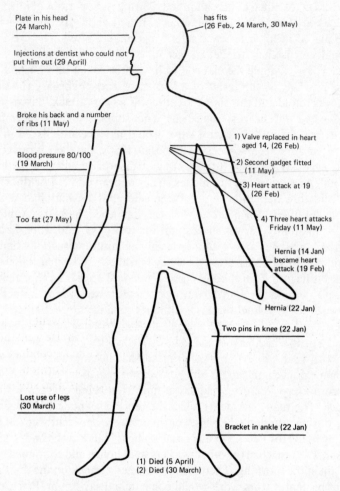

Plate in his head
(24 March)

has fits
(26 Feb., 24 March, 30 May)

Injections at dentist who could not
put him out (29 April)

Broke his back and a number
of ribs (11 May)

1) Valve replaced in heart
aged 14, (26 Feb)

Blood pressure 80/100
(19 March)

2) Second gadget fitted
(11 May)

3) Heart attack at 19
(26 Feb)

4) Three heart attacks
Friday (11 May)

Too fat (27 May)

Hernia (14 Jan)
became heart
attack (19 Feb)

Hernia (22 Jan)

Two pins in knee (22 Jan)

Lost use of legs
(30 March)

Bracket in ankle (22 Jan)

(1) Died (5 April)
(2) Died (30 March)

Note: Dates refer to the occasion when he told us of his problems.

Figure 4.2   Peter Martin's Health Problems

Health

Figure 4.2 shows those parts of Peter's anatomy which he claimed had created health problems for him. From the eighth meeting until the twenty-second, he discussed his health problems, which may be divided into those associated with organic malfunction and those which were the result of accident. It is difficult to make sense of his medical history. Peter's story is that he was the second twin to be born, that he was a weak baby and ill for much of his childhood. During these periods of illness he was looked after by his grandmother. Then at about sixteen, he had a valve placed in his heart, and later a pacemaker fitted. There is little internal consistency to Peter's accounts of his ill health. In early January, for example, he claimed to have been taken into hospital on Christmas Day as the result of a hernia; by early February the same story was retold and this time the cause was a heart attack. Discussions we have had with heart specialists have not supported Peter's accounts. It is extremely unlikely that a valve would have been replaced in the heart of an adolescent, especially in the late 1950s; and there is no record of his ever having been fitted with a cardiac pacemaker at the local hospital. An example of this inconsistency appeared in our fieldnotes in the following September: '... Peter said that he had had a new pacemaker fitted. When asked when this happened, he said, "A month ago". Apparently he was in hospital for two days, and when he was allowed home, he came with a letter giving strict instructions that he should not do anything other than stay in bed ....' Given his obsession about his health, if this had happened, it would appear strange that he made no mention of this event during other visits we made at this period.

The stories he told about his health grew steadily more dramatic; for instance, he recalled the time when he broke into a doctor's car in order to find a drug which he just *had* to have. He had levered the car window open with a pen-knife, found the drug, and had just injected himself with it, when a policeman caught him. Only his explanation that it was vital for him to have the drug had saved him from being charged with an offence. The many accidents which he reported tended to happen at work during a period when his workmates were apparently constantly sending home for Peter. On one occasion he told us how he had 'started work at 4.40 pm when the other workers went home, and continued until 1.30 am in the morning. There was sometimes a knock on the door and one of his mates from work would come in and say "right, Peter, they need you up at ...".' A month later he told us that as a mechanic he used to work from 8 o'clock in the morning until 4 o'clock the next morning before going home to sleep, only to be back at work at 8 am. He continually presented an image of being a central and indispensable figure in the labour force, be it mending television sets, cars, washing machines, or labouring. Such professed dedication to work must be contrasted to the reality of being one of the long-term unemployed, and in this the details of his ill health became a protective cover. Peter claimed that it was his tendency to overwork which had caused so many of his physical breakdowns.

Work

Peter claimed to be registered as a disabled person as a result of his heart condition. However, when we asked to see his card, his reply was 'I've thrown it away, as it's no use. Once you show the card, you are not given a job.' We checked with the disablement resettlement officer for the area in which Peter lived and he could trace no record of a Peter Martin ever having been on the register. Our best estimate is that he last worked two years before, sweeping floors at a local factory. Throughout the period of our involvement he did not work apart from one day, a day which ended disastrously for Peter because he fainted between two furnaces. He was taken to the medical centre where the doctor said, according to Peter, 'you're on drugs aren't you? "Yes", I said, "tranquillizers". The doctor then said, "I know what you need, you need some of this."' At that point, again according to Peter, the doctor injected him with some ZX (which is also a trade name for a well-known make of tyres) and after twenty minutes Peter was ready to return to work, though the firm sent him home in a taxi. This incident was part of another strange sequence. One Friday in March Peter told us that he was starting work at a Department of Employment training centre on Monday morning, a job for which he had been given a rail pass. The local employment rehabilitation centre is close to Bramwell, and Peter would not have required a rail pass to travel there. The following Wednesday he told us that he had spent Monday working in a factory and had had 'a fit'. After an injection of a drug he walked home 'supported on both sides by two old ladies'. A week later the factory had 'moved' and the journey home this time was by taxi. We asked him about the Department of Employment training scheme and Peter replied that, as he hadn't heard anything from them, he had started work on his own initiative.

Peter's Intellectual and Social Skills

Peter started school in the late 1940s. There was no remedial education in the secondary school and he joined the C stream, the class for the least academically able children. Peter's educational problems were sufficiently great for him to be transferred, with Paul, to a school for educationally sub-normal pupils when it opened in the area. They only spent two years and one term at this school, but one of their teachers remembers their being very interested in gardening. He commented, 'if only someone had picked this interest up and had developed it, then the Martins would have had a lot to contribute'. Though not able to read or write, Peter was able to paint reasonably well in a style reminiscent of the

'Eagle' comic of the 1950s, and had an interest in a wide range of mechanical and electrical gadgets. There were, however, limitations to his understanding of the world. Once we recorded a conversation about his eldest son's eyesight, particularly the vision in his left eye. The fieldnotes read: 'Sally and Peter were sitting opposite each other and Sally put her hand over her left eye to show me where Mark had bumped himself. Peter immediately contradicted her, saying it was the other eye and put his hand over his own left eye. Sally tried to explain that that was still the same side, but Peter insisted that she was holding the wrong eye. Eventually she got up and turned round to show him it was the same eye she was holding, but he remained unconvinced.'

Paul, the twin brother, moved with Sally and Peter into their house in Bramwell, but three months later left to look for work in Wales – allegedly taking with him the contents of the gas meter. Neither Paul nor Peter could read and therefore Sally had devised a complicated arrangement for communication. She copied out parts of a Ladybird 'Easy Reading Book', entitled 'Chicken Licken', and had given these to Paul. Soon after he arrived in Wales, Paul wrote a letter which Sally showed us. We had such difficulty in understanding this letter that we asked Sally to interpret it and we recorded what she said. The following is a transcript of the comments Sally made onto tape, the only time we recorded with any family.

Sally (reading): From Paul Lucky said we are on our way. You said Paul Lucky. Lucky hurry on to tell the King. Thanks. Schoolbook A. 1. Mr Paul Martin, (address), Welshpool. . . . I can't understand that word.
Researcher: Powys.
Sally: Powys. I am see you . . .
Researcher: Can you tell me what that means?
Sally: Well he's lucky, he's found a caravan and he's found his Uncle Tom out, and he's got a job, and he's settled down; that's all I can understand.
Researcher: That's great.
Sally: That's how we get to understand everything from the books, you know.
Researcher: So you don't have to have the same book, he just has a book and he copies . . .
Sally: No, it's the same book.
Researcher: Oh, he has the same book . . .
Sally: Well I wrote it down on sheets of paper for him, and we kept the book . . . and I put page 1, page 2, and so on, on the pages, and he carried

on from that. He picks it up from that. Picks words from it and that's how we carry on with it, and I've told him to do that, if he can't do a letter and I wrote him a letter back the same, and I haven't had a reply back.

Researcher: So when you write back, do you just write an ordinary letter back?

Sally: No, I do the same.

Researcher: You do the same.

Sally: We put ... em, like ... em, 'strong king', something such as 'we haven't moved' cause he understands 'haven't moved from here' and we put such as 'hurry back said Peter Lucky', and we put 'Peter somewhere there. Thank you for everything he's done for us'.

Researcher: Who's the king?

Sally: Well, it's like when he says anything ... is he going to tell the king ...?

Researcher: Is the king Peter?

Sally: Yes, oh yes, he's the king.

Researcher: Peter's the king?

Sally: Yes, 'cause he can't spell Peter, so he puts 'king thanks'. That's the only way ...

Researcher: When did you get this idea?

Sally: Well he brought some books that were given us, like, and Paul said, well, I like that one; a Ducky Lucky about ducks and that, Chicken Licken and all that; and he hit on that book ...

It is difficult to understand what is in fact being communicated and this example illustrates something of the problems we encountered in understanding the accounts given to us by the Martins.

Marital Relationship

Their marital relationship could best be described as volatile. Sally and Peter got married when Mark was a month old, Sally nineteen, and Peter twenty-six. They had known each other since Sally had been a small child. Mark was Sally's second pregnancy, the first having ended in a miscarriage. We remain uncertain as to who Mark's father was, though we know that it was not Peter. When Sally became pregnant for the second time, she had been living away from home, but decided to return to her parents' house to have the baby. It was then that Peter asked if he could court her and said that he did not want to marry her unless he could also look after the baby. After the couple were married, the family went to live with Peter's parents in Kindleton, but they soon moved into rooms out of the city: Sally had another miscarriage, but then shortly after she became pregnant with Ruth. At the time of Ruth's birth, Sally was not living with Peter. She had decided to leave him, and had taken Mark with her. At some stage she moved back to live with her parents because it was in her parents' house that Ruth was born. Peter started divorce proceedings, but Sally decided to return to him, bringing Mark and Ruth with her. She became pregnant again in the summer of the next year, though the pregnancy became complicated, and in November of that year Sally was taken into hospital where she remained, apart from a brief visit home at Christmas, until Gary was born early in the following year. A month later the family – mother, father, three children aged four, two and one month – moved into their first council tenancy, a ground-floor flat comprising kitchen, bathroom, lounge and two bedrooms.

In the middle of the next year they exchanged their flat for Ada Paterson's three-bedroomed house in Bramwell. However, seven weeks after moving, Sally left the family to go off with Harry Jenkins, a man with whom she had associated before she married Peter. We only learnt his name towards the end of fieldwork when Sally told us that she was scared to stay in the house alone because she was being bothered by men, particularly by Harry Jenkins, 'the man who split me up [from Peter] before Christmas'. He was the brother-in-law of a man she used to go out with before she met Peter. He had been coming to the house and insisting that she went out with him; when she had refused, he had threatened 'to cause trouble'.

Sally's account differed from the events Peter described at the same time. In October, Peter told us that Sally had left and that he had 'got the evidence'. He produced a diary which he opened at a page where we read: 'Geoff came – had his intercourse with me', and on another page: 'Geoff came in, felt me all over, and intercoursed me straightaway.' The name Geoff conflicted with the name Harry and it was uncertain how Peter knew what 'the evidence' meant as he could not read. It was possible that Sally had had affairs with both men. She also complained that one of her uncles had assaulted her. Throughout, Peter appeared phlegmatic about the various associations which Sally entered into, openly saying: 'if she wants a divorce, she can have one'.

Sally returned after being away for a month, saying to us on the first occasion we met: 'I was shocked how spotless the house was', and then added: 'apart from the dishes'. Two months later, their relationship had become more stable and they were displaying considerable affection towards each other. We saw them in the street, arm in arm, and Sally reported that they were much happier. Within four months, however, their relationship was again on the decline possibly as a consequence of Paul's return to Bramwell. Peter and Paul spent their day walking around Kindleton, to little obvious purpose. We saw them frequently. Sally was left at home alone.

Despite the varying strength of their relationship, Sally was prepared to support Peter's fantasy world. Thus Peter told us how he had come downstairs at 2 o'clock in the morning to see his grandmother sitting in the room. Sally joined in, saying: 'Yes, I came down behind him and went into the room and saw my grandmother.' Turning to Peter, she said: 'in fact your grandmother Dodd was sitting there, grandmother Marshall there and grandma Smithson sitting there', pointing each time to three seats as she mentioned each grandmother in turn. On other occasions she corroborated stories of Peter escaping from hospital and of having had three pacemakers inserted in his heart.

Child-rearing

The Martins had three children. The eighteen month period of our contact with the family covered the following age spans for each of the children: Mark, from five years, four months to seven years; Ruth, from three years, five months to five years, one month; Gary, from one year, five months to three years, one month. We acquired more information about the two boys than about Ruth: Mark (whose father was unknown to us and who had acute problems of soiling and enuresis) and Gary (who had been in two foster homes and whose return was uncertain, an uncertainty which persisted throughout most of our fieldwork).

Mark

Mark seems to be a pawn in the triangle between Harry Jenkins, Sally and Peter. While Harry was trying to re-establish his relationship with Sally, he enticed Mark away from school, saying to the boy that he was his father. Peter referred to Mark as 'the king-pin of the family', and on one occasion said that, if Harry took Mark away, Sally would follow. Peter also claimed that he had himself abducted Mark in the past when Sally had left. We gained some idea of how Mark viewed the situation when at one interview he arrived home with a piece of embroidery which he had done at school and gave it to Sally as a gift. Sally said that Mark gave it to her for staying with him for so long.

During our fieldwork we recorded two periods when Mark was frequently enuretic or encopretic. The first was just after Sally's return to the family, when Peter told us that Mark had been sent away from school for 'shitting himself'; Peter blamed the hard toilet paper supplied at the school. When he was about six, Mark was wetting the bed at night, causing 'two mattresses to have been soiled and burnt'. Mr and Mrs Martin had discussed the problem with the nurse at the school clinic and had been given a bed chart to record his progress. Our notes show some of the problems the parents had in using this chart: 'the child is awarded one blue star for each dry night, and a gold or silver star for three consecutive dry nights. No stars are given for wet nights. The last two-and-a-half weeks were full of blue stars with a gold star every third night. So I concluded that the boy had been dry for that length of time and asked for confirmation. "No", said Peter, "He keeps wetting himself; the stars are just to help him."'

The second period of enuresis started soon after Gary's return to the family. Mark had been taken to the clinic and had been given a course of Ethipram (the trade name for imipramine, an anti-depressant), a side effect of which is to dry up the patient (see Rutter, 1975, p. 292). Mark had also been given another Geigy bed chart and Sally claimed that since Monday when he had been given the chart, he had not wet the bed. Mark's enuresis was certainly linked with the two critical and emotional episodes of his mother leaving and coming back and of his younger brother, Gary, returning home.

Mark's headmistress said that he was a very aggressive boy in school. She described to us how he came out of classes to the playground with his fists raised to punch other children, though when he did hit them, he would complain if they hit him back. She also reported that when he first arrived at school, Mr Martin took him everywhere with him outside school hours and gave him a great deal of attention, but that since Gary had returned home Mark had become very jealous and aggressive, and the bed wetting had started all over again.

Apart from difficulties at school, Sally reported on a number of occasions that Mark was 'a devil for wandering away'. One summer's evening when Mark was six, his mother had found him more than a mile from home, playing with horses on a farm. She had been very worried because it had been very dark, after nine pm, and a four-year-old girl had recently drowned in the local canal.

Gary

When we first met the Martin family, Gary was in the care of the local authority. The first references to Gary were ambiguous. He was reported to be six months old and in the care of two nurses in the city, but the social worker would not tell them where the baby was. Gary, we were told, was six pounds, two ounces at birth, yet within a month he was reported to us as being eight pounds, one ounce at birth. Gary's physical development was poor after his birth, and he failed to gain weight. He had been fed on Ostermilk No. 2, but when he had vomited this, Sally had switched to National Dried, then to boiled sterilized milk and finally to pasteurized milk; but at each change Gary continued to vomit. The child was taken into care for non-wilful neglect three months after the family had moved into their flat in Cardale. He first went to live with a family in the south of Kindleton, Mr and Mrs Jones, and then, according to Peter, to live with two nurses in the north of the city.

As a baby, Gary was suspected of having cystic fibrosis, a suspicion which turned out to be unfounded. He had been a difficult baby in foster care and he had at first been given a short life expectancy. It was always envisaged that he would be returned to his parents as soon as possible. After living with Mr and Mrs Jones, Gary was moved to Mr and Mrs Walsh, a couple whose two daughters were nurses. Throughout his stay with foster parents, the Social Service Department maintained regular contact with the Martins, though Peter claimed that the social worker rarely visited and had not informed him of the change in Gary's foster parents. The family met their third social worker when the decision was taken to return Gary to his own home as soon as possible, although he would still be under the care of the local authority. The process was begun by his being taken to Bramwell every fortnight. At first he screamed continually when taken into the house, but gradually he began to approach Mark and Ruth, and then Peter, and finally Sally. Later in the year he was being brought by the social worker and another woman to visit every week. Our fieldnotes read: 'both Sally and Peter have taken an intense dislike to this other woman because she turns her nose up at them and refuses to let Gary go on to the floor, and makes comments about the dirt in the house. They have taken grave exception to this.'

Gary was finally returned home in late summer, which was earlier than had been planned, because the foster parents began to find the constant coming and going a strain. We have reports that during his last days with the foster parents Gary (now two-and-a-half years old) had fits, held his breath and turned blue. Interestingly, Peter interpreted this as symptomatic of Gary having the same heart condition as himself, and earlier, Peter had said of Gary: 'He's rather like me as a child; I was always in care.' On our first visit after Gary's return, we were shown a letter from his foster parents together with a photograph taken of Gary and the Walshs' eldest son, Nicholas. At first the foster parents visited Gary in Bramwell although Peter Martin discouraged them from doing so. At the same time Sally began to tell us stories to the effect that Gary had not developed while in care and that it was fortunate he had returned to the home of his natural parents.

Ruth

Compared with Mark and Gary, Ruth presented fewer problems. When Sally complained to the social worker that she, Sally, had been assaulted by her uncle, she let slip during the interview that Ruth had also been assaulted by the same uncle. The matter had been reported to the police who had not been able to establish a case against the uncle. On another occasion Ruth suffered a burn on her bottom, and again the social worker could not obtain a coherent account of how the accident had occurred. Ruth was seen by the headmistress of the school she attended as 'a nice little thing'.

In general, Peter Martin was nurturant towards his children; he looked after them when Sally left, picked them up from school regularly and played with them frequently. At times, Sally seemed unaware of the children, oblivious to their touching her, or pulling her skirt or otherwise demanding attention. In front of us she was anxious to appear caring; at one stage she changed Gary's nappy for no obvious reason other than to impress us with her maternal skill. In sum, the home is a caring one, though the quality of care is uneven and not reinforced by that attention to cleanliness which creates a positive impression with schools, health clinics and the like.

The family had to cope with the problems of Peter's health (though the exact nature of these remained uncertain), of caring for a sickly child, of a volatile marital relationship and of the fact that Peter and Sally had only low level skills which were not in high demand in the labour market. The social status of the family and its lack of political and economic power tended to amplify these individual problems, creating financial difficulties for them and it is to these that we now turn.

Finances

The family was economically dependent upon supplementary benefit. Table 4.1 gives the income and expenditure as described by the family and as calculated from official figures.

In December Paul Martin returned from Wales, and resumed living with his brother. He claimed £12.90 per week unemployment benefit, out of which he gave Sally £5. The total available income for the family was £37.95 per week, with rent and rates of £5.98 per week paid for.

Table 4.1 Sally Martin's budget for one week in March 1976

Income		Expenditure	
Supplementary benefit	29.95	18.00	Food for 3 adults + 3 children
Family allowance	3.00	1.80	Chicken[2]
Paul Martin's contribution to household	5.00	3.10	Coal
Total	£37.95[1]	1.00	Debt (Mrs Paterson)
		6.00	Peter – for decorating
		1.30	Gas and electricity
plus Rent/rates rebate	5.98	5.98	Rent/rates
	£43.93	£37.18	

(Thus £6.75 was left for household sundries, clothes, transport, entertainment, etc.).

[1] £33 (£37.95 minus Paul's £5) is 44% of National Average Earnings of £75 per week.
[2] Chicken. Sally insisted this was a separate item, although we never saw them eating chicken; their diet seemed almost totally starchy and fatty.

Official rates of supplementary benefit

Married couple	20.65	
Mark	4.35	
Ruth	4.35	
Gary	3.60	
	32.95	including family allowance
	5.98	plus rent and rates
Total	£38.93	

As Peter was officially classified as unemployed, he was not entitled to long-term benefit rates even though he had not worked for some years.

Food and fuel were the main items of expenditure; the £1 debt payment each week was to pay off a sum of £25 owing to the coal man. Peter and Sally alleged that Ada Paterson incurred the debt but as the coal man had only the number of the house and not the name of the occupant in his book he was charging the Martins with the debt. It is interesting to note that Sally referred to the £6 as Peter's 'decorating money'. In the first eighteen months the family lived in Bramwell, the lounge was decorated five times, the kitchen twice and upstairs at least once. Indeed, Peter claimed to have been 'told off by the housing welfare woman for decorating so much'. Sally was prepared to work and for a short period had a part-time job for British Rail, cleaning the toilets, and working alongside her mother. Her rate of pay was 55p an hour. She gave up the job, partly because it was too physically demanding for her and partly because Peter was talking of starting work at a training centre at that time.

At the time we calculated the Martin budget, local industry was paying £41.50 to unskilled labourers for a forty-hour week. As a point of comparison we thought it would be useful to see how the family income would have changed if Peter had been successful in getting a job. Table 4.2 shows his income; he would have been eligible for income tax at 1975/6 rates, paying slightly more in tax each week than he would have gained in family income supplement. He would still have been entitled to a full rent and rate allowance and, as the calculations were done before April 1977, to a family allowance of £3.00 per week. After 4 April 1977 the family would have been entitled to £1 per week extra child benefit. In sum, the family would have gained about £4 per week if Peter had been able to find a job. For all their poverty they were still generous enough to give away a table, some chairs and a dresser to a neighbour who was in a 'bigger mess' than themselves.

Table 4.2   Income if Peter were working as a local labourer

£41.50 Gross minus	2.38 national insurance =	35.67 net
	3.45 tax (estimate)	
	£5.83	3.25 FIS
		3.00 Family allowance
		£41.92

The family would have still been entitled to full rent and rate allowance.

Commentary

In the literature on the long-term unemployed (Jahoda, Lazarsfeld and Zeisel (1972), Veil et al. (1970) and Hill (1978) for example), reference is made to the apathy of those out of work for a considerable time. Veil saw as a general rule that, 'the unemployed person appears first of all as a defeated victim whose fall drags down with him the entire family group'. For Peter Martin there has never been anything to fall from. Like Mr Coxon in Marsden and Duff's (1975) study of unemployed men, Peter must endure the disparaging assessment of his worth as a human being consequent upon his lack of marketable skills. There are two important consequences of his unemployment; Peter's constant striving for status and secondly the effects on Sally's life.

Throughout our contact with Peter, discussions of work could be grouped into references to jobs he may or may not have had or into references to his dream. His dream was of a job where he was the expert. He talked about being self-employed, mending washing machines, training to be a doctor, being a television repair expert, and amazing the professionals with the speed with which he could diagnose faults. Peter was constantly striving for status. He was not the hard drinking, quick talking Vince Barker, whose natural home seemed to be the local pub. Peter could not impress by tales of his strength or his success with women. On one occasion Vince Barker, having noted that we were regular visitors to the Martins who lived next door but one to the Barkers, said to us: 'I hope you don't think we are like *them* (i.e. the Martins)'; he went on to explain that he viewed Peter Martin as incompetent and not a member of any social world in Bramwell.

There was a cultural norm within the Bramwell community that women did not visit another woman's home if 'the man' was there. Consequently, Sally was isolated from the world of women because of Peter's unemployment. Her only contact with women was with her own mother and with Gracie, her younger sister. She used to help Elsie Barker before the latter moved to Elsmore, but subsequently she was often in the house alone for long periods as Peter and Paul pursued their endless walks around the city. This isolation could have been partly the cause of her sexual adventures as she sought to relieve the boredom of her own life. She had worked, but considered the rate of pay she received from a nationalized industry to be so low as not to compensate her for her effort. Sally was also terrified at being thought incompetent as a mother and raced Gary to the doctor at the slightest sign of any illness.

So trapped was Peter in his fantasy world that we concluded that he would find it very difficult to enter employment where he had to display social competence. Our prognosis is that Peter will remain unemployed and increasingly unemployable as he moves more and more into his own private world where he can be important.

Perhaps his defence is that of playing the part of an incompetent, of someone who doesn't count and who has little contribution to make to a technological society. In an attempt perhaps to compensate he took a briefcase to his adult literacy class and told us that he 'was training for a doctor and today they were going to go round a hospital to see all the equipment'. He described fitting new brakes to an 850 cc motorcycle so that when a policeman tested the machine the brakes were so effective that it stopped instantly and the policeman flew over the handlebars. He also claimed to have instructed a gas board engineer on how to put liquid into the cooling system of a refrigerator and so earned himself £25. The examples were endless. The point we are making is that the stories that surrounded his ill health appeared to him to be acceptable explanations for his own unemployment. Peter had little to contribute to society, although an adult member of it. He was marginal to society, irrelevant to the world of work, and powerless to change his situation.

The picture of the Martin family is one of a family with few, if any resources, struggling to cope. Peter lived in a fantasy world which Sally reinforced. Berger and Kellner (1964) described the social construction of reality in marriage as partners present their experiences to each other and reach a consensus on the past. Peter's recreations of the past were so frequent that Sally had long since suspended any scepticism about his stories, and happily engaged with him in the current reformulation. Peter had no job, possibly because no job existed for him to do. The family tried to take a pride in their home, (putting up Christmas decorations or installing an aquarium for the children, for example) but the house was beginning to show the same structural faults as those of its neighbours; it was infested with cockroaches, and the lack of fencing around the garden made it vulnerable to the activities of neighbourhood children. One would have to be a strong optimist to see the point of spending a deal of care and attention on the home, and yet, as we have said, Peter spent a considerable amount of time decorating and redecorating the rooms. Interestingly in this connection, Petonnet (1973, p. 238) reported that most of the residents of a stigmatized housing estate in France 'repaint or repaper their walls frequently, as often as once a year . . . . The people focus their creativity on the walls.' No matter when we arrived at the Martins' home, we always found Peter repairing an old radio or fixing a child's bicycle or putting up a shelf for Sally. Marsden and Duff (1975, p. 244) described Peter's situation accurately when they wrote that unemployed men 'appeared to be pushed into doing masculine or otherwise self-justificatory activities about the home'.

Their income support was adequate to keep them alive, but allowed nothing for leisure, for travel, or for breaking the monotony of their everyday routine. Their existence was and continues to be a subsistence existence. The family did not experience either the violence which constantly threw a shadow over the life of the Barkers or the isolation of Ada Paterson. They were, however, seen as a 'dirty family'. Ada Paterson referred to the Martins as being dirty and Julie Barker certainly caught lice from Ruth Martin. Margaret, the gossip, claimed that the family were dirty and told Peter that they were better off without Sally. The dirt was a symbol of their lack of status within the neighbourhood.

Their house was kept clean and seemed more orderly than the homes of either the Patersons or the Barkers; the label 'dirty' indicated that the Martins were not acceptable within the community where they lived. They responded to the label by accusing others in turn of being 'dirty'; they claimed, for example, that, when they had exchanged houses with Ada Paterson, she had left the house 'in a shocking mess', which included blankets which were so soiled by her child's faeces that Peter had had to burn them. Local children still threw stones at their windows. In the short term, the strains on the family were likely to increase as the children grew older and more demanding. Mark was enuretic at seven. The Newsons (1968) reported that 11 per cent of their sample of four-year-old boys were wetting the bed most nights but provide no information for seven-year-old boys in their later study. The stability and consistency of care which children need were rarely present and the family could easily be placed in crisis should Sally decide to leave again. The Martin family, uncertain as their future was, would require continual support if the children were to gain the confidence to take responsibility for their own lives.

5 The Fieldings: Coming out of Deprivation

While Ada Paterson's garden grew or not as it pleased and was a place to dump unwanted carpets and oddments from the house, and while the Barkers' sported wizened rose bushes, transplanted but unwatered among the debris of prams and children's scooters, Dora and George Fielding, living in Aulton, surrounded themselves with a fenced oasis of french marigolds and green turf. Some other families in the same street tried to maintain their gardens, but mostly they were a wilderness of dried mud and thin weeds, while papers and broken glass poked their way under the gates. It was not a question of nature prevailing over culture, however, as for the most part a meagre top soil was too heavy with clay to encourage much growth or garden enthusiasm. In the nearby private estate where the top soil had been taken away by the building contractors, the same problem was sometimes solved by buying soil and having it delivered by the lorry-load: an expensive investment more suited to long-term ownership than to renting and 'exchanging', which was the pattern on the Aulton council estate.

Aulton is not a desirable area, although the houses are being converted and often have well-appointed kitchens and bathrooms and sizeable, well-lit rooms. Some people on the estate voiced the opinion that the council put people there if there were something wrong with them, but house allocation is more complicated than that, and it seems likely that those who are most desperate are more likely to take up the offer of a house in a less desirable area, and thus there is a tendency for those with the least resources and least power to congregate together.

Dora's mother, Enid Havelock, had lived before on the estate with her children, and Dora had chosen to come back there. Nevertheless, Dora had been married to a man who owned his own house in another part of Kindleton, and she and her second husband, George, were not satisfied with the environment in which their young family was going to grow up. Dora's mother was more at home in the area than her daughter, enjoyed going up to a nearby club in the evening, and had friends whom she went out with locally.

Our primary contact with the extended family was through Dora Fielding, her husband, George, and their two children, Nicola and Amanda. Dora was first contacted by us at a hairdressing demonstration organized by the Aulton Mothers and Toddlers Club. Dora was friendly and amusing in her conversation, and at first the most interesting element in it was her references to her next door neighbours, 'boaties', who had some of the classic attributes of the 'problem family'. Soon after, we visited Dora at home and began to ask her about her life history and family. The next door neighbours were evicted, while Dora's mother, Enid, began to talk about another and similar family in the next street – coal on the settee, boarded up windows, the smell of urine everywhere in the house, children anti-social and ill-clothed (but not badly fed), father never in work – they did indeed have a similar reputation, but were significantly different. Enid knew the mother quite well and liked her because she was a good sport and in spite of her size would have a 'knees up' at the club.

Introductions were again frustrated because this second family moved, this time not evicted but rehoused by the council in a bigger house on another estate. They were the subject of some bitter-tongued envy at the time, as families who considered that they kept cleaner houses and were more careful tenants felt that they should have been given the opportunity to move away from Aulton and its shabby roads and irritating vandalism.

In Aulton, the high proportion of young teenagers and the few public social amenities for them, apart from the youth club, went some way towards explaining the undirected vandalism which, for instance, would start fires and break windows in empty houses. The teenagers were not allowed into the school playing fields after school or during the holidays. When the Fieldings left Aulton for a house on a new small council estate in Drayford, near George's parents and many other of his relatives, their house was immediately vandalized: windows were broken, wallpaper torn from the walls, and a fire lit on the floor. When the next tenant came, she was unwilling to move in, and so the house remained untenanted for some time, risking further vandalism. The Fieldings felt they would be blamed for leaving the house in such a state, and in any case, felt some proprietary sense of loss at the damage done to their carefully decorated home. The same problems attended the Barkers' departure from Bramwell, where, after the first onslaught, their house remained boarded up and empty for months.

Dora Fielding's Biography

Dora was a big, attractive woman. When we met her, she was six months pregnant, and her normally ample size was augmented by a well developed lump which she called 'Fred'. She was looking forward to a boy, hoping, like many mothers, that wishful thinking would produce 'one of each'. In the event, Amanda was born, and no one appeared the least bit disappointed. 'We shall have all girls, shan't we, Nicola?' she said to her elder daughter, then two-and-a-quarter. Nevertheless, when Dora was expecting a third child, Nicola was encouraged to say that she only wanted a brother. Dora was a devoted mother, a woman with a heart big enough to encompass far more children than they could afford, as well as her husband, her mother and a rising population of household pets: at one stage, they included two dogs, a cat, a rabbit and a budgerigar. At the start of fieldwork, Dora was twenty-nine years old, and had been married to George Fielding for two-and-a-half years. They had a two-year-old daughter, Nicola, and Dora was expecting a second child the following September. She talked about herself as being extremely lucky in having a good husband and a healthy child, and she said that it had made her believe in God again, because He had been so good to her.

Nevertheless, she had not always been so happy. She said that she felt she had wasted her time between the ages of sixteen and twenty-seven when she had met George. She wished she had had some sort of training: to teach small children, for instance. Instead, she had left school – the same local secondary modern school which the others had attended as well as George Fielding, her future husband – and done all sorts of jobs, including work in shops and local factories, unable to settle to anything. When she met Denis Booth, her first husband, she was working in a factory. They knew one another for eighteen months before they were married. He was six months younger than she, and he timed the wedding so that they should both be eighteen years old. Photographs taken at the wedding show it to have been a grand affair with two sisters as bridesmaids and a long white dress with a train as wide as the room. There were eighty guests, but none of the family, according to her mother, Enid, really liked Dora's first husband.

Dora and Denis had their own terraced house in another part of Kindleton, but this was eventually condemned and the council rehoused them on one of the better estates. From there, they moved in with Dora's mother-in-law until she and Dora could not get along. Dora was working as the manageress of a shop, and with their combined wages

(Denis had his own business) they were able to buy an estate car, a cabin cruiser (with a mortgage) and a Land Rover. They were married for nine years, and their affluence was in large measure a result of their misfortune of not being able to have any children. Dora felt it deeply, especially as her husband blamed her for it and she was forced to see numerous doctors who were able to do nothing for her. In the event, she was told that her husband's sperm count was too low, and her own fertility was proven when their marriage had broken up and she immediately became pregnant by George.

Apart from the lack of children in her first marriage, there were other problems. They had gradually grown apart; Dora had become fat, and Denis did not care for this; there was some violence, and he had marked her face, broken her finger and dragged her by the hair; in the end he had gone off with another woman and said that he was fed up with marriage. In the emotional anxiety of the last few weeks before he finally left, after some considerable coming and going, she had twice taken an overdose of pills and had gone into hospital. It grieved her that her medical records continued to brand her as unstable because of this, because she felt that she was only unstable at that time. She felt that this could count against her should she ever want to foster children.

A year later, she divorced Denis and married George. She had gone to the Citizens' Advice Bureau to find out how to get a divorce. She already knew George from her school days and had gone out with him when she was fourteen. While she was living with her sister after the break-up of her marriage, she had met him again. Nevertheless, George's mother and sisters had disapproved of his going out with her while she was still married. They had lived together; Dora felt that they had done so, knowing that they were going to get married as soon as they could.

George Fielding's Biography
This was a first-time marriage for George, although he was nearly thirty. He was a quiet man and was living, as he always had, with his mother and father in the old part of Drayford in the midst of his relatives.

Like Dora's brothers and sisters, George had left the same school in Aulton without any qualifications and without much respect for education. He now wished that he had had some training, but he had left school as soon as possible, anxious to have money jingling in his pocket. At fifteen, he had gone to work in a brick factory: he had had to leave the house at 5.30 am and he had not got home until 7 pm. The work was very heavy and involved running with the bricks from the conveyor belt to the place where they stacked them. He had come home every night covered in dust from the brick-making, and so exhausted that he had fallen asleep without having his tea, and had woken to discover it was the following morning. His mother had told him he should not go back, and he had not returned. He earned £4 per day.

For five years he worked with an engineering firm, doing shiftwork. This had not been much of a life: he was working seven days a week and only had the August holiday. He drank a lot as there was little else to do and it was hot work. He was made redundant after five years, but had not been able to get any redundancy money, even though he had made quite strenuous efforts to get it. He said that his present job with the local authority was the best he had ever had. He liked being out of doors and there was no 'gaffer' to bother him; he was earning more than he earned seven days a week with the engineering company. Like his brother-in-law Ken, he did heavy, dirty work, with an element of danger.

George's father had been a miner, but he had not worked for twelve years. The doctors said it was bronchitis and not dust on the lung, so he had received no compensation. George's mother mentioned that they had gone through very hard times in the past, but such things were not often talked about.

After George and Dora moved to Drayford, they saw more of the grandparents, and old Mrs Fielding looked after the children if Dora had to go out. Before, when they lived in Aulton, George's parents used to walk the long way up to see their grandchildren without a murmur, and would joke about being able to run back downhill again. The visits were very casual and unfussed, almost like people walking quietly into their own home. Dora felt it was wrong that her father-in-law was uncompensated: in the old days, the pits were full of dust. The whole family felt strongly the injustice of the situation.

Both George and Dora came from families where money had been short and where education had not been seen as having any great value. George's family was local for generations and was well integrated into the local community. Dora's father came from a family which had been better off, local to the city and which owned a house there, but he suffered from ill-health which prevented his working while his six children were at school, and his death brought down a family which had long relied on the firmness of his hand to organize them all.

Enid, Dora's mother, was full of fun, but disorganized when left to her own devices. She was the child of a more violent and less organized household in a period of harsh economic circumstances. Although her mother had roots in the area, her father was from Ireland and thus unable to bring to the marriage his share of the family support system which seems to be important to life in Kindleton. Enid and her husband Jamie had had to move out of the area to get work in Birmingham during the War – and when they moved back to Kindleton, were, after a period with his mother, eventually obliged to live in Aulton, where they were again cut off from the family, particularly in terms of visiting, childminding, shopping and borrowing. The family did not have a car or a telephone by means of which Enid could have maintained closer contact with her family, but their common workplace provided a link with her mother until the latter died.

Marital Relationship
In spite of a bias which derives in some measure from Dora's articulateness, it is possible to assert that George's part in the home was very important. Even before they moved to the new estate, Dora and George had to some extent started to share the work within the home and went out together for social activities. There were some activities which were exclusively the domain of Dora and Enid, such as cooking, washing and cleaning the house, but in things such as care of the children and the making of constant cups of tea, George played a very large part. Furthermore, Dora often asked him to do things, which he usually accomplished with a considerable lack of grumpiness.

Our first impression was perhaps that Dora ordered him about, but at the time we first met Dora, she was six months pregnant and had high blood pressure. After the birth of the baby, she almost always had one or both of the children on her knee. Sometimes she said that George put much more into their marriage than she did, and she felt badly about it, as his work was so hard. When she went to work for a while, doing part-time evening work when Amanda was almost a year old, she felt immense pleasure at being able to contribute to the household expenses, and also in being able to buy the children extra clothes. Another aspect of this equality was also in having workmates and a social life at work which was quite independent of the home, just as George had his work and friends independent of his wife.

It might be true to say that they had achieved a balance between 'joint' and 'segregated' roles, and had agreed to participate jointly in infant care. Their relationship was very close and openly affectionate, and there was no doubt that they were completely committed to one another and to their children, helping one another at home with the children, both of them playing with them and disciplining them, going on holiday together and occasionally to a local night club. At the same time, there was some segregation of jobs at home and of entertainment. George would always go to his home village pub at lunchtime at the weekend, just as he had always done, and Dora stayed at home. She also had at Aulton a host of women friends, most of whom had considered it proper to avoid visiting when he was home from work.

When Aulton mothers did flock into the garden for cups of tea during one hot summer, George tended to keep to himself and not talk to them much. He was perfectly amicable with Dora's mother, Enid, with whom they lived, and was talkative with relations or close friends. He played with friends' children in a pleasantly gentle rough-and-tumble, which they enjoyed. Just as Dora had the support and the visits of her relations, so he was visited regularly by his parents and his brother and her girlfriend. There was a balance here, with each partner accepting the relatives of the other. In matters of principle, however, Dora often followed the example of her husband rather than that of her mother: he did not care for Aulton, or for too much living in one another's pockets, or for not paying one's way in everything, and these values predominated, especially after the move to Drayford.

Child-rearing

Dora was consistently affectionate and attentive to her children. She spent long periods with one or both of them in her ample lap, and was sensitive in dealing with any rivalry between Nicola and Amanda for her time and her attention. She was firm with them and did not allow long periods of temper-crying from Nicola: she would be told to go up to her bed until she got over it and only then would she be allowed to come down or else be brought down. A child would always be given a cuddle as soon as she was amenable again. The children were generally very good tempered and showed little frustration or emotional upset.

Nicola went through a period of disequilibrium, however, when her sister was born. This was in spite of the fact that the family had prepared her quite carefully for the arrival of a new baby. They had shown her the quantities of immaculate baby clothes, and emphasized that it would be *her* baby sister. There had been jokes about 'Fred' in Dora's stomach, but, when the time came for her confinement, Nicola was told that Mum had gone to work rather than that she had gone into hospital to have the baby. Dora instructed her mother to humour the child, but did not tell her the truth; there might have been some feeling of superstition that if she did, everything might not go well.

In spite of all the preparation, when Dora returned with a baby girl Nicola found the loss of attention difficult to accept. Relations, very much at Dora's bidding, were careful to bring Nicola a present too when they came with their gifts for the new baby, but of course everyone's eyes were on Amanda. Nicola regressed (the word which Dora used to describe Nicola's behaviour), asking for a bottle, a dummy and knickers at night. If Dora used a paper towel on the baby, Nicola had to have one too. Dora allowed her these attentions, so that she should not feel left out, and gradually the child adjusted. She played with her younger sister, and as the baby grew up, she changed from a mothering role to that of a more capable playmate.

Nicola occasionally had tantrums when she wanted either to stay at a friend's house or to do something which her mother did not want her to do. Dora sometimes hit her hard but regretted this afterwards. She said that she had sometimes hit her really hard (usually on the legs) and felt that it showed in a child's character when it was older. She attributed the fact that Nicola was rather quiet and closed within herself to this fact, although an alternative explanation could be that the child had the reserved and quietly self-contained disposition of her father. By the time the second daughter was a year old, her mother was remarking to people what a good little girl Nicola was, and characterizing the younger one as a 'little devil'.

Dora was concerned for her children's intellectual development, and had intentionally bought Nicola educational toys such as a plastic polyhedron into the sides of which the infant learned to fit all sorts of shapes. She mentioned the large number of books which the child had had from her cousins. She asked us what age she should start reading to Nicola and encouraging her to read. Although perfectly skilled in reading and writing herself, Dora did not read for pleasure and there were no adult books apparent in the house. She was, nevertheless, mildly anxious that her child should be as able as most children of her age at these skills. Dora spent time with her daughter, trying to teach her the alphabet, and remarked that the teachers in the local school did not care for parents to help their children, and thought it interfering. This upset Dora who wanted to help her child all she could. It also disturbed her that there would not be a place for Nicola at the local school until she was five. Pre-school provision in Kindleton is higher than the national average, but in Drayford there was nowhere for Nicola to go. Nicola's only contact with other children, therefore, was through the mutual hospitality of mothers: Dora would invite over some of her relations and their children, or she would visit or receive visits from local mothers and their children.

At Aulton, the visiting among mothers was constant, almost unremitting, and thus Nicola mixed a great deal. She was too young to play in the street, but she would go with her mother to other houses where there were children of various ages, and she would also play with them in her front garden or in the house. Dora said that Nicola was very mean with her toys, and she attributed this to the fact that other children played with her toys and sometimes broke them, while she did not play with theirs. Dora was very concerned that the child should have everything she could possibly need. This extended from clothing to a superabundance of toys. At both Christmases there were many expensive and elaborate toys for which the child had no interest; every weekend saw some small new toy to amuse her. The element of status was certainly present, and Dora mentioned that she had bought Nicola a new doll's pram, so that she could 'walk up and down the front' like the other children at Aulton.

Dora insisted on buying the baby entirely new outfits and a new pram. She did not want her to feel that she had Nicola's cast-offs, even though Nicola's clothes were still in good condition. Dora tended to give them away instead; she also gave away some of the surplus toys and encouraged Nicola to be generous about this.

Dora's attitude to toilet-training was fairly relaxed. When we first visited the family, Nicola was two, and was using a junior commode in the sitting room. She occasionally wet herself, and Dora would in general not make a fuss, even though she thought it was often laziness, but would change her pants and socks. When Nicola wet herself after Amanda was born, she sometimes cried, and Dora said 'Never mind', realizing that she was distressed, or sometimes she was annoyed. She started Amanda on potty-training gradually, when she could walk, by putting pants without nappies on her during the day. To begin with, there was laughter about the fact that Amanda had not quite got the idea, and thought that you sat on the potty *after* you had relieved yourself. These methods took quite a toll out of the carpet, however, and they had a new sitting room carpet in the new house, when the second child was about a year old. The children were kept very clean and always smelled fresh and pleasing.

Dummies were used, but generally only when the children slept. They were discouraged from using them during the day. The method Dora used would be to ask the child to give her a kiss, which of course she could not do with the 'dummy tit' in her mouth. They were referred to as 'titties'. The children were not put to bed in the evening, but went up later with their parents; the two girls slept on the settee or on a lap in the middle of the family. Dora said she would worry about them if they were upstairs. She thought middle class women who sent their children off to bed must be rather cold-hearted.

The children were not encouraged to be self-conscious about nakedness, and Nicola liked to wander about without clothes in the hot weather. The little girls could see their adult female relatives naked, but not their father or, by implication, other adult men. Dora felt that kissing was all right in front of the children, but that sexual activities were inappropriate if a child was sleeping in the same room. Dora was open in conversation about sexual matters, and liked to joke about such things too in a friendly, almost bawdy way, of which George did not always approve. She felt that sex education was the business of the parents and not the schools.

Dora was not only affectionate with and interested in her own children, but was generous and warm with her brother Ken's children, who were twelve and nine years old. She would have liked more children, and used to remark 'What's wrong with big families?' Nevertheless, particularly after the birth of Amanda, she disagreed with Enid who said she would have had more children if she had been able. The two sides of the question were always present in her mind: on the one hand she felt it was nice for children to have lots of brothers and sisters and cousins, and that however poor you were, you should have as many as you liked; on the other hand she knew that one's standard of living declined as family size increased, and for a while she was very reluctant to have a third child. She and George had never used contraceptives; Dora thought it made sex too premeditated and unromantic. When she became pregnant a third time, she was delighted; Amanda was a year and a quarter. It should be mentioned that when Dora made a defence of the large family, she was also defending friends from Aulton, who were mothers of large families, as well as defending her own natal family.

Health

Dora's attitude to post-natal clinics and health visitors was at the outset very dismissive. Her hospital experiences had been good, and she particularly appreciated nurses who themselves had had children or even grandchildren; she felt that no amount of book learning and watching of other people's experiences could make up for the individual experience of going through a birth. For this reason, she tended to have a poor opinion of the childless health visitors with whom she came in contact. She felt that the clinic was a waste of time and pointed out that they had weighed her baby wrongly on two occasions, giving her a false impression of whether Amanda was gaining or losing weight. She also blamed the health visitor for recommending Ostermilk No. 2 for the baby and then, when research as reported in the media suggested that it should not be recommended, telling her to use another dried milk.

We had evidence of a lack of respect and sensitivity from some of the local doctors. Dora and her sister, Evelyn, had changed doctors when their GP had allegedly refused to see the latter, after she was a minute late for her appointment. It was a long walk to the surgery from Aulton. During our period of fieldwork Dora's sister-in-law, Leslie, contracted appendicitis, which the doctor insisted was just colic, but it developed into peritonitis. While she was suffering painfully with this for two days at home, the doctor remarked 'There's no need for all this, Mrs Havelock', as if she were merely making a fuss. Dora's brother, Ken, eventually took his wife to hospital himself, where she had an emergency operation. The family, glad that she eventually recovered, did not complain. Enid Havelock also recounted several stories of the doctor telling her not to waste his time, when she went to see him.

Dora did not breastfeed her children. The predominant reason was that she thought it was 'not nice', a bit old fashioned and unsavoury, but as a more definite reason she said that there would be nowhere for her to do it – people were in and out all the time. The idea of breastfeeding in front of anyone, even her husband George, was so far beyond the realm of possibility as not even to be considered, and the idea of going upstairs out of the throng of family and neighbours was never considered either. Dora fed on demand, and did not leave her child to cry. The baby's health was good for the first year, apart from occasional bouts of influenza. When Amanda was about fifteen months old, Nicola caught measles and mumps, and the baby soon followed suit. Dora's attitude to welfare services for mother and baby gradually changed, and this seemed to happen more after the move from Aulton than before it, a fact which seemed to have some logical connection. She complained that the health visitor had only visited her twice in two years; her friend, Eileen, who had had her baby at the same time and in the same hospital as Dora, complained that the health visitor came every two weeks. It could be surmised that the health visitor was concerned with Eileen's problems: herself the child of a broken home, Eileen's husband had deserted her before her baby was born, and she was living with her own mother and her mother's girlfriend, with whom Eileen had a rather volatile relationship.

Eileen was not from Aulton, and her friendship with Dora gradually took the place of that with the Aulton mothers with whom Dora had spent her time before the move to Drayford. Although Dora had occasionally gone to the clinic with one of them, it was with Eileen that she made her fortnightly visits from Drayford. She was somewhat sceptical of the value of injections for the children: vaccination and immunization against an array of diseases did not appeal to her, especially when she read of cases of brain damage resulting from whooping cough injections. George agreed, and remarked that men at work who had been immunized against 'flu, had seemed to go down with it, so he could not see the point of it either.

Dora's attitude to the care of teeth was idiosyncratic. She did not believe in brushing her own teeth, and yet was ashamed when the dentist had to scale them. She did not believe that sweets and biscuits were responsible for her daughter's rotten teeth; instead she argued that they had come through rotten. She said that her own sister brushed her teeth and all hers were rotten, while Dora's were good. During our fieldwork, she suffered from unbearable toothache and had to have a tooth extracted. She said that the dentist had made her pay for this (even though she had a new baby and so would normally have been exempt from dental charges) because she had had it done immediately and not waited for her appointment.

The children were given sweets and biscuits frequently. Sweets were supplied as treats every evening when Enid, her mother, came home from work. When the ice cream van came round, parents and children had ices or lollipops. Dora said that it did not matter as the children always ate their tea, but in our observations Nicola did not always do so. George generally took sandwiches with him to work, and for tea the family would have something cooked, which might be eggs, beans and chips, or a meat dish with boiled potatoes, known as a 'potato dinner'; vegetable stew was a great favourite with Enid.

Finances

George handed over his take-home pay of forty-five pounds to Dora, receiving back from seven to ten pounds pocket money, which was for items such as beer, cigarettes, bus fares and dental charges. Dora said she knew how much he earned and what rises he got. She was receiving about thirty-five pounds per week from him to cover the expenses of the household; these included all the regular callers for clothes and furniture ordered from catalogues, food and gas and electricity bills. Her mother's contribution provided the rent. When she went to work in a local manufacturing firm, she was earning about twenty pounds for the same number of hours and piecework rates.

Dora and her mother bought consumer durables week by week, trying to be sure that they did not have too much of a burden of 'club money' to pay out every week, in case George should go sick. In this way they had bought a three-piece suite, an Axminster carpet, suits, a table and chairs and Christmas presents. Christmas presents especially involved considerable foresight because popular toys tended to sell out of catalogues, and consequently Dora would send away for things in October. Dora could not wait for Christmas Day, but showed Nicola *all* her surprises beforehand, and wrapped them again for December 25. It seemed quite impossible for her to keep secret any single present.

Enid took great care to be just in the giving of presents to all her grandchildren, and justice was secured by spending the same amount, six pounds fifty, on each child. Dora and George gave each other best suits, which they wore before Christmas on special occasions.

When the family moved to the new house with its smart white paint and light, airy rooms, they felt that their furniture looked tatty, and Dora and Enid spent a good deal more every week on furniture and carpets. Dora was aware that it cost more to buy through catalogues, hire purchase and Provident cheques (weekly contributions to a Friendly Society which are accumulated and exchanged for goods), but she thought it a positive advantage to have the article while you were paying for it, rather than to save. She said: 'We don't save', as if it were not something they commonly did or indeed aspired to do. Nevertheless, she saved regularly for the benefit of her children.

Some of the furniture which they bought was costly but shoddily made: tables and chairs were of cheap, and not durable, materials. Dora knew one could buy old things more cheaply, but she wanted her furniture to be bright and new. Before buying a carpet, Dora had assessed the advantages and disadvantages of different fibres, but had been limited by lack of money from getting what she knew to be a better and more lasting purchase. The family was tempted to another large expense arising from their move: they missed the wall gas-fire which had been the focal point of their old sitting room, so they bought an imitation log electric-fire with wooden surrounds. This cost them eighty pounds, and was necessitated because the house had been built without any fireplace or gas-fire fittings, and the occupier was intended instead to rely totally on central heating. In the event this left the household with no alternative source of heating when the central heating broke down over Christmas; they then realized that some kind of fire was a practical necessity.

The move itself involved them in expense as they had to budget for such things as the cost of a removal van and for the installation of a cooker. They had had to pay all their fuel bills together, and the new rent of £10.60 per week was higher than they were used to. The struggle of the first few months was alleviated partly by the fact that George and Enid were both wage earners, and secondly by Dora's starting to go out to work in the evenings too, even though this meant that she and George spent very little time together. They put up with this situation with very little grumbling and regret. George and Enid would go out before eight, and George would return in the early afternoon; at about five o'clock Dora would go off to work, and Enid would return at 5.30 to make the teas. Dora would come in again at 10.30 pm. Enid indeed, towards the end of our fieldwork, decided to remarry, and her future husband worked, as he always had, on nights while she, as she always had, worked on days. This did not seem to trouble her, because shiftwork was to her a fact of life, and so there was no use in grumbling at it. After Dora became pregnant for the third time, she decided to give up work, and only then did she mention the privation she had felt at not spending the evenings with George. She was still glad that she had been able to give her days to the children by doing the evening shift.

Dora's Extended Family

Dora's mother, Enid Havelock, is a vivid storyteller, and gave us a great deal of information about her family from the period of the First World War. Enid's father, Michael Donoghue, came to Kindleton from Ireland. He married her mother, Mary, a local girl, and they settled in Kindleton. She bore him seven children, of whom Enid was the last and only one to survive. She was born during the First World War, and when she was still a baby, her mother died of tuberculosis. Enid explained that Mary had fretted and scarcely ate while her husband was away fighting in France. Mary's next-door neighbour, Lilly, breastfed Enid, and later married Enid's father. The pattern of the relationship was already set by the proposal: Lilly refused him when he came home drunk to ask her hand, and she did not agree until he had blackened her eye. Lilly had seven children by her first husband (three surviving) and eight more children by Michael, none of whom survived. Enid described him as a good husband and father, but she also said that he used to drink and beat Lilly up, and that the reason why Lilly lost two lots of twins was that he knocked her down the stairs on two occasions. One child survived until the age of two, when she died of pneumonia. Enid blamed herself, as this happened soon after a street accident in which Enid and the little child were injured when the latter was under Enid's care. She and her parents lived through the hard times of the twenties, picking coal off the slag heaps and fetching soup when it was distributed. Michael's drinking stretched the family's slender resources uncomfortably. Enid told of one occasion when her father returned, having spent half the housekeeping on drink, and a fight ensued during the course of which Michael hit Enid's mother (Enid always referred to her stepmother, Lilly, as her mother), Enid knocked her father unconscious, and her mother hit her about, fearing that he had been hurt badly. A second anecdote described another occasion when Michael, again drunk, was discovered on the sofa with another woman; on this occasion Lilly broke a stone jar over his head and threw the woman out.

Enid described her stepmother giving birth to one of her own children at home, cleaning up, and immediately getting on with her washing. She painted a picture of a hard life made more difficult, but not more bitter, by the figure of the traditional drunken and belligerent father. Enid was, nevertheless, obviously very fond of her father and saw him merely as a different man when he drank. She did not know that Lilly was her stepmother until at the age of eight she was taunted about it by children in the street, and Lilly would not tell her the truth until her twelfth birthday. Enid recognized that it had been very difficult for her not to know the truth for so long, but fully expected her own daughter, Dora, to do the same with her own daughters, and not to tell them about her previous marriage until they were much older. Both Dora and her mother think that the eldest little girl, Nicola, would be upset if she knew that Dora had lived with another man. In spite of the growing number of divorces, and, indeed, the large number of divorces, liaisons and second marriages among their neighbours at Aulton, the family keeps alive an ideal according to which a woman is devoted to one man for her lifetime.

Enid said that she had not gone to school very much because of colds and 'flu; she felt that school was nothing to do with her. She could not read or write, but she was able to decipher the TV section of the evening newspaper without difficulty. She also had great problems in using the telephone. She left school at thirteen and went to work in a factory. She said it was very heavy work indeed, and for it she used to get ten shillings a week which she gave to her mother. In exchange she would be given sixpence a week pocket money.

When she was seventeen, Enid was injured by a motorbike which crashed into her bicycle from behind. She suffered a fractured skull, serious internal bleeding and a punctured right ear drum. As a result she had headaches and her hearing was affected.

When she was twenty-two Enid met a young man called Jamie Havelock and married him soon after, just before the outbreak of the

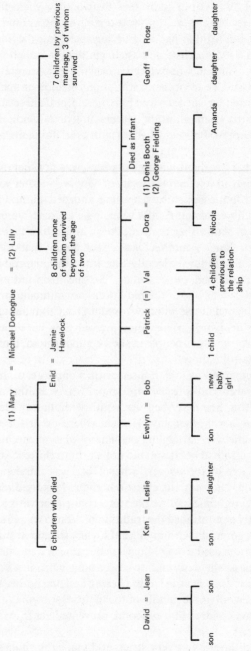

Figure 5.1 Dora Fielding's Family Tree

Second World War. Enid paid for the wedding breakfast with a Provident Society cheque; her father was so upset, weeping in the front room, that her stepbrother had to give her away. Enid was a Catholic, but Jamie was a Methodist, and their children were brought up as Protestants. Enid in fact conceived her first child on her honeymoon and continued living with her mother until Jamie got a job on the railway in Birmingham, and then she followed him there. Enid had seven children, one of whom died as an infant; the others all live in Kindleton, and all are married except for Patrick who lives with a girl by whom he has had a child.

Jamie's mother had her own house, which was not handed on when she died, but instead sold and the proceeds divided among her children. With his share Jamie bought a television and new clothes for all the family. By this time, he and Enid and their six children were living in a council house in Aulton, Jamie's mother's house having become too small for them. Jamie's mother was a member of a local voluntary association and had influence locally. She 'knew the council' which Enid thought had helped them to get a house. So they had lived in Aulton in what they described as one of the old houses, an unmodernized version of the semi-detached house where we found Dora and George Fielding at the start of fieldwork. When they arrived they were 'better', they considered, than the other people in the neighbourhood, and the estate was 'worse' than it is now.

Dora remembered the old houses with a mixture of horror and humour; they were rat-infested fire traps. She was nine when they arrived in Aulton. She described her youth without any glamour and without sparing her mother any criticism where she felt it was due.

Enid and Jamie were struggling financially when their children were young. Jamie had a bad heart and did not work for thirteen years before he died at the age of forty-seven, when Dora was thirteen years old, Patrick fourteen, and only the eldest daughter, Jean, had married and left home. Before, Jamie had worked as a coal-carter with a horse and cart. Apparently he continued the tradition of fathers who drank heavily and sometimes got nasty, although Enid loyally suggested that the fault was hers in that she used to nag him when he came in well-oiled from the pub. Nevertheless, she described two occasions when it was obviously too much for her: once she tried to gas herself and on another she tried to walk out on them all in the middle of the night. Her husband in the first instance, and her children in the second, prevented her from succeeding in these projects.

Her husband, Jamie, was very strict, and made the children do their own cleaning jobs around the house – something which they loathed – while Enid was kept on a tight rein and could not even say hello to another man in the street. He was violent with her too when he discovered that she was pawning his clothes until the end of the week. It is part of the family's explanation of Patrick's criminal behaviour to point out that during this period he was often punished by his father for things which the others did. Dora described him as a black sheep who truanted from school from his earliest days, and whom the other children, particularly his elder brother, forced into situations where he would certainly be punished. At the same time, Dora also felt that Patrick and Enid were alike in temperament and that, having been strongly controlled by Jamie during his lifetime, they both 'fell apart' after his death.

Dora felt that life was much easier for the older sister and brother, Jean and Ken, who were virtually grown up before their father died, and did not spend so long in Aulton. Dora thought that Ken glossed over the hard times that they went through and has now forgotten it in the midst of his present affluence. Money was very short both while Jamie was 'on the club' (national assistance because he was ill) and later when Enid was receiving the widow's pension. His national assistance was seven pounds per week, and later Enid's pension was four pounds. The younger girls remembered going to school with holes in their shoes, and they laughed to think of the socks whose lagging elasticated tops would sag under their feet. Dora remembered weeping on her bed when she could not go with other children on a school trip because the family did not have the money to pay for it. She mentioned several such sharp memories of childhood privations, and attributed her own generosity towards her children to a desire that they should 'have' where she had lacked.

Enid was evidently not able to manage the home as she had when her husband was there to keep a tight hold on their affairs. The family went downhill. Dora used to wash and iron her own clothes, and remembered the teachers at the local school asking her whether her brother, Patrick, could not be pursuaded to wash his neck. She said that they were a 'rough family', that her mother soon took to going out dancing until four in the morning and to having boyfriends back to stay, and that the whole family would sit down to share one tin of steak poured over potatoes. There were stories of Enid giving money to her boyfriends and of one who used to beat her up. On one occasion, Ken, who had married and left home, was called in to exact retribution when the man had beaten Enid, and he blackened his eye. On another occasion her boyfriend threw a brick through the window and hit one of her daughters.

In contrast to the strict regime which prevailed when father was alive – they tricked him into agreeing to Jean marrying at eighteen by getting him to write his permission when he was drunk – not only the mother but the children too were 'courting all over the house' after he died. Enid's anecdotes recalled that she once came back late at night to find Patrick sleeping with his girlfriend upstairs; but she drove them out. The freedom, however, also had its dark side. Dora married at eighteen and went to live in another part of Kindleton, but she recalled her youngest brother, Geoff, cycling the miles from Aulton in floods of tears, because Patrick was beating him up. Dora told her mother at one stage that she would be charged with cruelty if she allowed it to continue, and Geoff spent a lot of his time staying with Dora and her husband. Dora introduced Geoff to his future wife, Rose, and he married her at sixteen. Dora thought that he married primarily to get away from home.

Patrick: The Unsuccessful Sibling
During this period, Patrick was repeatedly getting into trouble, was sent to approved school and borstal, and became dirty and a heavy drinker. While all the other children, except Evelyn, married young and, after beginning their marriages at home, soon moved to their own homes, he clung to his mother in between periods of enforced absence. During fieldwork he was in prison, having completed one sentence for inflicting grievous bodily harm, and serving another for breaking and entering a house. Previous convictions suggested he had adopted a very violent pattern of behaviour. Just as was the case with his maternal grandfather, he was 'a changed man in drink'; charming in normal circumstances, he could turn very ugly when he had drink inside him.

One time when he lifted his hand to his mother, she had defended herself with the poker: she packed his bags. At that time he was paying her no board. A month later he took her out for a drink, called her 'the best Mum in the world', and they were on speaking terms again. Since that time he had been living with a married woman, Valerie, who already had four children. Val and Patrick have since had a child of their own. The family characterized them as spending their money, including the weekly postal order from the children's father, on drink and bingo and Dora felt that the children were ill-clothed but not neglected.

Pat and Val were not usually invited to family celebrations, because Pat would get drunk and difficult and Val would 'misbehave' and cause bad feeling between husbands and wives. In spite of such criticism, Dora had strong feelings of affection for her brother, was deeply moved when he reappeared from prison, and genuinely welcomed him and his family when they visited her home. Her affection was mixed with a resentment that he behaved as he did. Part of her could accept that he was 'not one for work', and that Val should work while he looked after the children, but when he stole again, she remarked angrily that he could get a job: he had 'two arms and two legs like anybody else' and he was 'thick'. He had promised her when he came out of prison that he would never get into trouble again, now that he had children, but he had slipped back into trouble.

In their attempts to understand Patrick's problems, the family singled out from their memories the fact that they were poorly dressed and that the teachers used to complain about his appearance. He was beaten at school; he also truanted a great deal. He was enuretic and wet the bed sometimes even when he was twenty, but this was attributed to his drinking. Bullied by his elder brother, he in turn bullied the youngest brother, Geoff, the delicate boy who was his parents' favourite.

Enid characterized him as 'hard' by the time his father died, that is at aged fourteen. To illustrate this, she cited the example of Jamie's funeral tea. They all had fish and chips, but none of them could eat, except for Patrick who ate all their teas. After his father's death, he 'went to pieces'. His criminal record adversely affected a close relationship with a local girl; he went through a period of visiting prostitutes. He kept contracting VD, and his close family were worried about infection from him. He drank and was dirty. A more settled period with a long-term relationship had not diminished his violence, and it was said that his 'woman egged him on' when he was drunk.

Ken and Jean: The Successful Siblings

The career of Patrick, the fourth child in the family, contrasted strongly with that of his elder brother, Ken. Ken had many of the same characteristics – he was tough, full of life and always had something funny to say – but he was evidently much more integrated into the community, his work and his family. When he was quite young, he married Leslie, a girl who like himself was very hard-working and who did a day's work in a factory to come home and accomplish all the chores at home as well. Her family did not 'lack' as the Havelocks had done as children, and Ken and Leslie saw to it that their two children did not lack for anything either. They were given a hundred pounds' worth of presents each for Christmas. They always had spending money for outings and money for sweets; gleaming bicycles, a portable television set, fishing equipment, and a toy electric organ attested to past generosity. The elder child, however, disdained and wasted these rich gifts. This family were aware that more children would mean that Leslie could not work and this would bring down their standard of living tremendously; it was a conscious decision that the number of children was limited to two. Nevertheless, ill health had recently stopped her working. Ken himself was a mechanic, and brought home a 'good' wage including a bonus coming from extra work done on the side in his spare-time. He worked hard and for long hours, but perhaps even more importantly, very consistently. He never took time off, unlike almost all the others whom v e interviewed and got to know: the occasional day off was a very usual and often very necessary part of worklife, but he did not have them, even though his work was very heavy and dirty.

Apart from his paid work, he was also working on improving his house in the evenings. They had bought a house with a mortgage on the new private estate near Aulton, and Ken was extending it. When he was not doing this, he was involved in local team games, supporting a local football club and playing in a football team and a pub skittle team. He seemed to have boundless energy and good health. He too liked his pint, and he and Leslie liked to go out dancing with Dora and George, and Leslie's sister and brother-in-law. Integrated as they were into the local community, in family, school, work, sport and entertainment, they were not interested in getting to know us as researchers or 'college people' from outside, and Ken's wife did not want to be interviewed. We met only by chance on several occasions, as they used to give Enid a lift home in the evenings, and once formally at a family christening.

Enid's eldest daughter, Jean, had the same outgoing personality and zest in her manner as her brother. She was large, pretty and vivacious, with lots of dyed blonde hair swathed up on her head. As a child she was the most successful at school and passed her '11 +' exam. Her father, however, would not let her go to the grammar school, as he believed they could not afford the uniform and books. She married at eighteen and had a son when she was nineteen before she actively wanted any children. She had a very difficult birth just after her father's death, and swore she would not have any more. When she was thirty, however, she wanted another child, and another son was born. Jean became the manageress of a large store, and she and her husband, David, saved £400 for a deposit to purchase a house, but they could not find a building society which would advance them the balance on a small older terrace house when they tried to buy one. So they spent the money instead on a car. Jean sometimes spoke in a middle class manner. She would like her elder son, who was academically able, to go to university, and to have the educational opportunities which she herself had missed. Jean would now like to train as a teacher.

Evelyn

Evelyn, Enid's third child, and her husband had a council house in Aulton near the house where Enid and Dora were living when we started fieldwork. Evelyn was first married to a man with a heart condition, who died suddenly and shortly after the wedding; she went through a stage of extreme shock and was unable to work for several years. She lived for a long time with her mother, who was working. Before she married her present husband, there was a period of instability, when he left her, and it was at this time that Evelyn had a 'breakdown'. She was in a psychiatric ward for a while. Dora considered that her boyfriend's departure and her 'breakdown' were related, while Evelyn gave a much more mundane explanation for her behaviour; she blamed the pain from a kidney infection.

Evelyn had a little boy who attended the Aulton nursery school. He seemed a little nervous, and Dora said that the child was easily brought to tears, but he had a very retentive memory and his relatives recounted admiringly that he could sing lots of nursery rhymes. The family had some reservations about the nursery school, and in particular resented the boy being made to sit in front of his dinner to force him to eat it, whether it made him sick or not. The point was made that the child surely had the right to refuse it, because his mother had *paid* for it. The question of who received benefits of various kinds and who 'stands on their own two feet' was a lively question within the extended family and in Aulton itself, where the large number of men out of work and the number of unsupported mothers meant that a large proportion of children at the local schools were entitled to free school meals.

Evelyn had had several miscarriages, but had worked consistently up until the arrival of her second baby. Her husband had been out of work, and Dora remarked that he went out drinking in Aulton quite a lot. Dora and Evelyn were close to one another both in age and affection, and Dora recognized that Evelyn and her husband worked things out in their own way.

Geoff: Early Marriage

The youngest sibling was Geoff, who was born shortly after Enid had lost a baby aged six months. Geoff weighed only four pounds, five ounces at birth, and was treated with the greatest care by both Enid and Jamie; this extended to not hitting the child, unlike the other children who were hit when they were naughty. Jamie in fact threatened to 'kick *her* arse' when she threatened the child in the same terms. The family 'wouldn't let the wind blow on him', and this favouritism attracted some jealousy from his brothers and sisters, and some bullying from Patrick.

He, like his brothers and sisters, went to the secondary modern school at Aulton. They were all beaten at school, but Dora says he was beaten so much he refused to go there. He married at sixteen, when Rose was expecting their first child, and now lived in a council house in another part of Kindleton with his wife and their two small girls. Dora said he was full of fun before he was married but at the age of twenty-one he was old for his age.

Geoff worked with Ken, following the same pattern as Evelyn and Jean: the younger sibling learning from the elder, and working in the same place. Enid worked at the same factory as her mother too, and this pattern of members of a family helping one another to find work and preferring to work together is traditionally common in Kindleton.

Relations with Neighbours at Aulton

When we first met Dora, she referred to herself and her two women friends, Irene and Heather, as 'the Three Musketeers'. It was they who had collected clothes together for a local jumble sale. The others would only go to the Mothers and Toddlers Club if Dora went. They would drink cups of tea together, and borrow Dora's washing machine, or lend one another pints of milk, give toddlers' clothes, or mind one another's children. There was, however, a certain amount of moving into and away from the street they lived in, and soon there were two clusters of friends with many lesser friends.

Straightaway, Figure 5.2 should make it obvious that Dora and Irene were strong characters, and that Dora also tended to attract satellites in the form of young mothers who used to come to her house for a good part of most days. Pam and Shirley had each a small girl and were expecting another child; their husbands worked intermittently and Pam's husband was an alcoholic and involved in petty theft. Maggie was expecting a baby, already had a large family and was soon to be divorced from her husband who did not provide for her; she and Rhona were less frequent visitors. Pam and Beatrice came to the street during the period of fieldwork, and gradually, as Dora asserted her independence from local values, Irene spent more and more time with Beatrice. These two had in common the fact that they were on social security and were living with (or having regular visits from) the father of their children, to whom in both cases they were not married. Beatrice had been married before

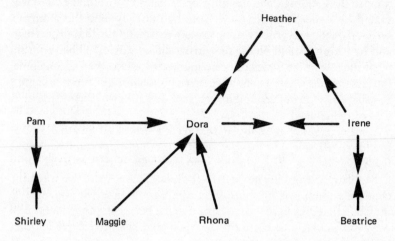

Figure 5.2   Patterns of Visiting

and had four children altogether; Irene had five children, the youngest being only a toddler. Heather also lived on social security, and she and Irene had children who were half West Indian. Heather and Irene's men knew each other and belonged to the same West Indian local culture.

Although Heather, Irene, Dora and Beatrice all kept immaculate houses, and did their best to furnish and decorate them to the best of their means, only Dora had a husband in work, who supported them solely and steadily according to the ideals of the wider society. The difference in Dora's values ('standing on your own two feet') became noticeable when there was an attempt locally to withhold rent from the council to protest about housing conditions. Dora alone of the Three Musketeers paid her rent, asserted that the conditions were adequate, and mentioned loudly that most people didn't pay their rent anyway – social security did.

Dora tried to justify her non-alignment partly in terms of not associating with a woman called Maureen, who, she said, was trying to boss everybody around. Dora said that a list had been made, last time there was community action, of those who would *not* take part: 'They can write my name in the sky, but I'm paying my rent', she said. Apart from the unacceptability of being ordered about by another mother on the estate, Dora's assertion that Maureen was the prime mover in it allied the rent strike with one of the most notorious families on the estate: she was an offshoot of the 'boaties' family who had lived next door to the Fieldings, had herself been brought up 'in a home', and was visited by a social worker now. Dora had already used this woman's position on the playgroup committee as a reason for not taking part in it, and by taking a stand on the rent strike she now divorced herself from what she saw as the undesirable people on the estate. At the same time, the fact that she wanted to be allocated a house on another estate cannot be ruled out as an understandable reason for wanting to stay on the right side of the council.

It seemed that by focusing on Maureen, Dora was trying to draw her friends to her side, but they, with little desire or opportunity to move from their houses, stayed in the opposite camp. A rift occurred. Dora had already justified her move from the estate at Aulton in two ways: the children's room was no more than a box-room, and she was able to maintain that they were short of space, and if her second child had been a boy, she would have been able to insist that she needed yet another bedroom, and therefore a bigger house.

Secondly, before the birth of her second daughter, Dora had been bitten by a dog in the street, and she insisted that the dog was always after Nicola. Doubtless, this held little weight with the housing department, but it served to justify to Dora's friends the Fieldings' desire to leave. The question of the dog was difficult, because Irene's neighbours had told the council that *her* dogs were savage and anti-social, and she was getting up a petition to say that they were harmless, always under control and that they did not bite. Now Dora was again in the opposite camp, as a complainant against dogs.

As Dora turned away from Aulton and its people, so her friends tended to dwindle too. The hot summer, in any case, had been a suitable time for visiting; in the autumn Pam and Shirley were visiting all day, but with the onset of winter the Fieldings rented a colour television as they drew more into themselves, waiting to be allocated a house. Christmas was very quiet and followed by bouts of 'flu. Dora felt neglected by her friends because no one had come in to help when she was ill. Not a soul had visited. At the same time, friendship with Eileen, whose baby had been born in the same hospital and at the same time as Amanda, was strengthened, and she came first to high tea and later to stay for a few days. As the other friends kept to themselves, Dora talked about Irene being better off supported by social security than by her 'husband' and preferring it that way, about Beatrice's husband being too idle to get work, about Shirley being lazy and dirty, and about Pam getting money and clothes from a social worker when she had an idle, thieving husband. By the early part of the next year, Dora was totally alienated from the culture and the people of her street, even though she tried to keep friends with them by having the occasional tupperware or other selling party. Her isolation was measurable in terms of the amount that mothers had been dependent on her before: Irene used to borrow her washing machine, Maggie, the children's swimming costumes, and Heather, the vacuum cleaner. Dora characterized Heather and Irene as real friends and the others as just borrowers. Apart from borrowing, there had rarely been an afternoon that we visited when a woman friend and her children were not also visiting.

Perhaps a critical event in all this was the fact that social security were informed that Beatrice was cohabiting, and Dora, because of her outspoken views, was mistakenly suspected of being the informer. The outcome was a closening of the relationship between Irene and Beatrice, and a further rift between Irene and Dora. Irene now used Beatrice's washing machine.

To give a proper perspective on the Fieldings' desire to leave, we should list some of the disadvantages, as they saw them, of living in Aulton, apart from its location on the outer edges of the city and consequent cost in terms of travel. Sometimes neighbours made 'unbelievable noise', and on one occasion, a wife came and threw bricks through her husband's window and shouted obscenities at him in the middle of the night, driving round and round in a car. Their next-door neighbours were in the habit of giving Dora's address to finance firms and even to the Electricity Board, and when their creditors came to re-possess furniture, they would come to the Fieldings' door. For this reason, Dora had had difficulty in the past in renting a colour television set. Women would come and spend all day in the house, making it difficult for Dora to get on with her work. The children caught lice off one another at the local school, and Dora had herself caught them twice, once from a neighbour's children – although 'it was easier than in the old days, when you could not get something from the chemist to deal with lice.' George felt it was useless trying to keep the garden clean and tidy when rubbish was constantly blown in or thrown in. He had no friends in the street and neither he nor Dora liked the 'atmosphere' in the local club or pub. They had not dared to put up a Christmas present of a holly wreath on the front door in case it was stolen.

On the credit side, there was a good deal of mutual helpfulness among women on low incomes: Dora, however, was more self-sufficient and was usually at the giving end. The abundant company of mothers and children was something which Dora was to miss in her new house, even though she said she did not want to see as much of other women as before. She lamented, nevertheless, that there was no fenced front garden where Nicola could play and talk to the other children. At four, she was still too young to play on her own in the street: there was a feeling – voiced also by Elsie Barker – that a child must be going to school before he can play outside. Danger from traffic was the stated and very valid reason.

The Move to Drayford

Halfway through our period of contact, the Fieldings left the noisy and notorious council estate of Aulton for a brand new house in a quiet cul-de-sac in Drayford, with newly turfed front gardens and trees planted by the council. When Dora moved to Drayford, she soon made new friends, but she continued to return to Aulton about once a week or a fortnight to keep in touch. But now her friends included several people with cars, and a woman with her own modern house, who gave her a lift to work every evening. George continued to go to the same pub in Drayford, and apart from that, mixed virtually only with relations and with one neighbour. He did not miss Aulton, but neither did he feel entirely at home in the new house. The street of detached houses, each with its own garden and garage, was not the same Drayford as the terraced street with its little butcher-grocer, bakery and post office, where people could shout from one side to the other and women would talk as they passed one another's doorways – the Drayford in which he was brought up. A year after the move, Dora talked wistfully of older houses and of the way in which a new house showed up your furniture. The house was almost too much to live up to.

The last important element in the social life of the Fieldings and in their ability to divorce themselves from the old estate, poorer as it was both economically and environmentally, was their relationship with their extended families. They had in effect moved from the centre of Dora's natal family to the centre of George's, and thus saw more of his parents and brothers, and were more available for mutual help (e.g. baby-minding or shopping). George's family were part of the older culture of Kindleton. Mrs Fielding had a parlour where she could have tea with friends, and Mr Fielding grew chrysanthemums; they were quiet and they stayed put.

Enid, who had often known poverty and its antidote, the 'good time', especially of a Saturday night at the pub, and whose only real roots for the last twenty years had been at Aulton, did not settle to the sobriety of Drayford. Unlike Dora and George, she had always gone to the Aulton

Club, and she continued to do so, in spite of the distance, after the move. The fact that she decided to go out with a former Aulton boyfriend, and that she wanted to marry and go to live with him in Aulton was the result of her desire to return to her old home. Enid did not want the quiet, detached cul-de-sac. The noisy, vandalized estate with its culture of a little beer, one-armed bandits, bingo and a knees-up at the weekend was what she missed; she did not return to the bottom of the estate, the most deprived area of houses, but to the more sought after area near the shops. The previous house was considered by many of the locals to be badly fire-proofed and dangerous. Dora kept in touch with her most successful brother, Ken, who lived nearby. He had already helped George to build a wall in the back garden. He and Leslie visited for tea every Saturday. Their daughter always used to visit Dora after school and would sometimes go shopping for her, and she still provided them with the invaluable service of a baby-sitter – something which many families on the newer estates lacked, if they did not live near their relatives.

Leslie bought susbstantial presents for the arrival of Dora's children. Ken was called upon whenever anyone was in hospital (births, miscarriages, operations) to ferry relatives to see whoever was a patient. He was called upon in emergencies because of his good sense, and also because he had a car and a telephone. He thus provided vital links between his family and hospitals, doctors and the police. When Dora was bitten by a dog in Aulton, Enid immediately telephoned not only the police but Ken as well. When Evelyn's baby was born, Ken took his mother to see them in hospital. Ken always gave his mother a lift home from work in the evenings.

Dora was now farther away from Evelyn than when she had lived at Aulton, and in fact she had applied for an exchange near Evelyn before she was allocated the new house. Dora went up to see her for the day, once a week, and it was Evelyn who provided them with cheap household goods from work, thus saving them a lot of money. Dora sometimes looked after Evelyn's little boy for her and had him to stay when Evelyn went into hospital to have her second child. Dora probably supported Evelyn rather more than vice versa because she was better off and had her more helpful husband and mother to help her.

Interaction with the other siblings was less frequent, but all of them visited at one time or another and exchanged presents at Christmas and birthdays. In addition, Jean, Leslie and Dora all had big family parties. Dora's party was on the occasion of Amanda's christening when all the family (except Patrick and Val) were invited as well as Irene, Heather and Eileen. (The other mothers were excluded on the grounds of not being real friends). At such occasions family played a stronger role in Dora's idea of her social world than neighbourhood. There were no neighbourhood parties of equivalent status, the only large get-togethers being selling parties to which only women were invited, and even then George had to go out for the evening. Unlike Enid, who went out to the club with her 'mate' and went on the annual outing to the seaside, Dora and George never went out with Aulton people, and their only trips to night clubs were with other family members. Enid, to conclude, was integrated into the Aulton neighbourhood as well as into her own family, while Dora maintained her family social links more actively and only a few links with Aulton mothers.

Relations with Wider Society
Before concluding this section on the Fieldings' social lives, we must add a reference to the broader society within which they lived. Dora took pride in the fact that they paid their way in everything and received nothing as charity; she was scathing about the fact that virtually all their neighbours were either on the 'dole' or on social security, saying that the men locally in Aulton were idle and did not try to get work. She assessed the families in the street, and said that when a salesman went round she could tell which ones would have goods from him and which not. She took pride in always paying her rent when it was due, and keeping up with her bills and 'clubmen', even when she moved.

In spite of her separation from the values prevalent among most of the people in her street in Aulton – their attitude to be one of alienation from the world outside whether it be the council, social services, industry or finance firms, all of whom they tried to outmanoeuvre – Dora was extremely loyal to her women friends who held different views. In particular, she did not divulge their secrets, for example, whether or not they were actually married or their financial arrangements, until friendship with us was well established – something which posed a difficult ethical problem. Because long-term anthropological fieldwork is not something which is much spoken about or televised in this country and 'surveys' are what most people understand by social research, Dora forgot how she came to know us at all, and asked us one day to remind her.

Dora and George cared little for politics, but George knew the name of their local councillor. Dora thought of the Royal Family as being so distant and unreal that you could hardly imagine them doing everyday things: she laughed about it. She believed in a benevolent God who would forgive you everything except murder. She did not think it necessary to go to church, except for christenings and funerals, and doubtless would have been happier if she could have married George in a church and not be considered to be living in sin by the clergy. On a more mundane level, she had no time for research into child-rearing, feeling instead that mothers knew best. She sometimes expressed the view, however, that her mother was old-fashioned. She read the local newspaper, watched the television and said she preferred 'real life' films. She was very touchy on the subject of social class, and very quick to get angry if she thought people were trying to make out they were better than she was. She felt that referring to 'tea' as 'supper' was an affectation, and that there were two sorts of people, 'moneyed' and 'ordinary'. She felt that 'snobs', 'big-heads' or 'moneyed people' were always trying to be different – in the way that Jean tried to put on a middle class accent. Nevertheless, she did feel that there were 'brainy' people. She felt that George worked extremely hard for the wages that he got, but although she had to struggle with the housekeeping, she did not think of themselves as being 'poor'. The idea of being 'working class' as opposed to 'middle class' was not one that she operated with, perhaps because her own family had fallen in status and were rising again. On the subject of her brother Patrick's misdemeanours, she sided with law and order and against him and his offences.

Commentary

Stated briefly, the Fieldings' norms and values were very much those of mainstream culture. If they had remained in Aulton, they would have begun to appear more and more deviant: not only would they have avoided the local entertainment centres and adopted, more scrupulously than was usual, a reciprocal agreement with the council and credit agencies (goods and services in return for regular money), but they probably would also have maintained a higher standard of living than most of their neighbours. These are the obvious differences between the Fieldings and most of the other families in Aulton. In Drayford the houseproud mother is not in the minority, and material possessions seem to be more ample than in Aulton. The choice of a small family and a higher standard of material culture is likely to be the norm.

The Fieldings were struggling after the move to Drayford with the problems of diminishing income and increasing expenditure. The next step for them, that of saving for their own home, like Ken and Jean, seemed impossible, because the rent on their council house was over ten pounds a week, and this left them with a very tight budget of £34.50 plus

£4 child benefit for food, clothing, fares and household goods. Nevertheless, various factors had worked in their favour in getting away from Aulton. Despite being married very young, Dora had only three children. She had never used contraceptives of any kind – was unsuitable for the pill because of her high blood pressure – but was prevented from having children by her first husband's infertility. She was not against having a large family, and might well have had one.

Her elder siblings, however, have limited their families, and they might have provided a model for her. The style of life maintained by Ken and his family provided a model which Dora admired and drew on for her own family. In this respect, the younger sibling had the advantage in following where the elder sibling had broken ground: Ken in turn was helped by his marriage to Leslie, who 'always had', by which the Fieldings meant that she had had experience of access to and use of more goods and services.

Jean's family showed some of the tensions which beset a family lying between sub-classes. Many writers have attested to the difficulties of the working-class child who is educated out of his local culture and out of his class. Jean did not leave her local environment or the network of her family, but she was skilled and had a position of responsibility. She showed certain leanings towards middle class values, in particular her stress on the importance of education and 'correct' speech, and the attempt to own her own house. She did not mix quite so closely with her family or the home area, and in this she formed an interesting contrast to Ken, who was unambiguously successful in material terms – owned a new house and modern furniture – and yet lived whole heartedly within the local community and family, having his children attend the local school. Although Jean and Ken were the more successful branches of this family, it is also worth recording how precarious that success was, and the hard toll in terms of family life and leisure which was taken by the struggle to make a better standard of life.

We had a little contact with all the brothers and sisters, husbands, wives and children except for Patrick and his family, either because he was in prison or because they were excluded from big, family celebrations. In a family where so much of life was shared with relatives – work, residential area, leisure activities – it must be seen as a deprivation that he and his family did not take part in the Christmas festivities and the *rites de passage* accompanying births, marriages and (one predicts) deaths, at which the whole family came together and saw itself as the Havelocks again, who ate, drank and enjoyed themselves in the same way, stood by one another and shared a common family culture.

One can view Patrick's life in terms of an interplay of personalities: the stern hard-drinking father and easy-going mother, the tough elder brother who used to get him into trouble, the sisters who also ganged up against him, the younger brother whom he in turn could victimize. The progression of Patrick's behaviour has also to be seen against a backcloth of poverty and low status ('we were a rough family then'), of a family whose standard of living was falling, and living on a disadvantaged estate. The escalation of sentencing is all too familiar, as Patrick followed the delinquent career of the hard-core offender from approved school to borstal and finally to prison. Although he was a hard worker, when he worked, he did not have a job after his release from prison. Drink could tip him into violence but even in prison he was in trouble and, it was said, never received remission for good behaviour.

Dora's position was complicated by the fact that she had already married once into relative affluence, and she returned to her sister and mother's estate only as a result of the breakdown of that marriage. Dora and George lived with Enid when they were first married, something which couples in Kindleton were accustomed to do until they got a house of their own. The family acted to some extent as a force upwards out of difficulties, and Dora and George benefited from their relatives as they moved to better neighbourhoods or more successful jobs. Here, the sibling group rose together.

It is important to note certain crucial factors: education has not played an important role in the family's rise. Jean, Dora and George all wished they had had training of some kind. The school appeared to have had a negative influence, especially in the case of the boys. Poverty interfered with opportunity as well as ambition. Obtaining well-paid jobs with considerable responsibility played an important part in Ken's and Jean's success. George's consistent employment has been important, but the fact that it was not even moderately highly paid was a constant barrier to home-ownership. Unlike the others, George was unskilled. Enid's period of short-time employment was problematic because Dora then became occupied with the children; Dora and George were at an earlier stage of the life cycle than Dora's siblings because of their late marriage, and this may well prove crucial. Among Dora's successful siblings, both husband and wife had long-term, full-time jobs, and their families had been limited to facilitate this. All the successful families worked extremely hard. Evelyn had the disadvantage of a husband in intermittent employment. Patrick, the least successful sibling, had a prison record to hinder his chances of getting a good job.

Dora's mother, Enid, decided to move back to Aulton when she remarried, as her husband had a house there. This meant that the council house tenancy was transferred to George's name; unfortunately, it also meant that Enid's contribution to the household income was lost. At the same time, a new baby meant extra expense, and Dora found it difficult to go out to work. George had timed his holidays in the past so that he could be at home to help his wife after the birth of a baby, but on other occasions when she needed help or was ill, he had to take time off work, and they lost a day's wages. If he overslept, the same thing happened. When he was ill, they received sick pay, but the doctor charged fifty pence for a note for work. When Enid left, there was no other wage to help tide them over such difficult patches, and at the very moment when their total income dropped, their expenditure increased. Even during the last year of fieldwork, their problems were exacerbated by a drop in Enid's wages: the firm where she worked was waiting for orders, and the workforce was put on a three-day week. This kind of change in wages was extremely difficult to budget for. George's steady council job seemed like security itself in contrast to the vicissitudes of industry; and yet he himself talked of extra men being taken on at the beginning of the summer so that regular men could take their holidays, and then sacked at the end when they were no longer needed. George was going to help the financial situation by not having pocket-money.

If the family is to manage on one wage, it must economize. It would be sensible, for instance, if Amanda's pram and cot clothes were to be used for the baby instead of entirely new items being purchased. Last year, far less was spent on alcoholic drink at Christmas (the only time when there is drink in the house). Dora had only one new dress and in any case she bought very few clothes and wore them summer and winter, whatever the weather. The family were talking of having to forgo their summer holiday. The Fieldings have usually had a week's self-catering holiday by the sea: in 1976 they paid £35 for a one-room chalet in Wales which had a bare floor and an outside lavatory. Having no car, they could not go and look for somewhere better.

The upward mobility, or 'coming out of deprivation', which we have asserted was taking place, was not just a matter of moving up the road to better housing. It also involved a moving away from the ideals and values prevalent in Aulton before the actual physical departure, and it involved a break with the strong women's culture of the group to which Dora belonged, whose conversation and gossip asserted common values and ideals.

Apart from regular, well-paid employment for skilled work and the help of an extended family all living in the same area, success has depended on a strong bond of mutual helpfulness between husband and wife: the wife's returning to work after the birth of her children and the sharing of responsibilities in the home are two important examples. They form a strong contrast to the life style of Vince Barker, for example, who enforced a rigorous division of roles in which he earned the money and spent nearly half of it on himself and his entertainment, while his wife was expected to extend the remainder to cover all the household expenses including rent, food, clothing, furniture, fares and tobacco for the whole family of eight people. At the same time, Vince preferred Elsie to stay tied to the home and even to continue to have babies, while she remained totally responsible for cooking, washing, cleaning, child-care and all the other work of keeping the home going. The contrast between these two types of family was obvious, not least in the house itself, where it was plain that the mother on her own was unequal to the double burden of housework and child-care imposed on her. Elsie Barker could not afford the rent of a better council house, nor the furniture which would look well in it. Nor, to obtain one, could she impress a housing inspector with an immaculate household, however much she tried, in the context of her six riotous and constantly attention-demanding children.

Jamie Havelock, Dora's father, provided another contrast. In spite of unemployment, Jamie ruled with a rod of iron – again contrasting to the inconsistent discipline and lack of participation which characterized Vince Barker's role. Enid's behaviour towards her children was perhaps most like Vince's – happy to increase the size of her family unendingly, given the opportunity, and yet anxious to go out and leave them, if there was good company elsewhere. Enid's response to widowhood was to throw herself into the more hedonistic aspects of local culture and to go out on the town, relinquishing to some degree her mothering role for that of the young unattached woman again. There is perhaps an analogy to be made with Ada Paterson here, where loneliness, disorientation and sudden release from the sexual and emotional constraints of marriage pushed the mother into a new, merry widow role quite unlike her previous *persona*. Thus at the very time when the family was suffering from a halving of parental affection, care and work within the home, the remaining parental contribution was weakened, and the children had to some large extent to look after themselves.

Enough has been said to indicate that personal factors and structural factors work together to create disadvantage, and, as with Vince Barker, Ada Paterson and Enid Havelock, in every personal factor a historical dimension with its own structural antecedents can be seen to have played a part.

Among the Havelocks, the individual chance of birth order and the age of each child when the family went to Aulton and when they lost their father seemed to have been significant factors. Ken and Jean were practically grown-up before the family moved to a disadvantaged estate; Jean was already married when her father died. The younger siblings, Evelyn, Patrick, Dora and Geoff, who experienced having to go to different schools in a new, highly deprived area and gradually falling into poverty and household neglect, have had more emotional difficulties. Dora told us that she and Geoff married young to get away from home, while for a time Evelyn became emotionally unstable and Patrick delinquent. In Dora's case, the further factors of low fertility and late remarriage have affected her situation; her present young family and George's relatively low pay have put a ceiling on their ability to improve their situation and increase their independence.

We have characterized the Fieldings as a family coming out of deprivation, a family who were also the offshoot, through their mother, of a family which had had considerable difficulties in the past. If one looked at the maternal grandfather and his forebears, however, one would characterize them as both going into a period of deprivation and later (most of them) coming out of it. They are, then, an example of discontinuities in deprivation.

6 Implications

In this chapter we shall discuss a number of alternative explanations for the experiences of the families we have studied, return to the question posed by our title of whether there is, in fact, a cycle of deprivation, and end by drawing out a few policy implications.

Alternative Explanations

In preceding chapters we have tried to give a dispassionate account of each of the families studied: we have presented the view which, as we saw it, most accords with the total circumstances of the family. The summary comments at the end of each chapter were arrived at after much discussion and debate amongst ourselves, and after much checking and rechecking of our conclusions with our fieldnotes and with the families. Alternative explanations are, of course, always possible and we wish to set out a number of beliefs which may be held about our families, but which we cannot accept for reasons we shall give. Some of the following ideas are not in the strictest sense 'alternative explanations': rather, they present shifts in emphasis or changes in the weighting given to certain factors.

As for the *Barkers,* it might be possible to see their problems being caused mainly or solely by Vince's personality defects or Elsie's inadequate mothering or both. Certainly, Vince's violent behaviour towards his wife and children and the consequent emotional stress, his lack of investment in the role of husband and father while living at Bramwell, and the small amount given by him to Elsie for housekeeping and clothing plus the resultant debt, all need explanation. Vince's personality might appear to be *the* fountainhead of many of his wife's and his children's problems.

Among our families, Patrick Havelock (Dora Fielding's brother) had also followed a similar path from delinquency in youth to prison in adulthood, and both had shown a certain amount of violence even when their home relationships became more stable than formerly. Both were said to have had problems in childhood – Vince was the neglected step-child of a family which had no time for him and Patrick the black sheep who was bullied by his elder brother and punished by his father, even for things which were not his fault. Both had volatile relationships with their mothers and had married, or fathered the children of women who already had one marriage and a child or children behind them. Both had difficulties in work, arising perhaps in part from their prison records, but although both of them would work hard, Patrick was happier looking after his children, and Vince needed a job which entailed a certain toughness and masculine glamour. The monotony of a nine-to-five job would bore him by its regularity; at the time of writing, he was taking days off sufficiently often for it to affect Elsie's budget.

In Vince, we saw a man with considerable skills (verbal, technical and social), who talked of the frustrations and monotony of his day-to-day life. Although in the past he was in intermittent employment, he seemed fairly settled at the time of our study, but he showed such an ambival-ence towards the pit that we could not predict whether he would always remain a miner: sometimes he spoke of it as a 'hell hole', at other times as his 'vocation'. The truth was probably no less paradoxical in that it was the danger and the arduousness of his work which most appealed to him. The impression which we were left with was that he sought a larger stage and a more demanding role in which to show his resourcefulness and skills, and that he was bored and cramped by the role allotted to the ordinary family man, a role which he performed with little attention or interest. Even the number of his children seemed to symbolize to him a masculine image which was part of his need to be better than average, to be more impressive, more daring and more generous. Unfortunately, he did not have the staying power and patience which success in our society demands, and he was left with the frustration of unspent gifts and energies. The educational system had not tapped his skills or given him any qualifications, and his prison record might have barred him from many possible positions of responsiblity. He, in turn, blamed his early life and his parents for the pattern of delinquency which had limited all his opportunities from his early youth.

The economic pressure of having to move about in search of work is a structural factor in family life which involves migration both within a country and across national and cultural boundaries. In this connection, mention has been made of Elsie Barker's family who came from an industrial area of high unemployment in search of work in the mines near Kindleton. Vince Barker's mother (from Wales) and stepfather (from southern England) travelled to the North for the same reason. So Vince and Elsie had in common shallow roots in Kindleton, an area where people's roots go very deep.

Apart from Elsie and Vince Barker's parents, the other geographically mobile people were Ada (who set off to hitch-hike to London, in all probability pregnant with her third child), Irene (who had left her child with her mother), Vince himself and Stan, who came from Wales in search of work. Enid Havelock's father, it will be recalled, had come from Ireland, and Ada Paterson's mother from Wales. It is noteworthy that all the newcomers we have mentioned came from those areas of Scotland, Ireland and Wales where there was heavy unemployment.

Such structural factors, exacerbated for Vince's generation by the disrupting influence of the War (with the fragile, unstable and short-lived relationships to which it gave rise), and the migration in search of work (with the consequent isolation of young parents from the support and culture of their extended families), are as much a part of the web of circumstances which affect growing children as is their parents' behaviour. Any undue concentration on Vince's personality, which excluded the wider factors that place his life in a meaningful social, economic and historical setting, would oversimplify the complexity of his current position. Similarly, any explanation which focused on the structural factors and omitted their very tangible effects on Vince's personality would tell only half the story. As we have stated often, it is only the dynamic interplay of both major sets of factors which, in our opinion, can in any way do justice to the complexity of the lives we are struggling to understand.

Any attempt, moreover, to see the Barkers' family problems as a result of Elsie's poor mothering would not stand up to close examination. Hilary Land's (1977, p. 174) argument fits Elsie's case: 'The impact of a low income, bad housing, and insufficient food, is not borne equally by all members of the family.... In particular, it is noticeable that in many respects the mother of the family puts the needs of her husband and her children before her own.' This is true of Elsie, whether we are discussing clothing or food or time or money devoted to herself. It was she who carried, almost single-handed, the burden of all the domestic work, the physical care and upbringing of the children and the worry of all their debts and budgeting. Certainly, she was at times irritable; she lost her temper with the children and slapped them – probably more in an effort to relieve her frustrations and tensions than to discipline them. But these reactions were not so much the result of a poorly controlled personality or of an inefficient or inadequate mother as the understandable response of a woman pushed close to the limits of her endurance.

We were asked a number of times by people who read earlier versions of this study why Elsie Barker continued to live with a man who used to beat her, and who made a scapegoat of their eldest boy. Why did she not sue for a divorce or simply get up and go? There were at least four reasons which encouraged her to stay. First, it was *she* who had walked out of her first marriage, which she regarded as a personal failure, and she continued to feel guilty about deserting her son. Secondly, she still 'worshipped' Vince in spite of the way he treated her. Thirdly, the removal of Tracy had caused Elsie's mothering skills to be publicly evaluated by officials and neighbours alike, and this had made her permanently vulnerable and terrified lest the children be taken into care if her present marriage were to break up. She twice mentioned to us that she would 'do herself in', if her children were taken away from her. She did, however, threaten rather frequently to walk out, and she *had* walked out on one occasion for a few hours. Finally, her structural role as housewife (as Oakley has analysed convincingly, 1976) had locked her into her present position – physically exhausted, mentally depressed and financially dependent on Vince.

It is possible to see *Ada Paterson* as an incompetent and uncaring mother, who was perhaps also educationally sub-normal and psychiatrically depressed, if not disturbed. Her widowhood had had and continued to have a deep effect upon her, and she still hankered after the days which she now considered halcyon, when she and Alf were living together in Bramwell. Depressed she certainly was, but we do not believe that she was educationally sub-normal. We know that she could both read and write, but no doubt she would have performed poorly on any formal tests of intelligence, literacy or numeracy; she gave us, however, ample evidence over the eighteen-month period of fieldwork that she was by no means stupid, although perhaps educationally backward. To give but one example from many possible, she was very skilful in rolling her eyes and appearing defeated and dejected, while recounting the latest misfortune to befall her. She would not look straight at us until our sympathies were engaged, and then she would bring her tale to a tragic climax, fix us suddenly with her eyes, and ask for a loan of a few pounds (which, incidentally, she always repaid promptly). This shows evidence of some social, not to say manipulative, skills which she used successfully with us and with the Social Services Department. The question remains to be asked: if she were so good at manipulating us and the Social Services Department, why was she not more successful at organizing other aspects of her life? Our tentative answer is that it was her virtually single-minded concentration on finding a man who would look after her and take care of her, rather than on deciding to look after her own child, which brought her into conflict with her relatives and her neighbours. In addition, her long-term health problems, her lack of self-confidence and her dependence on others, her isolation and loneliness (as a result of her widowhood) all appear to us to be better explanations of her present conduct than low intelligence or disturbed personality. Brown and Harris (1978, p. 286) have discussed the ability of an intimate relationship to reduce the risk of disorder among depressed women: 'The availability of a confidant, a person to whom one can reveal one's weaknesses without risk of rebuff and thus further loss of self-esteem, may act as a buttress against the total evaporation of feelings of self-worth following a major loss or disappointment.... The particular importance of the intimate relationship being with a man raises questions about the value of sexuality (or at any rate some sort of physical intimacy perhaps less sexual than nurturant)....' We feel it was this type of nurturant relationship which Ada was seeking in her dealings with Pete and Stan and, to a lesser extent, with Gwen, her neighbour. This type of relationship is accorded such a high priority in Ada's system of values that she is prepared to forgo her child, her financial security and her material possessions in order to obtain it.

Our explanation of the *Martin* family was in terms of Peter's low level skills and poor health contributing to his unemployment; his elaborate fantasies seem to be a compensation for his lack of status as a worker. An alternative explanation might be that Peter suffered from a psychiatric disorder. He certainly experienced hallucinations (for example, when he saw his dead relatives at his house in Bramwell), and he had delusions about his health, his own abilities and the outside world which made it difficult for us to obtain an accurate picture of his life, no matter whether he was telling us about the present or recounting past events. His instability could be coupled with Sally Martin's inability to explain what might be called the generally incompetent management of the household. The house was often dirty, the children unwashed and social relationships with neighbours almost non-existent. Yet this is too simple an explanation, because in the midst of what seemed to us at first glance to be neglect, there was care. For a time the garden was cultivated, there were trinkets elaborately arranged in the front room, Sally seemed to spend a lot of time washing and ironing and Peter was always busy repairing or improving some household object. We have evidence that Peter was interested in gardening while at school and he kept his first job at a local garage for nearly a year. For these reasons we have reason to doubt the extent of his illness and injuries, but it is even more doubtful that he has always been mentally ill; on the other hand, he was physically underdeveloped and often looked haggard and strained. During our period of contact he was never ill in bed when we visited, though there were several occasions when he claimed to have just returned from hospital. Within the Martin family Peter's employment opportunities were severely limited by his low ability and poor physical development, and the prolonged periods of idleness produced the fantasy world which the family inhabited.

Again, in relation to the extended family of the *Fieldings,* one could argue that the younger children (Evelyn, Patrick, Dora and Geoff) experienced more difficulties than their older siblings (Jean and Ken) because of defects in their personalities. As we have already argued, it is only when individual personalities are linked with structural factors and set in their historical and social context, that the complex interaction between all these factors in any one life comes alive to the imagination. We would explain the major differences between the successful older siblings and the less successful younger ones in these terms. Enid Havelock's children came to Aulton when the eldest, Jean, was old enough to leave school and the youngest a toddler. They were already a family of six children and two parents living on seven pounds a week, and after the death of their father (Jamie Havelock) they were living on four pounds, plus the wages of the older children. We were told that with his death, the problems in terms of Patrick's delinquency and the family's poverty became serious; they went downhill. Because they were a large family, they had had to move out of Jamie Havelock's mother's house and go to Aulton; because they were a large family on national assistance, they had financial problems. Before Jamie's death, it seems that his strong, even over-dominant personality had kept things running at home; his mother's help too had been a source of support in difficulty. With Jamie's death, a new freedom swept the family – not least for his widow, Enid – and in the unsettled period which followed, the financial and emotional stability of the family was rocked. During his life, there had been few opportunities for the acquisition or transmission of capital.

It is feasible to see their problems not only in the light of Enid's disoriented widowhood and inability to manage, but also in terms of a reaction to the harshness and strictness of what came before. Jamie's firmness in turn can be related to a necessity imposed by their straitened circumstances. Ultimately, it was his heart condition and inability to do the heavy work to which he had been accustomed, which brought poverty in its tow. Five of the six children were born before the family was fully dependent on assistance.

If we continue the sequence of events into the next generation, the older children, namely Jean and Ken, who were either independent already, or soon to be after their father's death, do not seem to have experienced to the same extent the deprivations suffered by Evelyn, Patrick, Dora, and Geoff. Dora told us that she and Geoff married young to get away from home, while Evelyn became for a while emotionally unstable and Patrick delinquent: those with most difficulties, Evelyn and Patrick, appear to have clung to their mother, while the others left as soon as possible. Evelyn was fifteen when her father died, Patrick fourteen, and they were eleven and ten years old when they moved to Aulton.

In sum, then, any discussion of the personality characteristics of Patrick or Evelyn would be shallow and superficial if it did not also give due weight to the problems of growing up in a large family, in which the father died at an early age because of poor physical health associated with years of hard physical labour; his death also resulted in a period of poverty and emotional instability for his widow and adolescent children.

General Implications

A cycle of deprivation? A change of metaphor
The major implication which stems from our fieldwork is that the cycle of deprivation is too simple an idea to explain the complex lives of these four families. We therefore wish to change the metaphor from one which suggests a straightforward, linear inevitability to one which will do justice to the complexity of the lives which we have described in the preceding chapters. The *web* of deprivation, rather than the *cycle* of deprivation, depicts more accurately the dense network of psychological, social, historical and economic factors which have either created or perpetuated problems for these families. Our repeated emphasis on the complexity and on the interacting and cumulative nature of the deprivations suffered by the families is *the* central, if unoriginal, point of this study. We would claim that no single hypothesis and no group of simple hypotheses could hope to explain the intricate mesh of factors which we have listed when summarizing the crucial features of any one family at the end of each chapter.

Such a conclusion immediately casts doubt on explanations which seek either to lay the total blame for deprivation on the inadequate personalities of the poor or to indict only the economic structure of capitalist society. Unfortunately, the debate is too often polarized into these competing but extreme positions; for example, William Ryan (1971) provided instances of what he called 'blaming the victim', while Paul Halmos (1978, p. 93) quoted the Director of the Central Information and Intelligence Unit, attached to the ten Community Development Projects in Great Britain, as claiming that 'the causes of deprivation have nothing to do with the characteristics of the deprived people who live in the areas. . . . Deprivation is caused, say the projects, by the structure of the capitalist society in which we live. . . .' It is our hope that the evidence we have presented earlier will make it more difficult in future for people to adopt either of these two extreme positions.[1]

Our main finding will not be welcome news to politicians and administrators for whom the notion of a cycle of deprivation has an appealing simplicity. One of the reasons why the cycle of deprivation has attracted so much attention is that, like Oscar Lewis's 'culture of poverty', it is such a captivating phrase. It appears to sum up in four words a number of conventional (but unexamined) wisdoms which have superficial validity for social workers, teachers and other interested professionals. Another reason for the popularity of the phrase is, in our opinion, that it suggests that there is a small, containable group of 'problem families' who are reproducing themselves in the midst of rising prosperity. Our research suggests, on the contrary, that there is no single group of families which can be readily isolated, labelled as 'problems', and given help. We have described the lives of four families who were in deprived but varying circumstances and their problems needed attention and amelioration, no matter what their parents or grandparents were like. Moreover, our families moved in and out of the established and official categories of deprivation at different times in their lives. However unwelcome this finding is, it suggests that the response in terms of policy will have to be just as complex and interactive as the problems are; but the implications for policy we postpone until later in this chapter.

To pursue the change in metaphor still further, the particular combination of adverse circumstances which made up the web of deprivation varied from family to family and varied within any one family at different times in the life cycle. There were also variations among the families in their ability to cut themselves out of whatever web

[1] Jacquie Sarsby feels that socio-economic factors play a larger part than this paragraph would suggest.

in which they had become entangled. Many members of our families, especially Peter Martin, created the impression of being powerless to change their lot, although some, like Elsie Barker, felt more trapped than others. The adults in general, and women such as Ada Paterson in particular, were prepared to put up with or to forgo much in case they lost something which they instinctively felt they needed – a man about the house, a father for their children (Elsie Barker, for example); and a neighbourhood environment which, by its very familiarity, gave them the reassurance they so badly needed. Most of our families suffered from a serious lack of confidence which explained much of their dealings with public officials, their reactions to a new and more respectable neighbourhood, and their fears and suspicions about the outside world generally. Their deference to officials is, in our opinion, best explained as a rational appreciation of other people's assessment of them and their realization that they had low status and were deviating from the middle-class norm. The social world of the Barkers, of Ada Paterson, and of the Martins was severely restricted and limited; this was less true of our more successful family, the Fieldings, for whom the extended family, neighbours and friends were the focal points of their lives.

The complex interplay of psychological, social and economic factors made it extremely difficult to generate any *one* theory about the causes of deprivation and the mechanics of its transmission. Our case studies lend support to the obvious, but not always accepted, assertion of Berthoud (1976, p. 13): 'It is not possible to explain deprivation either *solely* in terms of the personal characteristics of the individual, or *solely* in terms of the circumstances in which the individual finds himself' (1976, p. 13. Emphasis as in original). The complexity of the subject is such that all 'explanations', including our own, are bound to be partial and tentative; so we cannot look to research such as ours to suggest any form of social engineering which will prevent deprivation or its transmission in any certain way.

Moreover, it is worth remarking at this point that the British tend more than their European neighbours to believe that it is the poor themselves who are to blame for their poverty. In an EEC survey, *The Perception of Poverty in Europe* (1977, p. 72), 43 per cent of the British sample (25 per cent was the average for all nine Common Market countries) chose 'laziness and lack of willpower' as *the* cause of poverty, while only 16 per cent (26 per cent in the rest of Europe) blamed 'injustice in our society'.

Rutter and Madge (1976) illustrated the confusion over the term deprivation when they showed that it is used both to indicate a lack of

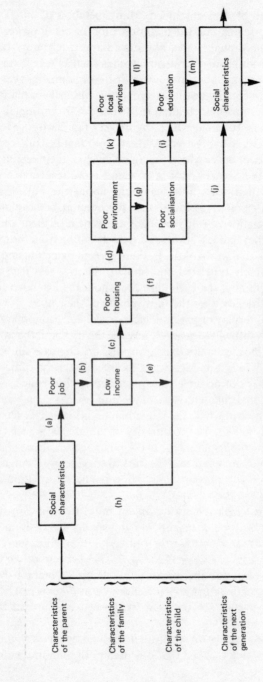

Figure 6.1 (226) *Berthoud's Representation of the Cycle of Deprivation*

Source: Berthoud, R. (1976), *The Disadvantages of Inequality*, London: Macdonald and Jane's, p. 108.

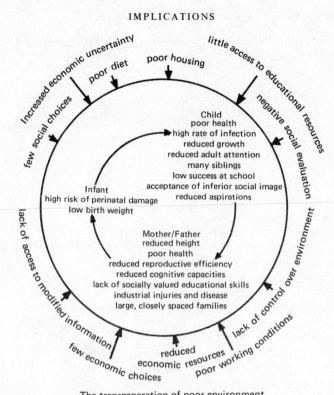

The transgeneration of poor environment

Figure 6.2   Richards' Model

Source: Richards, M. *et al.* (1972) in Richardson, K. and Spears, D. (eds.), *Race, Culture and Intelligence*, Harmondsworth: Penguin, p. 187.

something and an excess of something as well as deviation from an accepted norm. Our families lacked money, had an excess of environmental squalor and at times deviated from accepted norms of behaviour. To ask if this means our families were deprived is to assume that an essential or generally accepted definition of deprivation exists: there is no such definition.

The search for an all-embracing theory of deprivation is not new; we began this book by referring to Hurry who produced a series of models in 1921, using the phrase 'vicious circle' which goes back to De Gérando in 1839. More recently, Berthoud (1976) has produced a representation of the cycle of deprivation, Richards et al. (1972) a transgenerational model of poor environment, and Williams (1970) a model of the poverty cycle. We reproduce all three models in Figures 6.1, 6.2 and 6.3.

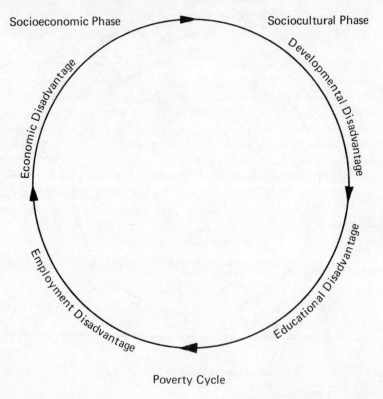

Figure 6.3   (227) Williams' Model

Source: Williams, F. (ed.) (1970), Language and Poverty, Markham.

Considerable time was spent in the middle of the project trying to distil the elements of each of our families into a general model, and the conclusion was eventually reached that there was no one path to deprivation. Although, for example, three of the families had children in residential care and had other common features, we were still unable to encapsulate each of these factors into one system of explanation. One way to resolve this difficulty is to generate a theoretical model of high generalizability but little predictability, where the antecedents of disadvantage are seen in global categories such as educational handicap, child-rearing patterns or low income. Each of these factors is part of the background to our families, but to include them as central elements in an explanatory framework is to miss the processes through which particular disadvantages are produced and sustained.

The models which have been developed tend to be descriptive of disadvantage; they outline what is considered to be the necessary features of the world of the deprived. Berthoud, for example, produced an illustrative framework (see Figure 6.1) of the cycle of deprivation, where he separated out the various links in the arguments which have been put forward by other researchers. He depicted poor jobs as leading to low income; a link which is in part tautological because one of the characteristics of 'a poor job' is that it brings in a low income; this in turn leads to poor housing, a poor environment and is transmitted through inadequate socialization and poor education to the next generation. The Inner Lambeth Area Study, however, would not support Berthoud's assumption that low income usually leads to poor housing, because Shankland et al. (1977, p. 64) found that 'income poverty and housing deprivation are not strongly associated with each other'.

Some models are propelled by simple economic determinism (that of Williams, for example), or biological determinism (Richards' model), where disadvantage is 'perpetuated through the permanent damaging of the mother's ability to produce healthy babies and her family's lack of resources necessary for normal physical – let alone social – development' (1972, p. 186). Stott (1973) presented a model which has pre-natal interpersonal tension as the key variable which leads to high child morbidity of all kinds and the continuance of disadvantage. A major difficulty with each of these models is that entry into or exit from the cycle is not explained; it would seem that once caught in the wheel, outcomes are certain. Social research, however, is not about causes and inevitability but about influences and tendencies.

Another attempt which tried to explain the process of transmission is the work of Jencks and his colleagues (1973). Using the technique of path analysis, they apportioned the contribution of factors such as father's occupation, child's educational achievement and occupational status in the variation of adult incomes. The striking finding of their study is how little any single factor contributes and how small a share of the variance in adult income is explained by all the antecedent factors chosen. Jencks's statistical approach, where the low correlations explain so little of the variation, is only another way of illustrating the complexity of a process which may sound too obvious when described by the labels 'cycle of deprivation' or 'transmitted deprivation'. At the conclusion of this study, our answer to the question 'Is there a cycle of deprivation?' must be that even to ask the question is to over-simplify issues of great complexity. There may be factors which increase the probability of a particular family being labelled as a problem, but the causal processes are many, complex and interrelated, the exceptions numerous, and the critical precipitating events different in each case.

Transmission

As for transmission, we have given an example of a family (the Barkers), in which the problems of one generation have already begun to reappear in the next. In Tracy and Steve Barker, we have a striking example of the problems of parents recurring among their children. Part of Vince's youth was spent in approved school, borstal and finally prison; Tracy has already gone from a children's home to a community (ex-approved) school. At a time when she was moving into adolescence and when she desperately needed affection and attention, she seemed to be going from one institution to another. Vince's own feeling was that if she went into local authority care, she would only get worse – as, of course, happened in his own case – and certainly there were already signs in Tracy of the influence of bad company in the bouts of shoplifting in which she became involved with older girls from the community home. On the other hand, her previous behaviour at home was clearly disruptive and her parents were not able to control her. Moreover, Steve Barker, although constantly picked on by Vince, looked up to his father and imitated his behaviour in a variety of ways. He insisted on a number of occasions that he was 'just like' his father. This raises the possibility of a transmission of values and attitudes through imitation of an admired role model (Bandura, 1970), but the boy was still too young for any firm conclusions to be drawn.

Elliot Liebow's (1967) study of adult Negro males in a blighted section of Washington's inner city during the early 1960s cautioned us against placing too much importance on children fashioning themselves in their parents' image: 'No doubt, each generation does provide role models for each succeeding one. Of much greater importance for the possibilities of change, however, is the fact that many similarities between the lower-class Negro father and son (or mother and daughter) do not result from "cultural transmission" but from the fact that the son goes out and independently experiences the same failures, in the same areas, and for much the same reasons as his father.' (p. 223).

We have also discussed the life of Ada Paterson whose account of her own parents suggested that they were not well off but were without the problems which have beset her life. Her siblings too appeared to be 'respectable' in the community, and she alone had become dependent on social security and the help of social services for a number of years, and passed through a series of relationships of varying stability. Her children in turn, delegated to the care of more capable hands, appeared to have lived in stable homes and to have had good jobs. It was too early for us to know how her son Michael would fare, although he was very lively and resourceful when we met him. The death of his father has led to the loss of his mother as well.

In Dora Fielding we see a person whose strength of character, assisted by her older siblings, has helped her to come out of the deprivations of childhood, but not without the emotional stress of a broken marriage and an attempted suicide. She in turn has been a support to her younger brother, who also used marriage to escape from their former home life. In comparing the adult careers of the four siblings who were still dependants when their father died, none of them has gone unscathed, although only Patrick has adopted the less respectable life style of unemployment, terms of imprisonment and living with a married woman.

We have also encountered transmission of a different kind: the continuance of a deviant pattern of relationships, broken marriages and illegitimacies. In particular, the illegitimate daughter who in turn has an illegitimate daughter was a pattern which we came across in Elsie Barker's elder sister, who gave birth to three illegitimate children, one (but only one) of whom repeated the pattern. Conforming to the norms of the community, which is the mark of the respectable family, involves the absence of any deviant patterns of behaviour such as adultery, promiscuity, criminality in theft or violence, or child neglect and idleness, and it is probable that any deviance from the norms of respectability restricts one's access to friendship with (and marriage to) those who fulfil all the norms. The transmission of such a lack of status is something which we noticed when Sally Martin, new to Bramwell, was associated with her 'dirty' family of origin. Dora, similarly, feared a lack of respectability if she should meet people who knew her before when she was married to her first husband. The combined stigmata of a prison record, broken marriages, intermittent employment, a child in care, marital violence, debt and long-term involvement with social services combine to make the position of the Barker family particularly difficult. The possibility of their fulfilling the norms of respectability was slight indeed, and for that reason the morale of both parents was often low. In Aulton, a certain toleration of deviance, particularly in parenting and marital relationships, made it easier for those who did not conform to the rules of 'respectable' society.

We are still left with the task of explaining why certain families, from all those in all social classes who lead complicated lives, come to the notice of the authorities and are labelled as public problems. In an attempt to answer this question, we would point to four main features and we shall discuss each of them in turn:

1. The families were overloaded with problems whose very complexity seemed to defeat them.
2. They had no resources, either material, emotional or social.
3. They had become stigmatized.
4. Their family patterns of early marriage, large families and child-rearing seemed to militate against them.

1. *The complexity of deprivation*   The Barkers, Ada Paterson and the Martins had more than their fair share of problems which interconnected and intertwined with one another. It was not so much that one of their problems created another in a simple, linear chain, as that they had so many problems to tackle simultaneously. The overcrowding, unemployment, low wages, poor nutrition, enuresis, depressions and family violence should not be looked upon as discrete areas of deprivation, but as interconnecting and cumulative forms of inequality. It is this interlocking network of inequalities – this web of deprivations – which was the families' greatest obstacle to coping in society. If they had had only one (or perhaps two) major disadvantages with which to cope they might have been able to overcome them, but we see little prospect of the Barkers, or of the Martins, or of Ada Paterson tackling the mass of problems which surround them or of significantly improving their status.

Rutter (1978, p. 50) identified a number of family variables (such as marital discord) all of which were significantly associated with child psychiatric disorder and concluded that

> ... even with chronic family stresses the children were not particularly at psychiatric risk if it was really a single stress. However, when any two stresses occurred together the risk went up no less than fourfold. With three and four concurrent stresses the risk went up several times further. It is clear that the combination of chronic stresses provided very much more than an additive effect. There was a striking *interaction* between stress factors which markedly inflated the risk to the child. (Emphasis as in original).

At times certain members of these families looked physically weighed down by their problems. Reflecting on the family lives of the Barkers, of Ada Paterson and the Martins, we came to realize that the cumulative effects of years of poverty and unstable circumstances have become ingrained in their personalities, in their physical and mental health, and in their modes of functioning. Ada Paterson could easily have been mistaken for an old-age pensioner, although she was only in her late forties. Elsie Barker had similarly aged prematurely and looked almost middle aged and exhausted from child-bearing. The lives they have led have taken their toll of them; there are human costs involved in poverty. Valentine (1968, p. 145), at the end of a sustained critique of Oscar Lewis's concept of 'the culture of poverty', still concluded that 'There can be no doubt that living in poverty has its own destructive effect on human capacities and that these impairments become part of the whole process perpetuating deprivation.' Herzog (1971) also argued that early and lasting experiences of poverty may permanently change (if not damage) the persons undergoing them. To take Peter Martin, repeated experiences of unemployment over long periods must suggest to him the likelihood of continued failure and this affects his present behaviour; witness the constant redecorating and the endless round of minor household jobs which he created for himself in his attempts to cope with idleness. Vince Barker similarly had suffered from a harsh childhood, having been rejected by his stepfather, and making his own way in life from a very early age.

Our case studies, moreover, have shown how the more social and economic problems (low wages, inadequate housing, poor employment prospects) are inextricably bound up with family relationships – between man and wife, between parent and child, between parent and step-child, between the children themselves and between the nuclear family and the extended family. One cannot dissociate the divorces, suicides or attempted suicides, the abortions, children in care, and accidents, the delinquencies, debts and family rows from their lack of money and lack of space, their low status and dirty jobs, their poor education, and poorer prospects, and their lack of power and control over their lives. Families from higher income groups experience many of the same or similar problems, although their genesis may be different, but because of their money and access to professional advice and services, they do not become public problems because they do not make demands on social agencies. *Their* problems may be just as serious, but they do not exercise the public conscience and no one talks of a cycle of deprivation in relation to *them*.

For all practical purposes, then, there is an almost indistinguishable complex of nature and nurture which influences the developing personality of a child; it is virtually impossible to separate out the individual, personal factors from the external, social factors which together affect how that child behaves and lives out his or her life. Nor can we make any easy division between structural factors on one side and individual factors on the other because part of the social structure is to be found inside people's heads. For instance, the way Peter Martin viewed the local job market (and he did so pessimistically, although our assessment was very different) tended to influence his behaviour; 'these impressions', wrote Marsden and Duff (1975, p. 232), 'are in themselves important social facts which must be taken into account'.

2. *Lack of resources* Whether one examined their material, social or emotional resources, our three families had no margins left with which to play. Ada Paterson, for example, had used up whatever fund of good will and friendship existed between her and either her family or her neighbours. She even destroyed some of the physical resources which had been given to her by social workers, by throwing out the furniture when she wanted to move from Cardale or by giving away her pension to encourage Pete to stay with her. Similarly, the Barkers with their large family used up with such speed the emotional resources of all who came into contact with them that they became a burden and a liability. In times of high inflation, such families fall quickly into debt, begin to impose on local shopkeepers and acquire reputations as bad risks. In sum, they lacked money, possessions to sell or pawn in times of difficulty, and emotional support.

Their general lack of resources was particularly apparent in relation to employment, low wages and housing, and we shall deal with each of these in turn. All our families were disadvantaged in what Marsden and Duff (1975) called the social contract which is struck between society and the manual worker. George Fielding was regularly employed, but his work was physically demanding, and a steady income depended upon his maintaining his strength. Vince Barker also relied on his strength to maintain his high earnings. Neither of them had the advantage of an incremental salary scale where rewards increase with experience; in their position, their earning power was more likely to decrease over time, as they grew older and their strength began to fail them. All the jobs available to Ada Paterson and Peter Martin were likely to demand too stringent a form of regulated and obedient activity. Neither seemed able to conform to the demands of the production line in terms of punctuality and consistent attendance at work. Both of them seemed to lack the social skills needed to get on with workmates and so keep monotony at bay.

In our wider circle of contacts, there were many others in the same boat: Ada's husband Alf and her two companions, Pete and Stan, were all part of the pool of unskilled labour, as was Peter Martin's twin brother, Paul, and many others who lived in Aulton. Probably the most successful family in conventional terms, namely Ken Havelock's, was similarly dependent on Ken's strength and physical fitness to maintain its standard of living. His brother, Patrick, was unemployed and seemed content to remain so. This may well be a rational decision in a world where work offers only monotony and drudgery in return for low wages.

Social isolation – something which Brown, Bhrolchain and Harris (1975), Brown and Harris (1978), and Gavron (1966) have commented upon among housebound mothers with children at home – was also a problem among the mothers whom we visited. Elsie Barker, for instance, wished she could get a job so that she could be out of the house and with workmates for part of the day. Dora Fielding also enjoyed having 'mates' when she worked, and the separate social life which work allowed: with her, however, the problem of childminding meant that she had to choose between being with her children and being with her husband. For Elsie Barker it meant perhaps neglecting her children and so incurring the disapproval of her social worker. Ada's isolation has been sufficiently emphasized – though it cannot be blamed on maternal responsibility – but the demands of factory work, the only work of which she had experience, prevented her from relieving her depression through going out to work.

In many of the families we contacted the inadequacy of the wage of the main income provider placed strong pressure on the other partner to obtain a job. Consequently, the provision of part-time work became an important supplement to the family income, and at various times, Dora Fielding, Elsie Barker and Sally Martin went out to work. Sally worked for a nationalized industry for a wage of 55p per hour, at a time when the average hourly rate for women manual workers was 80p. It is important to note that good, regular and committed workers such as Dora Fielding's husband *earn* their poverty and that he and Sally Martin were receiving their wages from nationalized industries or local government bodies. Christopher Jencks et al. (1973, p. 265), having shown that in America the richest 5 per cent of all families have incomes twenty-five times as large as the poorest 5 per cent, argued as follows:

> A successful campaign for reducing economic inequality probably requires two things. First, those with low incomes must cease to accept their condition as inevitable and just. Instead of assuming, like unsuccessful gamblers, that their numbers will eventually come up or that their children's numbers will,

they must demand changes in the rules of the game. Second, some of those with high incomes, and especially the children of those with high incomes, must begin to feel ashamed of economic inequality.

The quotation from Jencks also serves to make the basic point that the problems of poverty and low wages cannot be separated from broader questions about the distribution of wealth and income.

The problems of low pay have also been discussed in connection with the Fieldings and the great difficulty which they would have in accumulating sufficient capital for a deposit on a house. Dora's brother, Ken, who owned his own house, had a family of two children and a more highly paid job than George Fielding, and his wife also worked. Dora's sister, Jean, who accumulated enough for a deposit but was refused a mortgage, also limited her family to two, and she and her husband both worked. The small family thus enables an accumulation of capital which would not be so feasible with only the wages of one manual worker. Intermittent and under-employment has the effect of reducing overall earnings and of making it very difficult for the person on low pay to acquire any assets such as furniture and carpets or a car which would have to be paid for out of regular money.

Field (1975) warned that with inflation at the rate prevalent in the mid 1970s, the purchasing power of the poor was being eroded despite the regular increase in benefits. Families wholly dependent on benefits, such as the Martins, were becoming worse off. Even more disturbing, it was difficult to see what the family could have done to improve its position. Even if Peter had obtained a job, his wages would not have generated an income much above that which the family had at that time. The family was trapped at the bottom of the income distribution and they could do little about it. One of the continual problems of the low income family is to provide adequate food. Wilkinson (1976) has suggested that the low income diet is high in the wrong sort of calories and this leads to obesity. And people who are overweight die younger and are prone to heart disease, high blood pressure, strokes and diabetes. He further linked the lack of fibre, vitamins and trace elements and the excess of refined carbohydrates in lower class diets to diseases and to the difference in the death-rates between social classes. He also pointed out that the gap between the death-rates of the rich and poor widened between 1951 and 1961 when rationing was dismantled, and the diet of those on higher incomes began to differ greatly from that of the poor.

With regard to housing, when one recollects the overcrowded conditions in which the Barkers were living in Bramwell, and their even poorer accommodation earlier when in Castle Steet, it is hard to believe that the axiom of Tawney has been acted upon to their benefit: 'The duty of Governments is to create the environment which encourages the best, not the worst, in mankind.' On the brighter side, the local housing department has since informed us that there are no longer any families living in statutorily overcrowded conditions in Kindleton.

We noted that Dora Fielding's house was vandalized after she moved to Drayford and before the arrival of the new tenant. We are aware of the attempts of the local council to synchronize letting, and we sympathize with the management problem involved in long chains of tenants all moving at the same time. Our case study suggests, however, that the movement of tenants is a critical time if one is interested in preventing vandalism and loss to the housing stock. Other areas (e.g. see Benington, 1974, p. 267) report the need to board up empty houses on run-down estates.

Joint tenancies, in the names of both husband and wife, are already available to those who apply for them. Elsie Barker was unaware of this provision and her anxieties about being turned out of her husband's house might have been lessened if she had known. The existence of a joint tenancy will, however, not solve any problems if the husband and wife decide to split up.

The predicament of council housing departments faced with families such as the Martins is only too obvious: they are accused of forming ghettos if they allocate families with similar standards to neighbouring houses, but if they place them next to families who try to make the best of their homes and who are quiet and tidy, the 'good' families may be disheartened or annoyed, and want to move. The housing manager told us that there had been a policy of placing 'problem families' in between good tenants, in the hope that the good ones would influence the bad and help to lift their standards, but this had not achieved the desired effect. Nevertheless, we would agree with the Cullingworth Report (1969, p. 22) that even with the very small group of 'problem families', 'the provision of good housing is a base on which the other social services can build'. (Ministry of Housing and Local Government.)

3. *Stigma*   We came across a number of specific and general examples of stigma among the families we studied. In the former category was the effect the removal of Tracy had on the Barkers, not least in terms of Elsie's anxieties about any appearance of injury to or neglect of her children. Feelings of family stigma and failure were still very strong, years after the incident. We also feel that the terms 'transmitted

deprivation', and 'deprived' or 'problem families' may have a stigmatiz-
ing effect. The first term is not only ugly and unwieldy, but it also implies
some socially transmitted disease. Although the official title of our
research was the 'Transmitted Deprivation Project', we felt unable to
mention it to the families: they would all have been deeply insulted.
Instead, we talked to them of studying families who either had
experienced or were currently experiencing problems. Our families, and
particularly Dora Fielding's, thought that the term 'deprived' was
pejorative and derogatory. We suggest, therefore, that the terms
'transmitted deprivation' and 'problem family' be abandoned, just as
psychologists are increasingly giving up the single word 'intelligence'.
The phrase 'families with problems' is not much of an improvement, but
at least it encourages the user to specify the type and number of
problems, to say who defines the behaviour in question as a problem,
and to find out whether *the family* sees the same behaviour as a problem.
In the voluminous literature on the subject of the 'multi-problem family'
there is no one definition which is acceptable to us or to others; and yet
the term is bandied about as if we all understood or were agreed upon its
meaning. This is no semantic quibble; the use of such portmanteau
phrases as 'problem family' acted as a trigger with some of the officials
we interviewed and produced some rather stereotyped responses. A
decision to discourage the use of such terms would help to prevent such
oversimplified categorization.

Yet there was another, even more degrading term used by the people
in the areas we worked to single out a deviant or unusual family: it was
'the dirty family'. This phrase was hung round the necks of the Martins
like an albatross, and it followed them from one district of Kindleton to
another, isolating them from their neighbours. In our opinion, in
matters of cleanliness and hygiene, there was little difference between the
Martins and either the Barkers or Ada Paterson. Yet Vince Barker
pointedly commented that his family was not in any way like 'that dirty
family', namely, the Martins, who had recently become their neighbours
in Bramwell. In other words, the phrase 'dirty family' was not used
solely to describe the physical state of a neighbour's home; it was also a
term of moral disapproval and of social rejection.

An emphasis on smells and dirt as *the* distinguishing mark of the
'problem family' has a long history – see, for example, the classic
description of the archetypal 'problem family' in Wofinden (1944). We
ourselves in our early fieldwork did not remain unaffected by this
tradition. Such is the power of the image of the 'problem family'
conjured up by the literature that it coloured our earliest reports of visits

to families in Kindleton. Even being on one's guard against the wilder components of the stereotype did not prevent us from exaggerating the 'squalor' of the homes we visited. Only the evidence collected on repeated visits enabled us to dispense with our preconceptions; such is the compelling force of the traditional picture.

4. *Early marriage, large families and child-rearing*   We may ask at this point why certain people do not see children and marriage as something to budget and prepare for. Contact with our families gave us information on fifteen stepchildren and eighteen illegitimate children, and the numbers themselves provide some indication of the fragility of relationships. Why are there so many unwanted or haphazard pregnancies? The answer must be seen in the context of the incentives to early marriage, particularly for a woman, in terms of independence and status. What are her career alternatives? Levine (1977) has suggested that the process of industrialization has taken away the social controls on or disincentives to early marriage: such factors for example, as reaching peak-earning power early in life have encouraged early marriage. Also, as Ineichen (1977) and Land (1977) have pointed out, the birth of a child may even lead one via the uncomfortable intermediate phase of overcrowding to a council house of one's own and to adult independence.

The Barkers' problems are not only those of a large, closely-spaced family; their multi-faceted difficulties are also the legacy of former troubles and former marriages. Elsie, like Dora Fielding and Sally Martin, was first married before she was twenty. Like Sally Martin and Ada Paterson, she also had her first child before she was twenty. Ineichen (1975) found in his Bristol sample that it was teenage brides who were most likely to have married on a low income, without further education, in overcrowded conditions and with a child soon to arrive. Sarsby (1972) found that this pattern of early marriage prompted by conception of a child was a more typical expectation among the secondary modern schoolgirls (but not the private school or grammar school girls) whom she surveyed. Higher rates of divorce are also a feature of teenage brides (Rutter and Madge, 1976, p. 224). It is certain in Dora's case and probable in Elsie's that the low fecundity of their first marriages contributed to the breakdown of their marriages. Both are proud of the swift sequence of conceptions in their second marriages. Elsie's problems, however, relate both to her own previous marriage, with the guilt which she felt at deserting her son, and also to Vince's first marriage and the children which resulted from it. It is Vince's first marriage which is blamed for his unreasonable jealousy towards her, and it is the breakdown of that first marriage which eventually left Vince and Elsie with two extra children to cope with. Suddenly two children became five, with the birth of their own third child occurring a month after the arrival of Tracy and Nick.

Society in its present form is not structured to accommodate the large family, unless that family is very rich. A three-generation extended family can cope better with the large amount of child-minding involved, but the two-parent family, especially one in which the father keeps a rigidly masculine role, places a heavy burden on the mother. The problem is, of course, increased when the birth interval between the children is as short as is the case with the Barker children.

The other major problem for such a family is overcrowding, because large houses are, in general, expensive and the amount of local authority housing suitable for them is limited. Wages must also be stretched further than for the average-sized family as there are more people to feed and clothe; disadvantage in relation to smaller families on a similar wage is almost bound to occur.

Among the rich, those families who have numerous children do so presumably because they can well afford the pleasure of a large family or because they are not interested in such global problems as the population explosion. Among the unskilled and poorly paid, the pleasures of children are not tainted by monetary considerations: there is no feeling that one can better one's standard of living by planning one's family or saving; there is no career structure or incremental ladder which can make people in intermittent or unskilled employment feel that it will benefit them either to wait before they start a family, or to stop when they have had one or two children. In a world context, it is of course the carefully planning, non-professional middle class with their small families, who are deviant in not wanting as large a family as possible. In Britain where the middle class must be geographically mobile and in general made up of nuclear families, children cannot be counted on to be as great a support or blessing in old age as the paid up insurance policy.

In large families where the birth interval is shorter than two years, the advent of dried milk and a cultural repugnance towards suckling must attract some of the blame for the inordinate burden which such a family places on the mother. Suckling is believed to help prevent conception during the first year after the birth of a child. To have three children under five seems to be the most difficult aspect of having a family so close in ages. Child-minding is of course taken over by the schools as soon as a child reaches five, and the mother's task is greatly relieved. Elsie Barker was able to give more attention to her youngest child when all the others were away at school for at least part of the day.

We do not have comparable information on the child-rearing practices of all the families, as the children whom we got to know ranged in age from birth to fourteen; comparisons between the families can therefore only indicate certain general points.

We noted in Aulton on several occasions that the segregation of sex roles, or the imposition of gender, started straightaway. Dora Fielding, for instance, had selected two parcels of clothes from a shop before Amanda's birth, and George was to collect one of these according to the sex of the child. Blue was avoided for a girl; boys were dressed in little suits, girls in little dresses in pastel shades.

In the Barker family, a certain segregation of children's roles existed in such things as the elder girl, Julie, being encouraged to look after the baby. When she voluntarily started helping in the kitchen, Vince warned Elsie that she would soon be labelled a little 'Cinderella' by social services, just as Tracy had been described before she went into care. The Barker children were not dressed so scrupulously according to gender, although one felt that this was because things were worn by whichever child they approximately fitted and then handed down.

Both the Barker and the Martin family children appeared to have less gender role differentiation, but this impression is based largely on the fact that the girls tended to lack the typical 'feminine' characteristics of attention to cleanliness, quietness and lack of dominance or attention-seeking (Sharpe, 1976). All the children in these two families were wilder, grubbier and more demanding than Ada's boy or Dora's children. The Barkers also treated their youngest child permissively and with a lot of overt affection, and this was also true of the next oldest. Our overall impression was that toddlers were given more licence and affection.

We have discussed at length the Barkers' child-rearing practices, emphasizing the alternating shouting and coaxing, the bouts of temper and displays of affection, and we feel that the children have all adopted a similar pattern of achieving what they want. The usual sequence seems to be to demand something loudly straight away, and if it is refused, put off or modified, to sulk immediately and take some punitive awkward action (usually against their mother) or to cry; and then, when the awkwardness leads to shouting and loss of temper on the part of the parent, to weep loudly (sometimes to ask not to be hit) until the parent gives in. This sequence happens very frequently with one or other of the children. Vince has been seen to encourage them to be aggressive towards him and towards one another; alternating tears and aggression is a regular pattern among the children.

Affection for children tends to be described by our families in terms of buying them things. Dora Fielding's constant buying of toys and clothes, expensive Christmas presents, ice creams and sweets for the children, has already been commented upon, but she also discussed other people's fondness for her children in terms of things which they brought for them. Ada Paterson's boyfriend, Stan, remarked that he could not understand why people said that Michael was being ill-treated – was he not given pocket-money every day? The Barker children too expected their 'wages' when they came home from school, something for each of them to spend at the local shop. Instances in each family of these daily treats are too numerous to mention, but the underlying idea that it is a telling expression of love to a child was widespread.

In concluding this section on the general implications of our fieldwork, we want to emphasize the many positive and appealing qualities which we found among the parents of our families and the remarkable resilience of the children. It was amazing that, in spite of everything which had happened and continued to happen to them, they were mostly so loving, so generous and so friendly. On no occasion were we made to feel unwelcome in any of the homes we visited, and we have recorded the magnanimity of the Barkers in accepting the two children, Tracy and Nick, into their already overcrowded, rented room. It was no wonder that they fell short of the even-tempered, well-organized ideal. The pressures on them all were far greater than on those who had always lived in financial security and had stable, affectionate homes. We, however, noticed a division between certain parents, who had a very positive desire to make a better life for their children than they had themselves experienced, and those who were not oriented in this way. Such a desire was particularly true of George and Dora Fielding, but not so true of all her siblings as parents, nor was it especially true of Vince or Elsie Barker, and not at all was it true of Ada Paterson. The Fieldings' material indulgence of their children was very similar to the behaviour of the parents studied by the Newsons (1965, p. 249) in Nottingham. We also noted the resilience of the children in these families in the face of so many hardships. Michael, the son of Ada Paterson, remains a friendly, bustling, outgoing seven-year-old, in spite of the death of his father and subsequent rejection by his mother. The Barker children, for all their trying home circumstances, were not only coping at school but were actually doing rather well – a triumph of the human spirit over adversity. Our observation is not so much original as part of a growing body of evidence (for example, Clarke and Clarke, 1976) which has stressed the resilience of children in general, and of deprived children in particular.

Policy Implications

We do not wish to finish this study without attempting to suggest what the implications of our work are for social policy. We embark, however, on this section with trepidation and in the knowledge that considerable work has already been done in all the areas discussed; we are therefore aware that our suggestions are neither original nor immediately translatable into specific policy recommendations. Our attempts to understand the problems of our families as a whole have also led us into many areas where we claim to expertise and where we have no specialized knowledge. Townsend's point remains valid in this connection: 'Any statement of policy to ameliorate or reduce deprivation contains an implicit explanation of its cause. Any explanation of deprivation contains implicit prescription for policy.' (1974, p. 16). What follows, then, are suggestions about the general lines social policy should take rather than specific recommendations about how particular services might be changed to give more effective help to 'problem families'; and, if the problems are so numerous, interrelated and complex, then obviously no one single policy intervention will be sufficient on its own. Furthermore, our deliberate choice of families with different types of difficulty meant that our case studies did not converge on *one* set of problems, but instead they contained small elements of all sorts of problems.

1. *Health*

We wish to group together under the broad heading of health care a number of different observations we made about the lives of our families: namely the heavy or dangerous work undertaken by fathers and the incidence of early deaths and diseases, especially heart conditions, among them, the poor physical and mental health of mothers, the premature ageing of adults generally, the accidents and injuries to children and, indeed, to all other members of the families and the low standards of nutrition. If the recommendations of the Court Report (1976) were to be implemented (in particular, the provision of an integrated child and family-centred health service and a strong emphasis on *preventive* medicine), then the chances would be greater that our families and others like them would have more energy to tackle the other problems which beset them.

There was much poverty as a consequence of poor health among the families of men whose livelihood depended on heavy work – for example, the case of the Havelocks. We found it again in George Fielding's family, where his father had had to give up work as a miner because of the state of his lungs. Elsie Barker's father was also a miner with bronchitis and in addition, 10 per cent dust and heart trouble. Ada Paterson's father, who was a miner, also suffered progressively from bronchitis.

Although, according to Marsden's survey (1973), a widow with children is now less frequently in financial difficulties than other mothers with children, we could not fail to notice the large number of fathers in our families, who had died relatively young. Alf Paterson had his fatal heart attack while in his early forties, Elsie Barker's father had died in his late fifties, and Dora Fielding's father had died in his late forties of a heart condition.

In all of these, the importance of heart disease cannot fail to be noted. All the above men had been involved in heavy work either immediately before death or before they were incapacitated by illness. Alf had worked as a labourer carrying partially finished products from one part of the factory process to another. Elsie Barker's father was a miner; Jamie Havelock was a coal-man. Alf, whose work record was far less imposing than the other men's, had always been delicate. Of those fathers who had worked in the pit (Ada's father, Alf's father, George Fielding's father, Vince's stepfather and Elsie Barker's father), only George's father survived, and the majority were known to have suffered from bronchitis. The question of industrial disease and death is important, even though injuries in the mines have been much reduced, and miners are regularly screened for dust.

Another aspect of these families' lives was the frequent mention of serious and sometimes fatal accidents and injuries. Vince Barker's injuries include the most serious one which occurred when both his legs were broken in a pit-accident; in addition to the one who died, one of his children has scars from scalding on the chest. Ada Paterson's father died after falling from an upstairs landing, and four of her mother's brothers and sisters were killed in a fire one Christmas; Ada herself was knocked down by a bus at the age of three; her boyfriend, Pete, had suffered a bad accident and had a plastic bone in his leg. We cannot be sure about Peter Martin's history of accidents, but they were apparently numerous. Enid Havelock was knocked down while cycling at the age of seventeen, and has had headaches and impaired hearing since that time; Enid was also hurt by a car when she was a child, and she blamed herself for her little sister's subsequent death as a result of that accident.

This catalogue of accidental injuries is appalling enough, and it is particularly serious that so many of them occurred in childhood. In addition there were numerous examples of intentional violence, in particular Vince's attacks on Elsie and a fight in Kindleton one night, Enid's boyfriend's attack on her and the injury to Evelyn (and her brother Ken's reprisals), Ada's alleged rape incident, Patrick's attack on people in a pub, and many other accounts of violence from husbands to wives.

The number of people who were knocked down in the street is perhaps partly a reflection of urban life, but also, for working-class children, of the fact that life is conducted much more in the street, with games in the road and on the pavements and running in and out of one another's yards than it is among middle-class children, who tend to be 'kept in' or to play in each other's gardens. The culture of the street with all its dangers is much more available to the working-class child, who is not transported to and from school, or park, or friends, by car. We felt that the children of large families, close in age, were particularly at risk, because there was a great temptation for a mother on her own to send her children out alone while she minded the youngest ones at home, rather than always dress the little ones and take a pram or push-chair to and from school several times a day.

The vulnerability of our families is well caught by Carmichael's (1974 p. 27) analogy of society

> being like a plate and people like ourselves who have had good education and opportunities, who have had reasonably good health, who have stable jobs, who have some traditions of responsibility, who share most of the norms of society and have ties with society through things like paying mortgages, we are tucked quite comfortably in the middle of the plate, and, when things happen in the external world like massive unemployment or redevelopment of a city, the plate shakes a bit but we are never near enough to the edge that we need to fall off. But on the edge of the plate there are a whole lot of people just coping, either just coping economically or just coping emotionally, and these structural changes in society shuffle the plate and they go down into mental hospitals, prisons, model lodging houses, etc. Some of them manage to climb back up again, but for many of them that shake that society has made has tumbled them off, permanently.

Our families were certainly near the edge of the plate, and we became aware of how little it would take to knock them off the plate altogether. It would not need anything as substantial as 'massive unemployment or redevelopment of a city' to push our families off the plate. Their finances were so critically balanced that it only needed a small fire in the Barker's home to plunge them into debt yet again. It would only take a minor accident to George Fielding, which prevented him from working, to stop his family's rise from deprivation. In sum, their lives were precarious and shot through with insecurities; a concentration on their health problems should make them fitter for the fray.

2. Flexible, individualized services

We have argued that these families' problems are so varied and so complex that they cannot be easily categorized. In addition, the families are so rightly sensitive to the stigma of being set apart from the rest of society by being labelled 'deprived' or 'problem families' that any such categorization would be undesirable and perhaps even counter-productive. What these families need are more individualized and flexible rather than separate and specialized social services. It is not simply a question of pleading for more selectivity, or even for more positive discrimination, which would only give more of the same to those who seem most in need. Such social policies, directed towards the broad aim of greater social equality, continue to be needed, although they have their own problems of implementation: for example, they should be more sensitive to issues such as the poverty trap and the fact that many people do not claim benefits for which they are eligible because of the stigma attached to having to prove poverty. Such measures as Educational Priority Areas, Housing Action Areas, and Family Income Supplement are inevitably crude, and they are still inadequately co-ordinated with each other. They could also have negative as well as positive effects on some of our families, many of whose problems cannot in any case be *directly* affected by any form of government intervention. What our research suggests is that the social services, having moved from a nineteenth century charity model to a mid twentieth century model of universalist state intervention, should now advance to a third stage where more individual, more flexible and more imaginative schemes are devised to help these and other, similar families. For example, Ada Paterson's basic circumstances changed rapidly, not to say unremittingly, throughout the eighteen-month period of our fieldwork, as her boyfriends Pete and Stan came and went, and she herself was taken in and out of hospital. Her existence was anything but settled at that time and her needs changed from month to month and, at times, from week to week. The Social Services Department was, perhaps understandably, quite unable to respond to her sudden changes in circumstances; but as a result, she suffered. Another example where more effective, *indirect* help could be offered would be the provision of a weekly visit from a sympathetic person with whom Elsie Barker or Sally and Peter Martin could talk over their current problems. We found ourselves playing that role, and it appeared much appreciated by the families concerned.

3. *Area approach*

In describing the socioeconomic context within which the personalities of our families' members have to find room to grow, it is worth remembering that Kindleton has never been officially accorded the status of a depressed area or even an intermediate area. In terms of the variables measured by the 1971 Census, the city is not a deprived area in comparison with such cities as Glasgow, Manchester, or Leeds (Holtermann, 1975). As a consequence, Kindleton is unlikely to receive any substantial sum of money under the Urban Aid Programme, or any other programme (such as Community Development Projects or Comprehensive Community Programmes) designed to attack the blight of inner city areas. Yet the previous chapters have exposed a number of serious and interlocking deprivations in the lives of the families studied. This reveals, in our opinion, the shortcomings of any policy which is narrowly based on a priority area approach. In the midst of a spirited defence of the main advantages of priority area policies, Holtermann (1978, p. 34) acknowledged that 'although there is some spatial concentration of the deprived, only a small proportion of all the deprived live in the small number of areas likely to be covered by priority area policies'. We are here confronted with the paradox described by Barnes (1975, p. 7) in an educational context: 'most disadvantaged children are not in the educational priority areas, and most of the children in educational priority areas are not disadvantaged'. This line of thought suggested to Barnes that 'the focus of our thinking should not be small areas within the inner city but the inner city as a whole' (p. 7). Much as we agree with such an extension of the small area approach, it still would do nothing to alleviate the problems of the Barker children, the Martins, Ada Paterson or the Fieldings. Our case studies would suggest that, although social policy must of course concentrate on the appalling housing problems of Glasgow and elsewhere, there is a need for some mixture of both area *and* individual approaches in order to reach those people with problems who do *not* live in the chosen areas. Or to put the point in Halsey's terms (1977), there is no necessary opposition between work at different levels, such as regions, districts, schools and individuals.

4. *Family policies*

In conjunction with attempts to co-ordinate economic, social and environmental policies, we need more overt, explicit and co-ordinated *family* policies. Such policies start from an acceptance of the fact that the state cannot *directly* affect the all important familial relationships, and short of removing the children from their homes altogether (which must be done sometimes), the state can only help parents in their difficult and responsible task of rearing their children. Parker (1974, p. 16) made an important point in this regard:

> Policies that are mainly child-centred (for instance most of those connected with education) are likely to have slight effect on the rest of the family. Yet if we really want to aid the disadvantaged child we must assist his parents. It is they who must do the caring and the anguishing . . . we cannot have two sets of standards: one for helping children and the other for their parents – even though some of these parents will currently be classified as scroungers, workshy, inadequate or downright irresponsible.

It is possible that the sympathies of the general reader have been engaged by the plight of the children described in earlier chapters. But, as Parker argued in a different context, the children in these case studies all live in families and most of the deprivations we have listed continue to be borne by the whole family and not just by the children. Family policy has recently become a political issue between the major parties (see, for example, Phillips, 1978 and Land, 1978), and our work suggests that a more explicit family policy would require us to take a close and critical look at every major social service and not just those such as family planning and preparation for parenthood, mentioned by Sir Keith Joseph. Many of these major services, even when their aims are impeccable as, for instance, in health clinics and doctors' surgeries, could in their implementation be, as a matter of principle, more respectful, helpful and encouraging to parents than they often are at present. We came across example after example of times when Elsie Barker, Ada Paterson, Peter Martin and Dora Fielding could have been more sympathetically treated, particularly by members of the medical profession. Our research also joins a whole chorus of voices pleading for family income support to reach the mother (or nurturant parent) in a simpler, more identifiable and more regular flow of cash benefits, which would be related as closely as possible to the family responsibilities she was carrying at any one time. Whatever method of family income support is finally adopted in Britain, our small number of case studies at least have the virtue of making it clear that there are families who are falling through the large number of different holes in the social support system currently offered by society.

5. *The professionals and the poor*

A further implication is that there is a need for a wider acceptance of the limitations of what the professional services can in fact do *directly* for such families, who are such a complicated mix of private suffering and social casualty. Their problems are so multiple, so deep-seated, and of such long standing that simple solutions are ruled out. We have argued earlier for a more sensitive and respectful approach by social administrators and professionals (and not just social workers) in their contacts, whether direct or indirect, with all parents and children. We now wish to ask how much the training given to all social service personnel encourages a greater sensitivity to the way parents, and particularly those who have to battle against a concentration of problems, perceive and are able to make use of the very services from which they are supposed to be benefiting. We mean something much more here than the question of low take-up rates. A related point concerns the lack of communication among professionals. Stevenson, a member of the Maria Colwell inquiry in 1974, pointed out three years later, in relation to subsequent reports on cases of child abuse, 'the seeming inability of well-intentioned, hard working people to learn from the experience of others, despite high levels of anxiety and a spate of exhortations from on high, giving indications of child abuse and outlining basic elements of good professional practice'. She herself argued for new structural arrangements to improve the communication links between professionals and emphasized the role of the social worker as a prime agent in facilitating such communication. Despite these exhortations, we have to record that we ourselves could see gaps in the relationships between social workers and schools, and between schools and parents. The headteacher of the school which the Barker and Martin children attended complained of the lack of contact with social workers (even in serious cases) and the rapid turnover of social workers dealing with any one particular case. The speedy promotion of social workers from the field to positions of management within a modern, hierarchical and reorganized profession was partly responsible for the rapid turnover, which was, however, very unsettling to the clients. The introduction, however, of avenues of promotion to say, senior practitioner, may help to alleviate this difficulty, as would more investment in community workers. We also felt that the communication between the social staff and the teaching staff (at the residential school which Michael Paterson attended) could have been improved. The links between the school and the home could also have been closer, and the incorporation of educational welfare officers within the social work departments, a recommendation of the Seebohm report of 1968, would have strengthened such links. The Inner Lambeth Area Study also found poor co-ordination among professionals and proposed the establishment of multi-service centres staffed by multi-service teams 'to improve links between workers in different services, and between those workers and their clients' (Shankland et al., 1977, p. 179).

6. *Education*

Within each of our families it is possible to distinguish between aspirations and expectations, the former referring to their hopes for and dreams of the future, the latter to their assessment of what is likely to be the future pattern of events. To assert that our families sought immediate rather than deferred gratification is to show a misunderstanding of social structure not made by the families themselves. Their limited expectations ('to work in a local factory', 'to be like his dad', or 'to be like other kids round here') contrast with aspirations such as 'to be a pop-singer' or 'First Division football player', and they illustrate not a limited view of the future but rather a down-to-earth, realistic attitude to what was attainable in their area. A traditional escape route from low income and status has been through education, yet none of our families, including the Fieldings, had more than a sketchy knowledge of how the local education system operated, the possible alternative routes through it, or the market value of the certificates it issued at different stages. The move to a comprehensive system of education has, paradoxically, increased the level of complexity facing parents. While the education system continues its function of selection, the *process* of selection has become less visible and therefore less intelligible to our families. All their children now belong to a common school which continues to measure, select and label them for the occupational structure. This is not a call to abandon the comprehensive ideal, but an illustration of the dangers inherent in any apparent simplification of provision which unintentionally complicates an understanding of its nature. In other areas claimants unions and social workers have done much to publicize the rights of the individual to social security, and the Supplementary Benefit Commission has made an attempt to publish leaflets which explain in simple terms the basis on which payment is made. While there are exceptions, the education service has done little to explain itself to parents; guides need to be produced locally, as England has a uniform educational system in only a very general sense. The pattern of provision in our project area is different from that prevailing five miles to the west and different again from that five miles to the south. There is even one local education authority in England which has all six permitted forms of comprehensive reorganization within its boundaries. What are parents to make of such legalized variation? If we are to help families change their expectations into aspirations we must provide them with the detailed knowledge about how to make such a journey.

7. Poverty and wealth

The paradox which was highlighted in Britain by Sir Keith Joseph – 'in spite of long periods of full employment and relative prosperity... deprivation and problems of maladjustment so conspicuously persist' – challenges a basic assumption of social policy, namely, that through the achievement of economic growth social problems would be ameliorated if not eradicated. Hirsch (1977) has labelled this view 'dynamic egalitarianism', a view which sees not only Britain's domestic problems but also the international problems of poverty being solved by growth.

Hirsch attacked the metaphor, much favoured by growth theorists, of society as a marching column where the advantages of the privileged today become the common property of the majority tomorrow. The limitation within 'dynamic egalitarianism' is that it neglects the fact that for those at the tail of the column, the conditions of access to the advantages of those at the front have changed. The last family in a society to acquire a car faces vastly different roads from those driven on by the first; similarly the last child to obtain educational credentials finds his purchasing power within the occupational structure completely different from that of the first.

Each of our families is at the end of the column, but in asserting this we also wish to question the criteria by which such placements are made. Widely differing problems and inequalities are given the label 'deprivation', and it would be foolish to pause too long to think about the use or misuse of a word, except where the word is loaded with political ammunition. It is now used with such a wide reference as to be almost meaningless; and yet the question of whether those people, who benefit least from living in our society, and who suffer economically, socially, and psychologically, will in turn hand on their disadvantages to their children, is a question which exercises the governmental and the popular mind. No amount of semantic quibbling about the meaning of 'deprivation', 'disadvantage' or 'privation' can oust its relevance. No amount of quarrelling with the notion of 'transmission' can avoid the question of whether problems are repeated from generation to generation. Our case studies have shown the complexity and interrelatedness of problems, the crudeness and injustice of any stereotype of the 'problem family', and the callousness of branding the 'inadequate' mother or the long-term unemployed father as anti-social deviants, without trying to understand *their* accounts of their experiences and their attempts to cope with the world.

Our research strategy could not do justice to the importance of structural factors. An emphasis on curative, individualistic measures is a more likely consequence of our case study approach than an emphasis on economic or political change on a national scale. Policy of the latter kind cannot be derived from our study: we have not found the philosopher's stone which turns funds into facts, and reveals the true nature of deprivation and all its causes. What we have found is the more intimate working of suffering, the anxieties and privations of people who do not speak with a loud voice and whose need for help is too often caricatured as fecklessness and inadequacy. We have also described the constant links between external events (the demands, for example, of migration in search of work) and the quality of family relationships. To miss the compelling force of external circumstances on the performance of the roles of parent or child, and to imagine that the fragile household is not responsive to, and sometimes even torn apart by, the pressures of poverty, unemployment and insecurity, is to attribute to poor people a freedom of choice, and a control over their lives which does not stand up to enquiry.

Epilogue

We mentioned in earlier chapters how patterns changed *over time,* and indeed continued to do so as we were writing the preceding pages. All of our families lived highly complex, confusing and constantly changing lives. This point was forcibly brought home to us when, towards the end of August 1978, we decided to revisit each of the four families to see how they were progressing. About fifteen months had passed since we had last seen any of them and yet they were all most welcoming.

The *Barkers* were still living at Elsmore and Elsie had become convinced that the move had benefited the whole family. Although the afternoon was hot and sultry, there was a huge fire in the grate and the colour television was on. Vince was still staying in at nights, watching television or building complex mechanical toys: he had given up going to the pub every night, had started to brew his beer, but had yet to turn his attention to the garden. Elsie thought that a major contributory factor to this change of behaviour was Vince's ill health. He had been off work for the previous eight weeks with angina: he had been complaining for some time of pains in his chest and of his left arm going dead. One night he collapsed on the floor and had given the children a fright. He was now seriously overweight. A combination of lack of money (£53.50 per week for two adults and six children) and boredom had driven him back to work. Vince was now talking of finding work which was physically less demanding, as he was no longer as fit as he had been in the past. Their marital relationship seemed to have stabilized somewhat – Elsie told us that Vince had not hit her since she had attacked him in self-defence. 'I now stick up for myself', she said, and the support she was receiving from her own family may have helped to strengthen her resolve. On the other hand, Elsie's mother still came between them.

As for the children, Tracy continued to give them cause for worry. She had absconded so frequently from the community home (being absent for four weeks on one occasion) that she had been transferred to a more secure residential establishment; and from there she had been moved to a working girls' hostel. She disliked the work which had been found for her, considering it boring, and she was looking forward to her eighteenth birthday when she could return home.

Elsie also told us that Matthew, her eldest son from her first marriage, had been kicked out of the army and out of his father's home and had come to live with them, although Vince had not been keen on the idea at first. Matthew had then caused so much trouble in the house by eating everything in sight, staying out late, stealing, being 'cheeky' and associating with divorced women (who had young children and who were much older than himself) that Vince had told him to leave.

Steve and the other younger children were just recovering from an attack of chicken-pox and continued to quarrel and squabble as before, but they were still doing well at their new school. Steve had come eighteenth in his class in the first examination, fifth in the second, and his teacher thought him capable of coming first in the next one. The other children were as rumbustious as ever, with Julie and Alice being the only ones who were still wetting the bed regularly. Alice (now aged six) had been wetting herself at school and had been given drugs which, claimed Elsie, worked only for as long as she took them.

Financial difficulties still beset the family. For example, the damage caused by the fire a year previously to the ceiling tiles in the hall had not yet been repaired for lack of money. The Barkers were still involved with the social work department, but the family and Tracy's social worker had both been changed.

We were at first unable to contact *Ada Paterson,* but the Martins were full of information about her and they told us the following story. According to Sally and Peter, Ada had left her own flat in Cardale to go and live with a man who had subsequently turned her out into the street. She had then arrived at the Martins' front door one day before Christmas 1977 with two cases containing all her belongings and asked the Martins to look after them for her while she hunted for rooms. Some time passed and then, instead of Ada returning to collect her own suitcases, Mr Hunt, her former husband from Birmingham, arrived to pick them up. He apparently explained to the Martins that Ada had claimed that the local doctors had been planning to put her into a residential home; she had become so upset at this possibility that she had taken a train to Birmingham to try to contact him. While trying to find his house, she had been knocked down by a car and broken her collarbone, one arm and a leg. She had given the police Mr Hunt's name and they had traced him. He had then taken her back into his home and she had decided to settle down with him.

Shortly afterwards, we discovered that this story of the Martins bore little or no relation to the facts. We finally made contact with Ada Paterson, again with the help of the local social service department. Ada, as the Martins had told us, had moved away from her flat in Cardale, after Stan had 'left me in the lurch', with debts owing and with bad relationships between Ada and her neighbours. Apparently, Ada had told the neighbours that she preferred Stan to her son Michael and this had been the cause of the ill feeling.

Having left Cardale, Ada started to live with a 'gentleman' in Elsmore, but after a week he threw her out. She then moved to the home of one of her brothers in Kindleton. This arrangement did not last, and after about eight weeks she moved again to the rented room where we visited her.

She was then reunited with Stan and together they now lived in one room for which Ada paid £12 per week inclusive of heating. In the room there was a TV and a radiogram which belonged to Stan, together with some of the trinkets which we saw in the flat in Cardale. Ada was ill in bed, having just returned from a visit to hospital; Stan was at work, as he had found a manual labouring job some four weeks previously. The reason for the hospital visit was that Ada had collapsed on the floor that morning and the manageress of the rooms had taken her to the casualty department of the local hospital. Ada had strained her back while at work and was also suffering from a vaginal infection. She said that she was not getting on well with Stan, who thought her idle and who insisted that she paid the rent for the room, as it was not his responsibility to look after her because he was not married to her. She told us that Stan had 'a split personality' in that sometimes he was nice to her and at other times nasty; for example, he would come home drunk at the weekends after having left Ada alone all day.

The work to which she referred was a cleaning job at a local night club for which she took home £18; she worked from eight o'clock in the morning until one each day, including Sundays. The work involved a lot of sweeping which Ada said was too heavy for her, and it had caused her to strain some muscles in her back. She had been working for three weeks, she said she had enjoyed it and had got on well with the other cleaning ladies.

She had not seen Michael since Christmas, but knew that 'the welfare' had placed him with Alf's family on Michael's return from residential school. Ada's social worker told us that Michael was in voluntary care with Alf's relatives and, if all went well, he would probably be adopted by them.

Ada said that she had not seen the Martins for a long time. We asked if she had been knocked down by a car; she was amused at the suggestion, and assured us that she had neither been knocked down nor broken any bones during the year. She had telephoned Mr Hunt's family in Birmingham, and had been told that Mr Hunt had died of a stroke.

Ada looked very thin and poorly, her eyes were deeply set, and she said that she had been depressed ever since the death of Alf. She felt her life would have been better if she had never left her house in Bramwell. As it was, she had no doctor, she had lost her entitlement to a widow's pension because of cohabiting with Stan, and she had lost the rent rebate to which she had been entitled in both Bramwell and Cardale.

Little had changed with the *Martin* family since our previous visit. As we arrived outside the house, a child in the street called out: 'Which house?' and, on being told, replied: 'Oh, the dirty family'. Inside, the house *was* dirty, yet it also showed signs of being taken care of, which was more than could be said for the garden. There was a new three-piece suite which Sally said had cost £225 of which they had only £40 still to pay; there was a pile of clean washing which had been recently ironed, a tray with potted plants, trinkets in a cupboard, a coloured poster of Elvis Presley and some religious pictures on the wall. On the other hand, the remains of partially eaten meals, articles of dirty clothing, and other bits and pieces littered the floor.

Sally greeted us warmly at the door, but, as was typical of earlier visits, Peter, who had been in the living room as we approached the house, had moved into the kitchen by the time we entered the house. Only when we went to speak to him did he join us and soon he was dominating the conversation, just as before. He was still preoccupied with his health and told us that he had collapsed in a street in the city; he had been taken as if dead to the local mortuary. It was only when he was being cleaned on the slab that he woke up, questioned the attendants, and so realized where he was. His heart was still bad and he was taking aspirin to thin his blood in preparation for receiving a new and larger heart valve. He told one of us in confidence that when letters came from the hospital to invite him for a check-up he threw them straight into the fire so that Sally would not know and take him to hospital.

Peter was still unemployed, though he had worked for 'the cleansing compartment' (sic), until someone discovered his green card. He also told us that he had taken a driving test, during which an oil lorry in front of him 'let go a squirt of oil'. Peter managed to control his own 'wagon' and brought it to a halt to be congratulated by the examiner for passing a part of the test which was now given to everyone. Peter was shocked by the incident and tried to take one of his heart pills; however, in his concern not to let the examiner see him taking the pill, he mistakenly took two and passed out. He was again taken to hospital and, when Sally came to collect him, she told him that 'he had passed the test, but failed it because of his heart'.

We did not see the eldest boy Mark, aged eight, but were told that he was enuretic two or three times each week. Sally gave as a reason Mark's anxiety for Peter; apparently, hospital staff visited their home regularly to check Peter's pacemaker and Mark became worried when he saw the electric wires going into Peter's heart. Neither Ruth, aged six, nor Gary, aged four, wet the bed. Both children appeared very dirty and Gary had a strong smell of urine.

Sally looked much older, having cut her own hair short, and Peter looked unwell and talked of being surprised at a weighing machine recording his weight at over ten stone, when he knew it was normally between seven and eight stone. They were still in contact with the Mormon Church, though they had been unable to go on a trip to pay their last respects to Elvis Presley at a cost of £100 because of Peter's heart condition.

The visit to the *Fieldings* was as enjoyable and as friendly as ever. Dora now had three children, as she had given birth to a little boy some twelve months previously. Although a new pram had been bought for both Nicola and Amanda, the Fieldings had not been able to afford another new one for their young son. Money was tight and Dora had given up buying the best leather shoes for the children and was buying the cheapest instead. They have decided not to have any more children and George has had a vesectomy, losing two weeks' work as a result. He had also been off work for four months earlier in the year with a serious skin complaint; and they had both noticed that they received more money when George was 'on the club' than when he was working. Dora has been forced to take an evening job (three hours a night, five nights a week, for £12) 'just to pay the rent'. This had caused some unpleasantness between them because George did not like her having to go out to work, especially at night.

Dora's mother, Enid Havelock, remarried and returned to live in Aulton which she preferred to Drayford. Dora commented that, with a few exceptions, her neighbours in Drayford were not as friendly as her old friends in Aulton whom she still visited from time to time. Enid's new husband had recently suffered a serious heart attack, although he was still only in his late fifties. This reminded George that his father had undergone a serious operation which had left him very poorly. Patrick was still unemployed and, according to his sister, he was the type of person to go on having children just for the family allowances or just to increase the points he needed for a house.

When Enid left the Fieldings' home after her remarriage, they applied for a rent rebate and succeeded in having the rent reduced by twenty pence. When the third child arrived, however, the rent was reduced by two pounds. But shortly afterwards George received a wage increase of roughly that amount, and the rent was returned to the original figure. They both wondered how they could increase their standard of living in such circumstances.

Appendix: A Cycle of Deprivation? A Critical Review

We began Chapter 1 by discussing the speech Sir Keith Joseph made on 29 June 1972 to a Conference organized by the Pre-School Playgroups Association on 'the cycle of deprivation'. In this appendix we want to examine in some detail the evidence he advanced in support of 'the phenomenon of transmitted deprivation'. In all, Sir Keith listed and then commented briefly upon five research reports, which will be examined here at greater length, as they were the basis of his argument. In order, the five studies mentioned were:

1. Wright and Lunn's (1971) work on 120 problem families in Sheffield.
2. D. J. West's (1969 and 1973) Cambridge Study in Delinquent Development in an unselected sample of 411 London boys.
3. Davie, R., Butler, N. and Goldstein, H. (1972), *From Birth to Seven*.
4. Oliver and Taylor's (1971) description of five generations of ill-treated children in one family pedigree.
5. Urie Bronfenbrenner's observations on parental involvement with children in his book *Two Worlds of Childhood: US and USSR* (1971).

Sir Keith began by referring to the only major study completed in this country of problem families followed up over two generations. In a series of reports in 1955, 1967 and 1971, Wright and Lunn monitored the progress of 120 Sheffield families who were first judged by health visitors in 1954 'on very general lines' to be 'problem families'. Thirteen years later, in 1967, the married and single sons and daughters of 116 of the original 120 families who were 16 years of age or over were traced and visited. The principal findings were that:

1. More than 50 per cent of the sons and 75 per cent of the daughters were married and 59 per cent of the daughters had given birth to their first child at, or under, the age of 19 years.
2. The 116 families had produced 835 known descendants by 1967.
3. More of the married sons than married daughters were repeating the unsatisfactory parental pattern in their own marriages.

The 116 families were assessed on housing conditions, household possessions, employment, contacts with social agencies, juvenile delinquency, and broken families. The authors summarized all these assessments in a model (here presented in diagrammatic form in Figure A.1) which predicts that about 33 per cent of the families will escape from the cycle of deprivation and 'merge into the mass of average

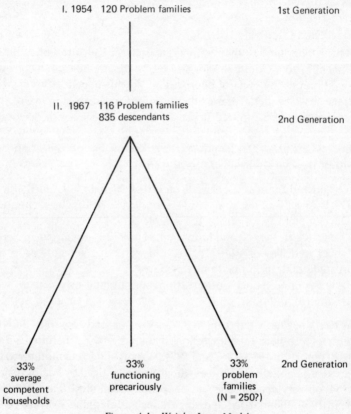

I. 1954   120 Problem families   1st Generation

II. 1967   116 Problem families
           835 descendants   2nd Generation

| 33% average competent households | 33% functioning precariously | 33% problem families (N = 250?) | 2nd Generation |

Figure A.1   Wright–Lunn Model

competent households. . . . It is certain that a further 33 per cent . . . are either already problem families in every sense of the term or have started on a course of involvement with helping agencies which is unlikely to be reversed' (1971, p. 319). A middle group of 33 per cent was characterized as 'functioning precariously' and could end up in either of the two other groups depending on the 'strengths and weaknesses of the parents' personalities'. In conclusion, their conservative estimate is that the number of unsatisfactory families which will arise from the 835 children of the original families, when all have married, will not be less than 250. This legacy of problem families which results in a doubling of the number of families requiring help in one generation is described as 'alarming'. Only one strategy is proposed to deal with the problem: a vigorous drive to promote contraception and so deal with the constant characteristic of these families, their 'fecundity'.

Wright and Lunn's study, although unique of its kind in this country, presents a number of difficulties, chief of which is the precise number of descendants who were interviewed and on whom the conclusions are based. Out of the total of 835 known descendants, only 577 were aged 16 or over. Of these, no information could be gained on 22, thus leaving 555. Only the 449 who were living *within* the city boundary were assessed, the other 106 being further afield in the armed forces or having emigrated. There may therefore be very good reasons to believe that the families living outside the city differed from the families which were assessed, although the authors suggested the direct opposite (1971, p. 319). So the 'alarming' conclusion about 250 new problem families is based on the findings from 449 children which have been generalized to the whole sample of 835. A more accurate estimate of the number of new problem families would have been reached by taking one-third of this figure of 449, namely 150; this is still high but far less alarming than the predicted doubling to 250.

A second difficulty with Wright and Lunn's work concerns the implicit attitudes towards these families which is revealed in the language used to describe them. An examination of the terminology used by researchers in this delicate area cannot be dismissed as an irrelevant or petty exercise for, as often as not, the words adopted are a reflection of theory – a point emphasized by Bowlby (1975, p. 454) in another context. For example, Wright and Lunn's work includes the following comments: 'Repetitive jobs provided no distraction from their [the girls'] instinctive drive towards marriage'; 'parenthood as irresponsible and inept as it is fecund'; 'Father psychopath, drunken bully, and oversexed'; 'deplorable standards of sexual morality.' Wives are 'feckless', husbands are 'lazy' or have 'a weak drive towards employment', horizons and aspirations are 'limited', attitudes to money 'irresponsible', hire purchase items are acquired 'thoughtlessly' and so on.

Another implicit attitude in the later reports is that an *individual* explanation of failure is being favoured: 'at a time of virtually full employment about 33 per cent of the males were poorly adjusted to work' (1971, p. 320). And indeed in the earliest paper, this view is stated explicitly: 'In each of these cases it will be noted that the fault resides in the individual and not the external circumstances.' (1955, p. 382). Dr Lunn (in a personal communication, 1977) has since stated that both he and Dr Wright 'believe that the genetic component of transmitted deprivation does tend to be much underestimated at present....'

A further difficulty concerns one of the limitations of the survey approach to social problems. Their statistical analysis suggested, but only marginally so, that parental involvement with social work agencies might lead to their children being involved with the same agencies. But the authors were unable to be definite about what mechanism or mechanisms explain the link, as they themselves admitted: 'Whether this is due to poor living conditions and poor social adjustment, to a family tradition of seeking help from some agencies, or to a combination of these factors, is hard to tell.' (1971, p. 316). Could it not also be that the social workers came to know the children and their problems informally by being involved in casework with their parents?

In general, the picture is not so bleak as the foregoing account and the authors' own conclusions appear to make it. For instance, Holman (1974) has pointed out that Wright and Lunn's research was possible only because the original families maintained such close links with their married children. In addition, 'the sons and daughters show a better employment picture than their fathers in that they are more commonly at work and more commonly in skilled jobs'. (Wright and Lunn, 1971, p. 307). In terms of housing conditions, the general impression of the interior, and of household possessions, the comparison between the married siblings and their parents 'is strikingly favourable to the former'. (Wright and Lunn, 1971, p. 304).

But, for all this criticism, these investigators have produced that most intriguing finding, mentioned earlier, that the married daughters had improved their position in life more than their brothers. Wright and Lunn themselves suggested three possible explanations. First, the girls appeared to be marrying out of their social class, while the sons, 'no doubt at a disadvantage among other eligible bachelors', (1971, p. 319) were marrying into families similar to their own. Secondly, it is possible that boys may be more vulnerable to the stresses attendant on being brought up in a 'problem family', and certainly Rutter (1970) claimed in a review of the relevant literature, that boys suffer more from all sorts of stress, both physical and psycho-social. Finally, they suggested that the fathers of such families provide very poor models for the sons as breadwinners and as heads of the household, and that their influence may be more damaging than 'the failings of a feckless mother' (1971, p. 319).

Sir Keith Joseph's second example of cyclical processes in operation was West's longitudinal study of 411 boys from a traditional, working-class area of London. A full account of this monumental and painstaking piece of research is given in the three books *Present Conduct and Future Delinquency* (1969), *Who Becomes Delinquent?* (1973), and *The Delinquent Way of Life* (1977), the last two written with Farrington.

Only three comments will be made about this splendid example of traditional criminological research which is predominantly psychological in orientation, with its clear aim of establishing that delinquents really are different from non-delinquents. Out of the 151 factors which were examined for their association with delinquency, five factors were judged to be of special importance: (i) low family income; (ii) large family size; (iii) parental criminality; (iv) low intelligence; and (v) poor parental behaviour.

The influence of structural, sociological factors is apparent throughout the study; to take but one example, low family income (and its close association with poor housing, overcrowding, large family size, etc.) appears to be the most important factor of all. And yet West and Farrington fight a heroic rear-guard action on behalf of psychological factors: 'Low income must to some extent have reflected incompetence, or at least lack of success. In modern times family income is not completely fixed by outside pressures, but is at least partly determined by motivation and ability.' (1973, p. 29). The conflict between psychologists and sociologists is at its most acute over this point, as Goldthorpe has argued: 'attempts to relate social inequality or particular aspects of it – say, in incomes – to differences in the so-called "natural" attributes of individuals have repeatedly failed' (1974, p. 37). In other words, this type of statistical study does not exclude widely different interpretations of the same basic findings.

Secondly, the statistical significance of the five factors listed above does not mean that they are the essential *causes* of delinquency. No simple, direct causal link has been established; the research has merely confirmed a relationship, an association. And no amount of sophisticated statistical operations can take the debate any further, as West himself admitted: 'It seems difficult to get beyond the observation that certain adversities are linked with delinquency, and that an accumulation of these adversities makes a delinquent outcome more probable.' (1973, p. 191).

Thirdly, one of West's five factors, parental criminality, suggests that there may be a continuity between one generation and the next in very much the way that Sir Keith Joseph maintains. But there are a number of different mechanisms each of which could explain the link: an hereditary predisposition to crime; a transmission of criminal tendencies through direct example and anti-authority attitudes, but of a more subtle nature than the rather unlikely Fagin's kitchen; the exercise of poor parental supervision; laxness in enforcing social rules; bad parent–child relationships seriously disturbing any social learning by the boy; and finally, as the influence of parental criminality appears to be important at adolescence but not before, it may be that the standards of a highly delinquent neighbourhood are having their effect on the boy's behaviour just as they did on his father's a generation earlier. It is also possible to explain this intergenerational continuity without any reference to internal family dynamics at all. The police may pay far more attention and be far less lenient to the children of parents whom they know to be criminal; and so a link is forged between two generations in much the same way social workers become involved with children from 'problem families', as suggested in the earlier discussion of the Wright and Lunn study. Subsequent analysis by Farrington, Gundry and West (1975) provided evidence of such a link, whereby selective prosecution by the police of boys from families where other members have a criminal record was shown to be *one* important factor in the 'familial transmission of criminality'. Knight and West (1977) then enlarged the scope of their enquiry to include not only criminality but also welfare dependency in two generations. They concluded that the habit of making unusually frequent social security claims was transmitted from one generation to the next, and was a characteristic feature of the delinquent minority. Rutter and Madge (1976, p. 171) summed up this whole debate neatly: '. . . the mechanisms underlying these continuities remain ill-understood and it should be emphasized that even when both parents are criminal about half the sons do *not* become delinquent'. (Emphasis as in original).

It will not be necessary to deal in such detail with the other three studies referred to by Sir Keith, as they do not bear so directly on his central thesis of transmitted deprivation or are relatively minor pieces of research. As a third example, Sir Keith Joseph chose Davie, Butler and Goldstein's *From Birth to Seven* (1972), which is the second report of the National Child Development Study. In 1958 information was gathered on virtually every baby born in England, Scotland and Wales during the week 3–9 March. This cohort of children, numbering some 17,000 at birth, is a representative national sample, selected only by date of birth, and information on the children has been collected at birth, and at the ages of 7, 11 and 16. But, although *From Birth to Seven* lists in grim detail the severity of the disadvantages suffered by certain children from birth onwards, nowhere does it provide direct evidence of a cycle of deprivation operating in 'a clear sequence of social disability from parent to child', as Sir Keith claimed. The report on the children at 11, *Born to Fail?* (Wedge and Prosser, 1973), highlighted the *overlap* between problems by pointing out that 6.2 per cent of these children (i) came from a one-parent family or a family of five or more children, *and* (ii) lived in a low-income family, *and* (iii) suffered from poor housing.

Despite these multiple and interlocking deprivations, some of the most socially disadvantaged children in the country were found at the highest levels of measured attainment in reading and in maths; and almost 50 per cent of them were found to be well adjusted at school. The fact that one in seven of the disadvantaged children had some 'outstanding ability' in science, sport, music, chess, etc. is a most hopeful finding which should do much to counteract any brutal pessimism about the ineluctable transmission of deprived status from parents to children. This is not to forget that the attainment of underprivileged children on the whole deteriorates in relation to national standards as they grow older; and this is depressingly true whether examined longitudinally (Douglas, 1964; Douglas, Ross, and Simpson, 1968) or cross-sectionally (Payne, 1974). So there is no inevitable connection between parental disability and school failure. On the contrary, the evidence presented by the National Child Development Study indicated that some groups of children do *not* reproduce the problems experienced by their families. Indeed, Peter Wedge, one of the authors of *Born to Fail?*, accepted in 1976 (in a personal communication) that their work '... has not demonstrated a causal relationship between the circumstances of the two generations'.

Fourthly, Sir Keith Joseph incorporated into his argument a study by Oliver and Taylor (1971), which has since been augmented by further reports by Oliver and Cox (1973), and by Oliver, Cox, Taylor and Baldwin (1974). In the first two papers, the families of babies who had been battered were examined and it was found that there were numbers of seriously ill-treated or neglected children among the relatives and antecedents, stretching back as far as five generations. Their data also indicated that 'socially incompetent people who ill-treat their children have themselves suffered poor mothering (although hereditary factors are not excluded)' (1973, p. 89). Some of these families have become a 'burden on the community', receiving extensive social and medical help over long periods of time, but nevertheless 'distress and social dependency within these kindreds is perpetuated through the generations, with certain lines at serious risk of continuing the pattern' (1973, p. 90). This is the strongest evidence so far advanced in support of a cycle of deprivation. The total numbers involved, however, were small: forty-nine in the first report, and forty-one in the second. Moreover, the basic findings are open to a wide variety of interpretations; for example, information on members of the earliest generations consisted of remarks such as 'Remembered by descendants as being "Very peculiar"'. (1971, p. 476).

Finally, Sir Keith added two quotations from a book by Urie Bronfenbrenner, Professor of Psychology and Child Development and Family Studies at Cornell University. The book, entitled *Two Worlds of Childhood: US and USSR,* argued that adults in Russia are far more deeply involved in the lives of children than their counterparts are in the United States. In only one paragraph (p. 116) of this book does Bronfenbrenner refer to England, which is characterized as 'the only country in our sample which shows a level of parental involvement lower than our own, with both parents – and especially fathers – showing less affection, offering less companionship and intervening less frequently in the lives of their children'. The article by Devereux, Bronfenbrenner, and Rodgers (1969) on which this sweeping generalization is based turns out to be a cross-national comparison of child-rearing in England and the United States, and it is suitably guarded and cautious. So it needs to be; for the paper describes a sample of 741 eleven-year-old children, all from a single county in England, who filled in a questionnaire on their parents' behaviour. The responses of the English children were then compared with those of a sample of 968 American children who all lived in one county in the state of New York. Moreover, the discussion is confined to arithmetical means which obscures the extensive variation within each sample on all the variables tested. While the differences between the two samples are statistically significant, in absolute terms they are very small: 'so perhaps our most substantial finding is really the basic similarity in patterns of child-rearing in both countries' (1969, p. 266). No more need be said.

Since June 1972, Sir Keith Joseph has returned to the theme of the cycle of deprivation on a number of occasions – in speeches to the Association of Directors of Social Services (March 1973) and to the National Association for Maternal and Child Welfare (June 1973). In all, the evidence for an inevitable 'cycle of deprivation' is precariously thin in the five studies examined above, all of which were concerned with different types of disadvantage. Furthermore, only Wright and Lunn's research could be said to have been directly concerned with establishing intergenerational continuities. No further evidence for the theory was advanced in Sir Keith's subsequent speeches apart from the testimony of an anonymous director of social services, who was quoted (1973b) as saying: 'We have 20,000 households in the city. Nearly all our problems – delinquency, truancy, deprivation, poverty and the rest – come from about 800 of them. And I think that most of the families have been known to us for five generations.' Social policies need to be based on harder evidence than the extemporaneous musings of unidentified officials.

It was, however, Sir Keith Joseph's Birmingham speech of October 1974 which sparked off a national controversy. Towards the end of his address, Sir Keith drew upon an article of Margaret and Arthur Wynn in the Summer 1974 issue of *Poverty,* the journal of the Child Poverty Action Group. He introduced this section with the highly emotive words 'The balance of our population, our human stock is threatened.' He continued by claiming that the article showed that

a high and rising proportion of children are being born to mothers least fitted to bring children into the world and bring them up. They are born to mothers who were first pregnant in adolescence in social classes IV and V. Many of these girls are unmarried, many are deserted or divorced or soon will be. Some are of low intelligence, most of low educational attainment.... They are producing problem children, the future unmarried mothers, delinquents, denizens of our borstals, sub-normal educational establishments, prisons, hostels for drifters. Yet these mothers, the under 20s in many cases, single parents, from classes IV and V are now producing a third of all births. A high proportion of these births are a tragedy for the mother, the child and for us. Yet what shall we do? If we do nothing, the nation moves towards degeneration....

The furore which these words provoked at least had the value of establishing the fact that Sir Keith's conclusions were based on a misunderstanding of two tables in the Wynns' article; these tables are produced separately here. The Wynns combined (for reasons which are nowhere explained) social classes IV and V in Table A.1 and so concealed a wide disparity between them: class IV produced 22.9 per cent and class V only 2 per cent. In other words, unskilled workers had proportionately even fewer illegitimate babies than the professional workers of social class I. The real bunching occurs in classes III and IV

Table A.1   Illegitimacy and social class: Scotland 1972

Social Class	% of all births that were illegitimate
I	2.7
II	4.3
III	6.9
IV and V	13.1

Source: Annual Report of the Registrar General for Scotland 1972, pp. 108–9.
457 out of 6661 illegitimate births were not classified by social class.

and is caused by the rather out-of-date and crude classification of occupations than by any variation in moral standards among the mothers concerned. (*The Sunday Times,* 27 October 1974).

Exception was also taken to his statement that 'these mothers, the under 20s are, after all, likely in due course to be the mothers of perhaps over 35 per cent of all British people'. The 35 per cent was, therefore, a reference to an *age* group and not to a *social class* group. It would appear that Sir Keith had mistakenly, but understandably, applied the Wynns' conclusion to the final two rows in Table A.2.

Table A.2   Pregnancy under 20 and social class: Scotland 1972

Social Class	% of all births to mothers under age 20
I	4.4
II	4.1
III	11.7
IV	15.7
V	20.0

Source: Margaret and Arthur Wynn, 'Can family planning do more to reduce child poverty?' *Poverty,* Child Poverty Action Group, no. 29, Summer 1974, p. 17.

But a more serious challenge to Sir Keith Joseph's and the Wynn's argument came from the figures of a falling birth-rate which had been released only for Scotland (Registrar General Scotland, 1973). The number of births in social classes I and II actually increased by 5 per cent between 1969 and 1972; in social class IV there was a decline during the same period of 24 per cent, and in social class V a decline of 20 per cent. Figures which have subsequently been released for England and Wales show much the same pattern of a falling birth-rate which is mainly a lower working class phenomenon (Registrar General, 1974, p. 45).

A DES report (1978) quoted a study by the Office of Population Censuses and Surveys to the effect that, for the period from 1970 to 1975, the average annual rate of decrease in legitimate live births was 0.8 per cent for social classes I and II, while that for other classes was 6.6 per cent.

There have been a number of more fundamental objections to the cycle of deprivation advanced by people like Eysenck (1973b), Townsend (1974), Holman (1973b, and 1978), Rutter and Madge (1976) and others such as Wilson (1974b), Wilson and Herbert (1978), and Jordan (1974). Before examining each of these in turn, it is worth remembering Horton's cautionary words about such competing perspectives: 'All definitions and theories of deviation and social problems are normative. They define and explain behaviour from socially situated value positions.' (1966, p. 702). The great danger in Horton's opinion is that social scientists may mistake their normative categories for 'objective' fact. Horton then classified normative theories into two ideal types – order and conflict theories. These two over-simplified models of society, both of which, according to him, have their roots in the nineteenth century, are then contrasted in detail. In brief, order theories presuppose a society with shared culture and values, where social problems result from anomie and are explained by social disorganization and/or inadequate socialization. Solutions to social problems are seen in terms of more social control, more or better administration, and adjusting individuals to the needs of the system. In direct contrast, conflict theorists picture society as a continual political struggle between groups with opposing goals and values. For them, social problems reflect 'the adaptive failure of society to meet changing individual needs' (p. 704) and are caused by 'the exploitive and alienating practices of dominant groups'; the only acceptable remedy is a radical transformation of the existing system. Such a classification provides a useful framework within which to place the wide variety of responses to Sir Keith Joseph's notion of a cycle of deprivation.

Eysenck was one of the first to do public battle over this concept which, to his mind, created an unnecessarily lugubrious picture of society by neglecting the fundamental fact of genetics, namely, 'that heredity can produce *differences* between parents and children, as well as similarities'. (1973b, p. 203. Emphasis as in original.) According to Eysenck, the deep-seated social problems listed by Sir Keith Joseph as reproducing themselves from generation to generation are susceptible to a single solution, heredity, which, through the law of regression, 'will break "the cycle of deprivation", if not in one generation, then in two or three. The offspring of the "lumpenproletariat" will not remain "lumpenproletariat" for ever, and the offspring of the "deprived" will not remain "deprived" for ever.' Such faith in the power of heredity is not seen by Eysenck to be connected in any way with his own political beliefs. Writing about the charges made against Sir Cyril Burt in *The Sunday Times* in late 1976, Eysenck dismissed ideological assumptions as red herrings; for him, belief in the importance of heredity is quite unrelated to a person's political stance. His prime concern in this highly sensitive area is to remain the dispassionate scientist who will continue to uncover the 'facts' with ever increasing precision. So he argued in a political, social and historical vacuum against the possibility of society congealing into IQ castes, and in direct opposition to Horton's contention that all such social theories are normative and socially situated. Eysenck is not.alone in pleading for a neutral, empirical, and scientific approach to social problems.

But no such quarter was asked for or granted by Townsend, who in a speech to the British Association of Social Workers in March 1974 called the thesis of a cycle of deprivation 'a mixture of popular stereotypes and ill-developed, mostly contentious, scientific notions. It is a conceptual bed into which diverse travellers have scrambled for security and comfort.' (1974, p. 8). His more reasoned objection to Sir Keith's thesis was that four separate steps of selection had been taken:

1. Certain *types* of deprivation had been chosen. No mention had been made, for example, of redundancy, dismissal from work, dangerous or dirty working conditions.
2. Certain *causal* factors had been selected. Poor schools, poor housing and poor community services were omitted from the argument and yet may be as responsible for the emotional and intellectual impoverishment of children as poor child-rearing. Only the latter was emphasized by Sir Keith.
3. Certain *interpretations* of the term 'transmission' were chosen. Sir Keith talked only of the biological inheritance of personal attributes and of particular child-rearing patterns being copied by the second generation. But 'transmission' could also mean continuities in customs or traditions in a national or local population.
4. Certain *remedies* were selected. Only the most inexpensive, interventionist measures were supported by Sir Keith who ignored *both* major redistribution of resources and reorganization of institutions and services *and* less bold strategies for supporting parents.

Townsend summed up his opposition by claiming that, not only was the thesis 'a piece of ideological special pleading', it was also a diversionary tactic for 'it diverts our concern, and our research endeavour, from treating deprivation as a large-scale structural phenomenon to treating it as a residual personal or family phenomenon; it diverts us from considering potentially expensive to considering comparatively inexpensive policy measures; and it diverts us from... blaming the Goverment to blaming... the victim' (1974, p. 10). This final remark is rather exaggerated for it is difficult to see how an emphasis on familial factors necessarily leads one to 'blame' the families concerned.

Holman was less overtly hostile but no less opposed to Sir Keith Joseph's concentration on one explanation to the virtual exclusion of all others. In a book of readings, he and Butterworth (1975) advanced three competing explanations for the large scale persistence of social deprivation. First, the problem can be seen in terms of individual malfunctioning or maladjustment, as Boyson did in his book *Down with the Poor* (1971). Jordan (1974), however, claimed that there was no evidence to link poverty with maladjustment and that the equating of the poor parent with the inadequate and neglectful parent is nothing other than an official, middle-class stereotype. Secondly, the blame can be laid at the door of inadequate social services and social policies, as Jenkins proposed in *What Matters Now* (1972). Both of these analyses of the problem were considered by Holman to be seriously defective because:

1. Attempts to change deprived families will achieve little 'if the causes of deprivation rest mainly in the social structures of society rather than in the personalities of the poor ...' (Holman, 1973b, p. 436).
2. Reducing poverty may only be possible by reducing wealth and privilege.
3. The social services themselves may actually reinforce poverty by containing the discontents of the poor.

In direct opposition to the explanations of Boyson and Jenkins, Butterworth and Holman proposed another model of poverty which focuses attention on the social and economic structures of society. In this view, poverty has the major function in a highly stratified society of helping to preserve the existing divisions and inequalities; and the latter will only be successfully challenged by collective action by the poor themselves.

These conflicting explanations, based as they are on competing political and ideological beliefs, were treated and named differently by different authors. Wilson, for example, preferred the terms the 'consensus', 'pluralist', and 'conflict' models, and furthermore, she explicitly rejected 'the traditional conception of social deprivation as mainly, if not exclusively, the result of cultural or psychological deficiencies in the individuals and groups concerned' (1974b, p. 4). She could not accept Sir Keith's pleas for more preparation for parenthood or even his admission that 'Good parenting cannot be possible where living facilities and work opportunities are inadequate' (1973c, p. 14). Her study of fifty-six families in a Midland city claimed to show that 'good parenting', as the phrase is normally understood, was irrelevant to the tasks of bringing up children and preventing them becoming delinquent in deprived areas. Parents were forced against their own better judgment to insist on a strict regime which severely limited their children's freedom: '... in the world of poverty the material preconditions necessary for child-centred parenting do not exist' (1974a, p. 246). In other words, what was missing from Sir Keith's analysis, according to Wilson, was 'the dynamics of the decaying city centre' (1974b, p. 7).

Later, in 1976, there appeared the survey of the literature on the cycle of deprivation which was commissioned by the DHSS/SSRC joint working party. Rutter and Madge in *Cycles of Disadvantage* reviewed the vast literature in this area and concluded by clarifying the options open to researchers. They began, however, by showing that the term 'deprivation' has been used to cover so many different forms of disadvantage that 'the word almost functions as a projective test in which each person reads into the concept his own biases and prejudices...' (1976, p. 2). Accordingly, they dropped the concept 'deprivation' altogether in favour of the phrase 'cycles of disadvantage'. Although the omission of the adjective 'transmitted' and the move to the plural 'cycles' are improvements on the original phrase used by Sir Keith Joseph, just as many objections can be raised to the term 'disadvantage' as to its forerunner. Rutter and Madge continued by censuring Sir Keith for focusing too narrowly on the family. After all, continuities in various forms of disadvantage could be evident in regional groups, schools, inner city areas and other social and cultural institutions as well as in families. Furthermore, what appears to be an inter-generational continuity may not be familial in origin at all, but the result of the second generation facing exactly the same social or political inequalities as its predecessor, a point trenchantly made by Liebow in *Tally's Corner* (1967). They also argued that the study of *discontinuities* may be as valuable, if not more so, than the more frequently found study of continuities; by which they meant that 'a surprisingly large proportion of people reared in conditions of privation and suffering do *not* reproduce that pattern in the next generation' (1976, p. 6. Emphasis as in original).

They then turned to more specific methodological considerations, including different measurements of disadvantage, intra- and inter-generational continuities, the need for knowledge of the causal processes or mechanisms underlying bald estimates of continuities, etc. Interestingly, the powerful attack of Townsend is neither discussed nor even mentioned; and the objections of Holman, Wilson and others are similarly passed over in silence. Instead, Rutter and Madge adopted the following position: 'Although others have felt more confident in their analysis of the motives and meanings behind the 1972 speech, we have not considered it either appropriate or fruitful to engage in these speculations.' (1976, p. 4). At least we have here an admission that there *were* 'motives and meanings behind the 1972 speech'. We only wish to ask why these should be omitted from consideration. What could be more important than 'motives and meanings'?

We object to this stance of Rutter and Madge because it is one of the main contentions of this appendix that the speeches of Sir Keith Joseph on the cycle of deprivation must be seen in their political, social and historical context. For the ideas which informed these speeches, the 'motives and meanings', did not spring fully formed and fully armed from the mouth of Sir Keith as the goddess Athena did from the head of Zeus. Rather, these ideas are part of a long, cultural tradition, the development of which is best seen in a detailed historical framework before motives can be assessed. Ideological issues have always been inextricably intertwined with attempts to deal with deprivation and poverty, as Jordan (1974), Holman (1978) and many others have demonstrated. Indeed, there is a long, unbroken tradition of attitudes to the 'deserving' and the 'non-deserving' poor in this country. Smout (1969, p. 90), writing about the establishment of the Scottish Poor Law in 1535, claimed that the distinction between the 'deserving' and the 'non-deserving' poor had been recognized even earlier by the medieval church and state in the fifteenth century. That such a distinction should have survived so long is offered as evidence of the best 'continuity', the most perfect 'cycle' in this whole debate. Jordan (1974, p. 15) even referred in his historical analysis to a 'cycle of official deprivation of the poor', by which he meant that the principles of the English Poor Law of 1834 had recently been reintroduced to deal punitively with the 'undeserving'. Consequently, all of us who study 'transmitted deprivation' are involved, whether we like it or not, in the political and social implications of our own conclusions or those of others.

Bibliography

Argyris, C. (1968), 'Some Unintended Consequences of Rigorous Research', *Psychological Bulletin*, Vol. 70, no. 3, pp. 185–97.

Askham, J. (1975), *Fertility and Deprivation*, Cambridge University Press.

Bandura, A. (1970), *Principles of Behavior Modification*, New York: Holt, Rinehart and Winston.

Barnes, J. (ed.) (1975), *Educational Priority, Vol. 3, Curriculum Innovation in London's E.P.A.s*, London: HMSO.

Benington, J. (1974), 'Strategies for Change at the Local Level: Some Reflections' in Jones, D. and Mayo, M., *Community Work: One*, London: Routledge and Kegan Paul.

Berger, P. L. and Kellner, H. (1964), 'Marriage and the Construction of Reality', *Diogenes*, Vol. 46, no. 1, pp. 1–23.

Berthoud, R. (1976), *The Disadvantages of Inequality*, London: Macdonald and Jane's.

Bowlby, J. (1975), *Attachment and Loss, Vol. II, Separation: Anxiety and Anger*, Harmondsworth: Penguin.

Boyson, R. (1971), *Down with the Poor*, London: Churchill Press.

Bronfenbrenner, U. (1971), *Two Worlds of Childhood: U.S. and U.S.S.R.*, London: Allen and Unwin.

Brown, D. (1975), 'Shiftwork: A survey of the sociological implications of studies of male shiftworkers', *Journal of Occupational Psychology*, Vol. 48, pp. 231–40.

Brown, G. W., Bhrolchain, M. N. and Harris, T. (1975), 'Social Class and Psychiatric Disturbance Among Women in an Urban Population', *Sociology*, Vol. 9, no. 2, pp. 225–54.

Brown, G. W. and Harris, T. (1978), *Social Origins of Depression*, London: Tavistock.

Butterworth, E. and Holman, R. (1975), *Social Welfare in Modern Britain*, London: Fontana/Collins.

Carmichael, K. (1974), 'The Cycle of Deprivation', British Association of Social Workers' Conference, Manchester University, March 1974.

Chazan, M. (1964), 'The Incidence and Nature of Maladjustment among Children in Schools for the Educationally Subnormal', *British Journal of Educational Psychology*, Vol. 34, pp. 292–304.

Clarke, A. D. B. and Clarke, A. (1976), *Early Experience: Myth and Evidence*, London: Open Books.

Cohen, S. (1979), 'Community Control – A New Utopia', *New Society*, Vol. 47, no. 858, pp. 609–11.

Cooper, J. D. (1976), 'The Closing of the Training Schools in Massachusetts' *Community Home Schools Gazette*, Vol. 70, no. 5, pp. 221–4.

Cornish, D. B. and Clarke, R. V. G. (1975), *Residential Treatment and Its Effects on Delinquency*, Home Office Research Study, no. 32, London: HMSO.

Court, D. (1976), *Fit for the Future, Report of the Committee on Child Health Services*, London: HMSO.

Davie, R., Butler, N. and Goldstein, H. (1972), *From Birth to Seven*, London: Longman, for The National Children's Bureau.

Davis, D. R. (1970), 'Depression as Adaptation to Crisis', *British Journal of Medical Psychology*, Vol. 43, pp. 109–16.

Department of Education and Science (1978), *Higher Education into the 1990s*, London: HMSO.

Department of Health and Social Security (1974), *Report of the Committee on One-Parent Families*, Finer Report, London: HMSO.

Devereux, E. C., Bronfenbrenner, U. and Rodgers, R. R. (1969), 'Child-Rearing in England and the United States: A Cross-National Comparison', *Journal of Marriage and the Family*, Vol. 31, no. 2, pp. 257–70.

Douglas, J. W. B. (1964), *The Home and the School*, London: Panther.

Douglas, J. W. B., Ross, J. M. and Simpson, H. R. (1968), *All Our Future*, London: Panther.

Downes, D. M. (1966), *The Delinquent Solution*, London: Routledge and Kegan Paul.

EEC (1977), *The Perception of Poverty in Europe*, Brussels.

Eysenck, H. J. (1973a), *The Inequality of Man*, London: Temple Smith.

Eysenck, H. J. (1973b), 'The Triumph of the Average', *New Society*, 25 October, pp. 201–3.

Farrington, D. P., Gundry, G. and West, D. J. (1975), 'The Familial Transmission of Criminality', *Medicine, Science and the Law*, Vol. 15, no. 3, pp. 177–86.

Field, F. (1975), 'Raising the poverty line', London: *The Guardian*, 3.6.75.

Gavron, H. (1966), *The Captive Wife*, Harmondsworth: Penguin.

Goffman, E. (1968), *Asylums*, Harmondsworth: Penguin.

Goldthorpe, J. H. (1974), 'Social Inequality and Social Integration' in Rainwater, L., *Social Problems and Public Policy*, Chicago: Aldine, pp. 32–40.

Halmos, P. (1978), *The Personal and the Political*, London: Hutchinson.

Halsey, A. H. (Ed.) (1972), *Educational Priority, Vol. I: E.P.A. Problems and Policies*, London: HMSO.

Halsey, A. H. (1977), 'Whatever Happened to Positive Discrimination?', *Times Educational Supplement*, 21 January, no. 3216, pp. 23–4.

Hawthorn, G. and Carter, H. (1976), *The Concept of Deprivation*, SSRC paper.

Helling, I. (1976), 'Autobiography as Self-Presentation: The Carpenters of Konstanz' in Harré, R., *Life Sentences*, New York: John Wiley, pp. 42–8.

Herzog, J. D. (1971), 'A Review of Valentine's Culture and Poverty', *Harvard Educational Review*, Vol. 41, no. 3, August, pp. 375–85.

Hess, R. D. and Handel, G. (1974), *Family Worlds*, Chicago: University of Chicago Press.

Hill, J. (1978), 'The Psychological impact of unemployment', *New Society*, 19 January, pp. 118–20.

Hirsch, F. (1977), *Social Limits to Growth*, London: Routledge and Kegan Paul.

Holman, R. (ed.) (1970), *Socially Deprived Families in Britain*, London: Bedford Square Press.

Holman, R. (1973a), 'Poverty, welfare rights and social work', *Social Work Today*, Vol. 4, no. 12.

Holman, R. (1973b), 'Poverty: Consensus and Alternatives', *British Journal of Social Work*, Vol. 3, no. 4, pp. 431–46.

Holman, R. (1973c), 'Supportive Services to the family' in Stroud, J. (ed.), *Services for children and their Families*, Oxford: Pergamon Press.

Holman, R. (1974), 'Social Workers and the "inadequates"', *New Society*, Vol. 29, no. 622, 5 September, pp. 607–10.

Holman, R. (1978), *Poverty: Explanations of Social Deprivation*, London: Martin Robertson.

Holtermann, S. (1975), 'Areas of urban deprivation in Great Britain', *Social Trends* no. 6, London: HMSO.

Holtermann, S. (1978), 'The Welfare Economics of Priority Area Policies, *Journal of Social Policy*, Vol. 7, no. 1, pp. 23–40.

Horton, J. (1966), 'Order and Conflict Theories of Social Problems as Competing Ideologies', *American Journal of Sociology*, pp. 701–31.

Hurry, J. B. (1921), *Poverty and its Vicious Circles*, London: Churchill.

Ineichen, B. (1975), 'Teenage Brides', *New Society*, 7 August, pp. 302–3.

Ineichen, B. (1977), 'Youthful Marriage: The Vortex of Disadvantage' in Chester, R. and Peel, J. (eds.), *Equalities and Inequalities in Family Life*, London: Academic Press, pp. 53–69.

Jahoda, M., Lazarsfeld, P. F. and Zeisel, H. (1972), *Marienthal*, London: Tavistock Publications.

Jenkins, R. (1972), *What Matters Now*, London: Fontana.

Jencks, C. et al. (1973), *Inequality*, London: Allen Lane.

Jordan, B. (1974), *Poor Parents: Social Policy and the 'Cycle of Deprivation'*, London: Routledge and Kegan Paul.

Joseph, K. (1972a), 'The Cycle of Deprivation', Speech at Conference of Pre-School Playgroups Association, 29 June.

Joseph, K. (1972b), 'The Parental Role', *Concern*, no. 11, pp. 4–12.

Joseph, K. (1973a), 'The Cycle of Deprivation', Speech at Seminar of Association of Directors of Social Services, 27 March, *Community Schools Gazette*, Vol. 67, no. 2, pp. 61–72.

Joseph, K. (1973b), 'The Family Way', *The Guardian*, 4 June.

Joseph, K. (1973c), 'The Cycle of Deprivation and the Importance of Parenthood', Speech to National Association for Maternal and Child Welfare, 27 June.

Joseph, K. (1974). Speech in Birmingham, 19 October, London: Conservative Central Office News Service.

Keller, S. (1975), *Male and Female: A Sociological View*, New Jersey: General Learning Press.

Knight, B. J. and West, D. J. (1977), 'Criminality and Welfare Dependency in Two Generations', *Medicine, Science and the Law*, Vol. 17, no. 1, pp. 64–7.

Lafitte, F. (1973), 'Income Deprivation' in Holman, R. (ed.), *Socially Deprived Families in Britain*, London: Bedford Square Press.

Lambert, R. (1964), *Nutrition in Britain 1950–60*, Occasional Papers on Social Administration, no. 6, London: Bell.

Land, H. (1969), *Large Families in London*, Occasional Papers on Social Administration, no. 32, London: Bell.

Land, H. (1975), 'The myth of the Male Breadwinner', *New Science*, 9 October.

Land, H. (1977), 'Inequalities in Large Families: More of the Same or Different?' in Chester, R. and Peel, J. (eds.), *Equalities and Inequalities in Family Life*, London: Academic Press, pp. 163–76.

Land, H. (1978), 'Who Cares for the Family', *Journal of Social Policy*, Vol. 7, no. 3, pp. 257–84.

Leacock, E. B. (1971), *The Culture of Poverty: A Critique*, New York: Simon and Schuster.

Leissner, A., Powley, T. and Evans, D. (1977), *Intermediate Treatment*, London: National Children's Bureau.

Levine, D. (1977), *Family Formation in an Age of Nascent Capitalism*, London: Academic Press.

Lewis, O. (1964), *The Children of Sanchez*, Harmondsworth: Penguin.

Lewis, O. (1965), *La Vida*, New York: Vintage Books.

Lewis, O. (1966), 'The Culture of Poverty', *Scientific American*, Vol. 215, no. 4.

Lewis, O. (1969), *Pedro Martinez*, London: Panther.

Lewis, O. (1970), *A Death in the Sanchez Family*, London: Secker and Warburg.

Liebow, E. (1967), *Tally's Corner*, London: Routledge and Kegan Paul.

Lunn, J. E. (1961), 'A Study of Glasgow Families Rehoused', *The Medical Officer*, 10 February, pp. 73–7.

Marris, P. (1958), 'Widows and their Families', *Institute of Community Studies Reports, no. 3*, London: Routledge and Kegan Paul.

Marsden, D. (1973), *Mothers Alone*, Harmondsworth: Penguin.

Marsden, D. and Duff, E. (1975), *Workless: Some Unemployed Men and Their Families*, Harmondsworth: Penguin.

Miller, W. B. (1958), 'Lower Class Culture as a Generating Milieu of Gang Delinquency, *Journal of Social Issues*, Vol. 14, pp. 5–19.

Ministry of Housing and Local Government (1969), *Council Housing Purposes, Procedures and Priorities*, London: HMSO, (Cullingworth Report).

Mitchell, S. and Shepherd, M. (1966), 'A Comparative Study of Children's Behaviour at Home and at School', *British Journal of Educational Psychology*, Vol. 36, pp. 248–54.

Morgan, L. A. (1976), 'A re-examination of Widowhood and Morale', *Journal of Gerontology*, Vol. 31, no. 6, pp. 667–95.

Newson, J. and Newson, E. (1965), *Patterns of Infant Care in an Urban Community*, Harmondsworth: Pelican.

Newson, J. and Newson, E. (1968), *Four Years Old in an Urban Community*, London: Allen and Unwin.

Newson, J. and Newson, E. (1976), *Seven Years Old in the Home Environment*, London: Allen and Unwin.

Oakley, A. (1976), *Housewife*, Harmondsworth: Penguin.

Oliver, J. E. and Taylor, A. (1971), 'Five Generations of Ill-treated Children in One Family Pedigree', *British Journal of Psychiatry*, Vol. 119, pp. 473–80.

Oliver, J. E. and Cox, J. (1973), 'A Family Kindred with Ill-used Children: The Burden on the Community', *British Journal of Psychiatry*, Vol. 123, pp. 81–90.

Oliver, J. E., Cox, J., Taylor, A. and Baldwin, J. A. (1974), *Severely Ill-Treated*

Children in North-East Wiltshire, Research Report no. 4, Oxford Record Linkage Study: Oxford University Unit of Clinical Epidemiology.

Packman, J. (1968), *Child Care: Needs and Numbers*, London: Allen and Unwin.

Parker, R. (1974), 'The Implications for Social Policy', *Concern*, no. 13, pp. 15–20.

Parry, W. H., Wright, C. H. and Lunn, J. E. (1967), 'Sheffield Problem Families – A Follow-up Survey', *The Medical Officer*, 8 September, pp. 130–2.

Payne, J. (1974), *Educational Priority, Vol. 2, E.P.A. Surveys and Statistics*, London: HMSO.

Pétonnet, C. (1973), *Those People: The Subculture of a Housing Project*, Westport: Greenwood.

Phillips, M. (1978), 'Family Policy: the Long Years of Neglect', *New Society*, 8 June, pp. 531–4.

Philp, A. F. (1958), 'The Problem Family and the Social Services', In *The Problem Family*, London: I.S.T.D. publication.

Piachaud, D. (1974), 'Do the poor pay more?', *Poverty Research Series 3*, London: Child Poverty Action Group.

Polsky, H. W. (1962), *Cottage Six*, New York: Russel Sage Foundation.

Popper, K. R. (1969), *Conjectures and Refutations*, London: Routledge and Kegal Paul, 3rd edn.

Radin, R. (1933), *The Method and Theory of Ethnology*, New York: Basic Books.

Registrar General (1974), *Quarterly return for England and Wales for 2nd Quarter 1974*, no. 502, London: HMSO.

Registrar General Scotland (1973), *Annual Report 1972, Part 2, Population and Vital Statistics*, Edinburgh: HMSO.

Richards, M., Richardson, K. and Spears, D. (1972), 'Conclusions: Intelligence and Society' in Richardson, K. and Spears, D., *Race, Culture and Intelligence*, Harmondsworth: Penguin.

Rutter, M. L. (1970), 'Sex Differences in Children's Responses to Family Stress' in Anthony, E. J. and Koupernik, C. (eds.), *The Child and His Family*, New York: John Wiley.

Rutter, M. L. (1975), *Helping Troubled Children*, Harmondsworth: Penguin.

Rutter, M. L. (1978), 'Early Sources of Security and Competence' in Bruner, J. and Garton, A. (1978), *Human Growth and Development*, Oxford: Clarendon Press, pp. 33–61.

Rutter, M. L., Tizard, J. and Whitmore, K. (ed.) (1970), *Education, Health and Behaviour*, London: Longman.

Rutter, M. and Madge, N. (1976), *Cycles of Disadvantage: a review of research*, London: Heinemann.

Ryan, W. (1971), *Blaming the Victim*, New York: Vintage Books.

Sarsby, J. (1972), 'Love and Marriage', *New Society*, Vol. 21, no. 521.

Schur, E. M. (1973), *Radical Non-Intervention*, Englewood Cliffs, N. J.: Prentice-Hall.

Seebohm Committee (1968), *Local Authority and Allied Personal Social Services*, London: HMSO.

Shankland, G., Willmott, P. and Jordan, D. (1977), *Inner London: Policies for Dispersal and Balance*, London: HMSO.

Sharpe, S. (1976), *Just Like a Girl*, Harmondsworth: Penguin.

66666

Smout, T. C. (1969), *A History of the Scottish People, 1560–1830*, London: Collins.

Social Trends (1976), no. 7, London: HMSO.

Spencer, K. (1973), 'Housing and Socially Deprived Families', in Holman, R. (ed.), *Socially Deprived Families in Britain*, London: Bedford Square Press.

Stott, D. H. (1973), 'Follow-up Study from Birth of the Effects of Prenatal Stresses', *Developmental Medicine and Child Neurology*, Vol. 15, pp. 770–87.

Stevenson, O. (1977), 'Social Services and Child Abuse: Some Dilemmas and Opportunities', *Royal Society of Health Journal*, October.

Tawney, R. H. (1932), *Land and Labour in China*, London: Allen and Unwin.

Tonge, W. L., James, D. S. and Hillam, S. M. (1975), *Families Without Hope*, British Journal of Psychiatry Special Publication, no. 11, Headley.

Townsend, P. (ed.) (1971), *The Concept of Poverty*, London: Heinemann.

Townsend, P. (1974), 'The Cycle of Deprivation – The History of a Confused Thesis', British Association of Social Workers' Conference, Manchester University, March 1974.

Valentine, C. A. (1978), *Culture and Poverty*, Chicago: University of Chicago Press.

Veil, C. et al (1970), 'Unemployment and Family Life', in Anthony, E. J. and Koupernik, C. (eds.), *The Child in his Family*, New York: Wiley–Interscience.

Wedge, P. and Prosser, H. (1973), *Born to Fail?*, London: Arrow Books.

West, D. J. (1969), *Present Conduct and Future Delinquency*, London: Heinemann.

West, D. J. and Farrington, D. P. (1973), *Who Becomes Delinquent?*, London: Heinemann.

West, D. J. and Farrington, D. P. (1977), *The Delinquent Way of Life*, London: Heinemann.

Whyte, W. F. (1955), *Street Corner Society*, Chicago: University of Chicago Press.

Wilkinson, R. (1976), 'Dear David Ennals...', *New Society*, Vol. 38, no. 741, pp. 567–9.

Williams, F. (ed.) (1970), *Language and Poverty*, Chicago: Markham.

Wilson, H. (1974a), 'Parenting in Poverty', *British Journal of Social Work*, Vol. 4, no. 3, pp. 241–54.

Wilson, H. (1974b), 'The life and death of the cycle of deprivation and some unresolved problems', *Poverty*, no. 30, pp. 3–8.

Wilson, H. and Herbert, G. W. (1978), *Parents and Children in the Inner City*, London: Routledge and Kegan Paul.

Wofinden, R. C. (1944), 'Problem Families', *Eugenics Review*, Vol. 38, pp. 127–32.

Wootton, B. (1959), *Social Science and Social Pathology*, London: Allen and Unwin.

Wright, C. (1955), 'Problem Families: A Review and Some Observations', *Medical Officer*, 30 December, pp. 381–4.

Wright, C. (1958), 'Problem Families', *The Eugenics Review*, Vol. 50, no. 1, pp. 35–9.

Wright, C. H., Lunn, J. E. and Parry, W. H. (1967), 'Sheffield Problem Families – A Follow-up Survey', *The Medical Officer*, 8 September, pp. 130–2.

Wright, C. H. and Lunn, J. E. (1971), 'Sheffield Problem Families. A Follow-up

Study of their Sons and Daughters', *Community Medicine*, no. 3304, Vol. 126, no. 22, pp. 301–7.

Wynn, M. and Wynn, A. (1974), 'Can Family Planning do more to reduce child poverty?', *Poverty*, no. 29, pp. 17–20.

Young, M. and Willmott, P. (1962), *Family and Kinship in East London*, Harmondsworth: Penguin.

Young, M. and Willmott, P. (1975), *The Symmetrical Family*, Harmondsworth: Penguin.

Index

Index of Names

General Index

Aulton, 4, 8, 9, 19–21, 122–3, 171, 175

Barkers, 6, 8, 11, 12, 13, 15, 23–71, 72,
119, 155, 165, 170–74, 177, 179
  biography: Elsie, 32–7, 57–9; Vince,
  26–9
  child rearing, 49–55, 57, 181; Tracy,
  24, 38–41, 48, 54, 57, 70, 71, 160,
  170, 177; Nick, 38; Steve, 24, 37,
  42, 53–4, 56, 63, 170; Julie, 24,
  25, 37, 41, 53; Tom, 24, 31, 37,
  51, 52–3; Eddie, 24, 37, 49, 50, 51,
  52, 62, 68; Alice, 24, 25, 36, 37,
  43, 51, 52, 62, 64; John, 24, 37,
  42, 49, 50, 51, 52, 57, 64
  commentary on, 60–71; alternative
  explanations, 157, 158–60
  Elsemore, 55–7; and fire, 56
  epilogue, 192–4
  finance, 30, 44–9
  housing, 23, 24, 25, 55; and overcrowding, 23, 25, 49
  marital relationship, 41–4, 56–7
  social worker (see also Minton,
  Hilary), 59–60
  work and life style: Elsie, 37–8;
  Vince, 29–32
Bramwell, 6, 15, 16, 21, 23–55, 72, 101

Cardale, 16, 21, 79, 87–90, 102, 103,
174
Child rearing, 179–80
  Barkers, 49–55
  Fieldings, 128–31
  Martins, 113–16
  Patersons, 83–6
Culture of poverty, 10, 164
Cycle of deprivation
  concept of, 1–3, 163–5, 199–214
  interconnections of, 172–4
  and local officials, 4, 178
  and resources, 174–7
  and stigma, 177–9

  and transmission, 165–71
Cystic fibrosis, 115

Drayford, 123, 125–6, 129, 148–50,
177

Education, 190–1
  Barkers, 27, 71
  Fieldings, 129, 153
  Martins, 104, 109, 114
  Patersons, 99
Elsmore, 18, 21, 47, 55–7, 192–4
enuresis, 63, 113, 121, 194

Fieldings, 9, 11, 12, 13, 122–56, 165,
171, 174, 176, 178
  biography: Dora, 124–5; George,
  125–7
  child rearing, 128–31; Nicola, 123,
  124, 128–31, 134; Amanda, 123,
  124, 127, 128, 131
  commentary on, 151–5;
  alternative explanations, 157,
  162–3
  Drayford, 126, 128, 133, 148–50
  epilogue, 197–8
  extended family, 139–44
  finance, 133–5, 151, 152
  health, 131–3
  housing, 123, 148–50
  marital relationship, 127–8
  neighbours, 144–8
Families
  alternative explanations of, 157–63
Family planning, 66, 152
Family policies, 188–9
Family size, 180–1
Finance, 175–7

Havelocks
  Enid, 122–3, 126–7, 133, 134, 135–9,
  154, 159, 162
  Jamie, 136, 138, 162